# Brunei

# WORLD BIBLIOGRAPHICAL SERIES

General Editors:
Robert G. Neville (Executive Editor)
John J. Horton                            Ian Wallace
Hans H. Wellisch              Ralph Lee Woodward, Jr.

**John J. Horton** is Deputy Librarian of the University of Bradford and currently Chairman of its Academic Board of Studies in Social Sciences. He has maintained a longstanding interest in the discipline of area studies and its associated bibliographical problems, with special reference to European Studies. In particular he has published in the field of Icelandic and of Yugoslav studies, including the two relevant volumes in the World Bibliographical Series.

**Ian Wallace** is Professor of Modern Languages at Loughborough University of Technology. A graduate of Oxford in French and German, he also studied in Tübingen, Heidelberg and Lausanne before taking teaching posts at universities in the USA, Scotland and England. He specializes in East German affairs, especially literature and culture, on which he has published numerous articles and books. In 1979 he founded the journal *GDR Monitor*, which he continues to edit.

**Hans H. Wellisch** is Professor emeritus at the College of Library and Information Services, University of Maryland. He was President of the American Society of Indexers and was a member of the International Federation for Documentation. He is the author of numerous articles and several books on indexing and abstracting, and has published *The Conversion of Scripts* and *Indexing and Abstracting: an International Bibliography*. He also contributes frequently to *Journal of the American Society for Information Science, The Indexer* and other professional journals.

**Ralph Lee Woodward, Jr.** is Chairman of the Department of History at Tulane University, New Orleans, where he has been Professor of History since 1970. He is the author of *Central America, a Nation Divided*, 2nd ed. (1985), as well as several monographs and more than sixty scholarly articles on modern Latin America. He has also compiled volumes in the World Bibliographical Series on *Belize* (1980), *Nicaragua* (1983), and *El Salvador* (forthcoming). Dr. Woodward edited the Central American section of the *Research Guide to Central America and the Caribbean* (1985) and is currently editor of the Central American history section of the *Handbook of Latin American Studies*.

VOLUME 93

# Brunei

Sylvia C. Engelen Krausse
Gerald H. Krausse

CLIO PRESS

OXFORD, ENGLAND · SANTA BARBARA, CALIFORNIA
DENVER, COLORADO

British Library Cataloguing in Publication Data

Krausse, Sylvia C. Engelen
Brunei.—(World bibliographical series; 93).
1. Brunei. Bibliographies
I. Title    II. Krausse, Gerald H.
016.9595'5


ISBN 1–85109–029–0



Clio Press Ltd.,
55 St. Thomas' Street,
Oxford OX1 1JG, England.

ABC-Clio Information Services,
Riviera Campus, 2040 Alameda Padre Serra,
Santa Barbara, CA 93103, USA.



Designed by Bernard Crossland.
Typeset by Columns Design and Production Services, Reading, England.
Printed and bound in Great Britain by
Billing and Sons Ltd., Worcester.

# THE WORLD BIBLIOGRAPHICAL SERIES

This series, which is principally designed for the English speaker, will eventually cover every country in the world, each in a separate volume comprising annotated entries on works dealing with its history, geography, economy and politics; and with its people, their culture, customs, religion and social organization. Attention will also be paid to current living conditions – housing, education, newspapers, clothing, etc. – that are all too often ignored in standard bibliographies; and to those particular aspects relevant to individual countries. Each volume seeks to achieve, by use of careful selectivity and critical assessment of the literature, an expression of the country and an appreciation of its nature and national aspirations, to guide the reader towards an understanding of its importance. The keynote of the series is to provide, in a uniform format, an interpretation of each country that will express its culture, its place in the world, and the qualities and background that make it unique. The views expressed in individual volumes, however, are not necessarily those of the publisher.

## VOLUMES IN THE SERIES

*To
the memory of
May*

# Contents

# Contents

# Contents

# Preface

This bibliography presents an inter-disciplinary country profile of Brunei up to, and including, 1987. No other reference work, published in English, has treated this Bornean mini-state in such detail. Existing works are either unannotated checklists or focus on one particular subject, a period of time, or cover several political entities together, typically Brunei, Malaysia and Singapore. Although this bibliography does not claim to be definitive, it does cover a wide range of recent research and historical works, and will be of interest to the general reader and information specialist, as well as the student and scholar seeking to discover more about Brunei.

Almost forgotten by the rest of the world and regarded as something of an anachronism, Brunei has quietly emerged as the wealthiest state in Southeast Asia after nearly a century of British protective rule. As a young sovereign nation with extensive oil reserves, this country, the smallest in the region, is rapidly gaining international attention. By the same token, the government is quite concerned about its image as presented by the foreign press, and, in particular, their portrayal of the Sultan. This may partly explain why Brunei is not a popular destination for tourists and why few Western scholars are permitted to engage in field research. However, many Brunei students who do study abroad carry out their research at home, and the results of these efforts, in the form of theses and dissertations, are becoming much more widely available from selected British and American universities.

This bibliography is divided into thirty-one main subject headings, four of which are further sub-divided. Within each chapter, entries are arranged alphabetically by title. Each entry gives complete bibliographical details and is fully annotated. In making our selection, we have taken into account not only the editorial guidelines of the World Bibliographical Series, but also the quality of research and the number of publications available on a given subject. A particular wealth of material exists on the history, culture and natural sciences of Brunei. By contrast, the reader will find sources on the legal system, literature and religion under-represented, since, in Brunei, publications on these subjects are primarily in the Malay or Jawi languages. Occasionally, a Malay-language source has been included in this bibliography on the grounds that it was most relevant and not available in English.

Until recently, Brunei had no academic or cultural organization dedicated to the collection of archival material. In fact, the country had been intellectually looted for the best part of a century. Currently, the Brunei Museum is a major depository for local publications, yet many items remain uncatalogued.

Government documents are almost exclusively published in Malay and, consequently, have been excluded from this bibliography. One of our objectives was to produce a reference work primarily for an English-speaking audience. The Economic Planning Unit of the Ministry of Finance produces bilingual publications, such as development plans and census reports. The unit was established in 1973 in an attempt to improve the quality and efficiency of data collection and analysis. Each ministry and government department also produces a wealth of publications, but no central depository exists in Brunei which houses them all. A widely used government publication is the monthly newsletter, *Brunei Darussalam*, issued, in English, by the Broadcasting and Information Department of the Prime Minister's Office.

As to the spelling of Malay words, considerable variation may be found in the citations due to regional language differences and changes in the spelling system recently instituted by the Malay-speaking countries. In the annotations, no attempt has been made to provide uniform spelling of place-names, titles and ethnic terms; rather, each entry makes use of the spelling as presented in the original work being annotated.

*Acknowledgements*

Many institutions and individuals have generously contributed to the preparation of this bibliography. Due to their guidance and professional assistance, we finally completed the manuscript with great satisfaction. Special thanks are due to Ms. Patricia Lim Pui Huen and the staff of the Institute of Southeast Asian Studies in Singapore; Ms. Sophie Kuah and the staff of the library at the

# Preface

National University of Singapore; Pengiran Haji Idriss, Brunei Ambassador to the United States in Washington, DC; Ms. Nellie Haji Sunny, Dewan Bahasa dan Pustaka in Bandar Seri Begawan; Mr. Haji Matussin Omar, Director of Museums in Brunei; Ms. Linda Shboul, University of Sydney; Ms. Helen Stephens, University of Hull; and the staff of the British Library in London.

In the United States we wish to express our gratitude to Mr. Charles Bryant and Ms. Lian Kho, Yale University; Mr. William Badgley and Ms. Miko Yamamoto, Cornell University; Mr. Lee Dutton, Northern Illinois University; Mr. William Tuchrello and Mr. Kohar Rony, Library of Congress; Ms. Joyce Wright, University of Hawaii; many inter-library loan librarians throughout the country; and especially those at Ohio State University, Northern Illinois University and the University of Hawaii.

We would like to thank the following scholars for sharing with us their writings on Brunei and their expert advice: Dr. Donald E. Brown, University of California, Santa Barbara; Dr. Allen R. Maxwell, University of Alabama; Dr. Lewis Hill, University of Hull; and Dr. A. V. M. Horton, Loughborough, England. We are particularly grateful to the Alumni Foundation, University of Rhode Island, which has provided partial funding for a visit to Brunei.

Finally, our sincere appreciation must go to our family and friends, and colleagues at the University of Rhode Island for their special interest in, and sustained support of, the project: Mary Tate and Susan Myette for the word processing; Vicki Burnett and her staff for the smooth handling of hundreds of inter-library loan requests; all my colleagues at the University of Rhode Island Library; and my good friend, Karin Negoro, for her research efforts in England. Needless to say, no bibliography is ever complete, and for any inadvertent errors or omitted references we remain responsible.

*Sylvia C. Engelen Krausse*
*Gerald H. Krausse*
*Kingston, Rhode Island*
*August, 1988*

# Introduction

The Bornean Sultanate of Brunei, under British protection since 1888, finally achieved independence on New Year's Day, 1984, and emerged as the world's 169th sovereign state and the sixth member of ASEAN (Association of South East Asian Nations). Today, the new nation is characterized by an oil-dominated economy, an absolute monarchy, a strong Islamic tradition and a welfare system that has become the envy of its more powerful neighbours. The magnitude of the country's wealth is tied inextricably to the continued exploitation of its oil and gas resources. The fact that Brunei is a small country, both in terms of area and population, places significant limits on future development, and options for defence and foreign policies.

While these observations may presuppose no 'real' history before nationhood and the discovery of oil, Brunei is, in fact, one of the oldest countries in Southeast Asia. Archaeological excavations have provided evidence which suggests that connections between Brunei and China existed as early as the 6th century AD. In later centuries the Sultanate became a powerful Muslim kingdom, playing a major role in maritime trade and the spread of Islam throughout Southeast Asia. With the arrival of the Europeans in the 18th and 19th centuries, however, Brunei gradually lost its influence over the region, until only very limited control of its ancient domain remained. Its former territories were either conquered or passed in one form or another to the 'White Rajah' of Sarawak or the British North Borneo Company. Those who moved upon Brunei justified their actions by claiming that the Sultanate had not only decayed to the point of near extinction, but, also, imposed intolerable burdens on its subjects. Such claims, along with the very real obscurity of Brunei during much of this century, make it difficult to produce a fair account of the country's past and its situation today. This bibliography is

**Introduction**

a first step towards providing useful and readily available references for a study of Brunei, its environment and society.

**Geography**

Brunei Darussalam is located on the northwestern coast of the island of Borneo, only 440 kilometres north of the equator. As such, it has a climate which is characterized by uniformly high temperatures and precipitation throughout the year. Its total land area of 5,765 square kilometres, with a coastline of 130 kilometres, is slightly larger than the state of Delaware in the United States. Nearly two-thirds of that area are still covered with tropical forests in which mixed Dipterocarp predominate. Extensive swamp land surrounds Brunei Bay where nipa palms and mangroves are the most abundant flora. Approximately one quarter of the country may be regarded as arable land, but at least half of this is on steep slopes and subject to erosion if cleared. The coastal zone in Brunei is the most productive eco-system, providing not only marine resources but also timber, coal, silica sand and agricultural land. Consequently, more than 85 per cent of the population, and almost all major economic activities, are confined to the coastal plain. At the present time, the country's natural resources, apart from oil and gas, are not yet heavily exploited. Brunei's economy is, however, moving into a new era, by embracing a strategy of diversification rather than depending on oil. Forestry, fisheries and agriculture will play an increasingly important role in the economy. There are an estimated 20 million tons of silica sand deposits which are potentially useful for glass production. The government has an ambitious target of becoming self-sufficient in rice during the 1980s. Peat production, freshwater aquaculture and paper pulp mills are other options. Environmental pollution will, however, surely magnify, as the use of pesticides, deforestation, sewage discharge and oil spills are inevitable consequences of rapid economic development. The oil well blowout in 1981 which resulted in some shoreline contamination and the smaller spill which occurred in 1984 are evidence of the potential for environmental degradation. Brunei is fortunate to be well-endowed with natural resources, but only a sensitivity and gradual adaptation to changing conditions will allow it to remain so.

Historically, a profusion of labels has been given to the

Sultanate and its dependencies, particularly as they changed hands among competing foreign interests. European writers and cartographers have used a variety of place-names to identify the early kingdom and its domain, among them, Bruni, Brunai, Burney, Borneo, Borne and Burni, from which, ultimately, two words crystallized – Brunei and Borneo. During the 'golden age' of the Sultanate the two terms were synonymous, but as its power declined the word 'Brunei' came to be associated only with the remaining territory ruled by the Sultan, while 'Borneo' was applied to the whole island. In the 1600s, the Portuguese and Spaniards most frequently used Borney or Burney for 'Brunei', which was probably a corruption of the native word 'Bruni'. The name Brunei only became current in English in about 1840, apparently popularized by the writings of Rajah James Brooke. Today, there is no longer a political entity referred to as Borneo. The dependencies known as 'British Borneo', a concept used purely for convenience with no constitutional sanction, included all territories under British control. The first territory to come under British influence, rather than control, was a portion of Sarawak, also known as Sarawak Proper, governed by the Brookes. Eventually, British control extended over all of Sarawak, North Borneo, Brunei and the island of Labuan. As British Borneo was firmly established, protectorate status was given to Sarawak, North Borneo and Brunei, while Labuan remained a colony. Although Sarawak and North Borneo became British crown colonies in 1946, Brunei never actually became a British possession even though it was always part of British Borneo. At present, Sarawak and Sabah (formerly North Borneo or British North Borneo) make up the two eastern states of the Malaysian Federation and Indonesian-controlled Borneo is known locally as Kalimantan. As for Brunei, the official designation of the country, glorified by the honorific Arabic title, Daru'L-Salam, is fully expressed as Negara Brunei Darussalam (the Abode of Peace).

## History

Brunei's written records date from the 15th century, with the introduction of the Arabic script by Muslims. What is known about the pre-Muslim kingdom comes from Hindu and Chinese chronicles and scattered archaeological evidence discovered in Brunei since the early 1950s. Chinese annals of the 16th century

**Introduction**

contain reference to a kingdom known as Po-'ni or Fo-'ni which sent tribute to the courts of China in AD 518 and 523. Similar missions were subsequently sent to emperors of the Sung dynasty in AD 977 and 1082. With the decline of the Sung dynasty, Brunei transferred its allegiance to Hindu Majapahit in Java, then back to China again, and finally made contact with Muhammadan Malacca. Some of the evidence of this regional diplomacy comes from the 'Nagrakertagama' a Javanese script of 1365, which refers to 'Buruneng' (Brunei) as a vassal state of the Majapahit empire. During the time of the Ming dynasty, Chinese emperors once again demanded tributes from the king of Po'-ni in 1405 and 1425. After this period, contact with China and Java became less frequent due to the disruption caused by the arrival of the Europeans.

As to archaeological evidence in Brunei, two sites, Kota Batu (Stone Fort) and Kupang, have produced indications of contact with Chinese and Indianized civilizations. At Kota Batu, one of Brunei's earliest capitals, research uncovered old Brunei and Chinese coins, as well as Chinese ceramic artefacts. Most of the coins date from the dynastic periods beginning in AD 960 and ending in 1450. Two dated tombstones found at Kota Batu were from the early Ming dynasty. Near Brunei, at the town of Limbang, recent finds include a stone figure of a Hindu deity and a horde of gold 'Indian' ornaments. Some of the gold objects appear to resemble those of the Majapahit period (*circa* 1300-1450) of Java. Chinese objects, found at sites in Brunei, Sarawak, Malaya and China, demonstrate not only the kingdom of Po-'ni's antiquity, but also its span of influence and level of development before the arrival of the Europeans.

Brunei had reached its zenith in the 16th century, when the Europeans arrived in Southeast Asia. Its authority and commercial control extended over many tribal and Muslim communities throughout the Malay Archipelago. From his court the Sultan's control reached outward along the coast and along rivers as far as tax collectors could penetrate, and his royal title won considerable respect. The Sultanate of Brunei never actually colonized; instead, it stationed a chief (*pengiran*) at the mouth of a major river where the Sultan's forces would collect tolls and which would act as a trading centre. The coastal Bruneians imported Indian cotton, Chinese pottery, silk, porcelain and firearms which were bartered for camphor crystals, gold, wax, honey and other agricultural commodities with people from the interior. It was a highly satisfactory system, for if either party was not getting its value, they simply stopped trading until an agreement was reached. The transactions were, however, highly dependent on a powerful fleet which could fend off intruders and pirates commonly found in Bornean waters. While Bruneian mariners were sometimes thought of as warriors, more realistically they were, primarily, merchants – the 'Venetians' of the South China Sea. As the Sultanate reached its height in commerce and prosperity, its sovereignty, in all probability, embraced much of Borneo (as far as Sambas and Pontianak), as well as overseas dependencies which included the Sulu Archipelago and the southern islands of the Philippines. The description of Brunei in its heyday, as portrayed by Antonio Pigafetta, the historian of Magellan's expedition in 1521, glows with oriental splendour, the elaborate trappings of state and 'chariots drawn by elephants'. The glamour and power of the kingdom in Pigafetta's time should not, however, be exaggerated, as the Sultan's hold over his territory was always tenuous. Indeed, the arrival of the Spanish in the Philippines in the early 16th century may have set in motion a prolonged period of decline, which was not effectively brought to a halt until this century.

Aside from sea trade, the Brunei kingdom was equally interested in spreading Islam to its outlying dependencies, bringing them into direct conflict with the Spanish forces in the Philippines. After a Spanish attack on Brunei's capital in 1578, warfare continued for many decades (known as the Moro Wars) between Muslim communities and the Spaniards in the southern Philippines. In time, the Sultan's dependencies throughout his empire fell away. The Spaniards established themselves in Cibu in 1565, evicted Bruneians from Manila Bay and the Sulu Sultanate became independent in 1660. The power vacuum created by the decline of Brunei was rapidly filled by the maritime activities of the Sulu Sultanate. Slave raiding and piracy contributed significantly in making Sulu a powerful state during the period 1750-1850. Piracy was primarily practiced by Muslim seafarers, the Bajau, who raided commercial fleets and coastal settlements formerly under the influence and protection of Brunei. Finally, Brunei's possessions on Borneo were partitioned between Sarawak and Sabah, while the Dutch gradually asserted their claim to the rest of the island. To make matters worse, there were internal disputes between loyalists and rebel rajahs, who fought over the succession to the throne well into the 19th century. At this point in time, the Sultanate was depicted as a disunited and corrupt principality, politically weak and in a state of anarchy. In short, Brunei had suffered the same fate as other maritime states in Southeast Asia when European mercantile practices came to bear on the region.

During the 19th century the island of Borneo became an arena for the struggle of power among the British, Dutch, Portuguese and Americans. The British turned their attention to the northwestern coast of Borneo for two reasons: Brunei's position on the India–China trade route, and the fear that other European rivals might take advantage of Brunei's political instability and establish a foothold there. The British sphere was initiated by the private efforts of a Victorian adventurer and empire-builder, James Brooke, in 1839. He landed in Kuching, helped to end a local rebellion there and, in 1841, was rewarded with the title of Rajah over Sarawak Proper by Sultan Muda Hashim. Subsequently, Rajah Brooke began an intensive effort to wipe out piracy in northern Borneo, often with the aid of British naval power. During the ensuing fifty years, James and his nephew, Charles Brooke, had extended, by force or diplomacy, the boundary of Sarawak to include the district of Limbang, thus splitting Brunei into two parts.

The 1847 Treaty of Friendship and Commerce with Great Britain was to prohibit the Sultan of Brunei from giving away any more of his territory without the consent of the British government. In 1853, however, Brooke succeeded in acquiring the Baram River area in defiance of the 1847 Treaty, claiming that he had always considered himself to be an independent ruler. In addition, the Sultan, in a dramatic gesture of independence, signed a treaty of commerce with the United States, in 1850, granting America 'most-favoured-nation' status. The occupation of parts of Brunei's northern frontier was America's first attempt to colonize territory in Borneo. For Great Britain, the American presence was considered to be a threat to their strategic interests. A private venture, later to become the British North Borneo (Chartered) Company, purchased a large tract of land for commercial purposes from the Sulu Sultanate in North Borneo with strong support from the Foreign Office in London. As to the attitude of Brunei toward the loss of its former possessions, few of the sultans objected because many were paid handsome cession monies from both Sarawak and North Borneo.

Unable to resist powerful external influences or the rivalry of petty chiefs from within, the Sultanate was virtually non-existent as a political entity by 1880. In 1888, the British authorities placed Brunei under the Protectorate Agreement in an effort to eradicate anarchy, piracy and the expansion efforts made by the Brooke family and the North Borneo Company. However, very little changed in Brunei apart from the fact that it was saved from extinction. The new protectorate status allowed the Sultan to continue ruling and Charles Brooke managed to annex the Limbang River Basin in 1890. Two important events in the 20th century contributed to the salvation of the Sultanate and its resuscitation. In 1906, Brunei accepted the first British Resident advisor to assist the Sultan in all internal affairs except Muslim and native law. Under the Resident system, law and order was established and an administrative structure was initiated with central control over the entire country. The other significant event was the discovery of oil in commercial quantities which added to Brunei's general prosperity during this period, but was to be of even greater consequence later. Oil production was not actively pursued at that time because of the economic recession in Great Britain and the onset of World War II; explorations were fully resumed after the war.

Under the dynamic leadership of Sultan Sir Omar Ali Saifuddin III, a new form of government emerged from the Brunei constitution of 1959. Later, in 1962, the Sultan began negotiations with the prime minister of Malaya to join the Malaysian Federation, along with Brunei's neighbours, Sarawak and Sabah. The British government, in the meantime, realized that the interests of Royal Dutch Shell, in which it had a substantial stake, might be jeopardized if Brunei entered the Federation. Once again, under British pressure, the Sultan called off the negotiations on this issue. In the meantime, under Brunei's new internal self-rule and constitution, political parties became active and elections were contested. The Brunei People's Party (Partai Ra'ayat Brunei, or PRB) was a product of political change which favoured nationalism and independence. Although the PRB claimed it was fighting British rule, the Sultan believed it posed a threat to the throne, which the royal family had managed to preserve despite centuries of colonial encroachment. During the first election, the PRB won overwhelmingly on a platform of independence from Britain and a federation with neighbouring states. The Sultan, however, had no desire to share power with the elected representatives, Azahari and Zaini Ahmad. On 7 December 1962 the PRB launched a rebellion and held Brunei at ransom until British troops, flown in from Singapore, crushed the uprising. Although the Sultan survived the revolt, it succeeded in damaging Brunei's relations with the

## Introduction

Philippines, Indonesia and Malaysia, who supported the efforts of the PRB. After the abortive rebellion, a state of emergency was declared which is still in effect today.

In 1979 Brunei signed another treaty of friendship and cooperation with Britain which made independence by 1984 a certainty. A lay period of five years was given to the Sultan to allow him to adjust to the withdrawal of British protection. Negotiations during this time centred on the question of whether Britain should provide basic security in exchange for continued access to Brunei's petroleum resources. It can be argued that the oil–security linkage is asymmetric since the Gurkha regiment has only limited fire power and back-up and is, therefore, no real deterrent to external aggression. The Sultan's government has also built up its own defence force, now one of the best equipped in the region. At the same time, Brunei has emerged as an important oil supplier, the revenues of which cover defence expenditure, which can amount to 40 per cent of the nation's budget, the highest in the world. Thus, while Brunei's foreign policy prior to 1979 had been based on security through alignment with an extra-regional power, after 1979 it was concerned with the consolidation of security through the attainment of international legitimacy. If one condition for nation-building is to 'have the opportunity to age in the wood', then the four years of nationhood to date have certainly given Brunei a measure of internal stability and regional cooperation. It is to be hoped that this young nation can live up to its name, the Abode of Peace.

## The sultans

Several sultans played a pivotal role in the cultural and political history of Brunei, their royal genealogies dating back nearly 600 years. According to the Brunei chronicles, the first Muslim ruler was installed around 1365 by the Sultan of Johore. Awang Alak Betatar assumed the title of Sultan Mohammad after embracing Islam, following his marriage to a Johore princess. The teachings of Islam were further spread by Sharif Ali, a Persian missionary and direct descendant of the Prophet Mohammad. He succeeded to the throne as the third Sultan and assumed the title, Paduka Seri Sultan Berkat (the Blessed). As Sultan, he ruled vigorously, built mosques and constructed the first defence barriers at Kota Batu and across the Brunei River. Sultan Bolkiah, by far the most renowned sovereign, reigned at the height of Brunei's 'golden age', and made the names Brunei and Borneo almost synonymous. His fleets took him on numerous voyages to Java, Malacca and the Philippines where he seized Seludong (Manila). Sultan Bolkiah died on one of his voyages while returning from Java and is now buried in Kota Batu.

The most revered 20th-century ruler of Brunei was Sultan Omar Ali Saifuddin III, more familiarly known as 'The Seri Begawan' (1950-67). His reign was highlighted by two major events: the civil rebellion by the People's Party in 1962, which he crushed with the assistance of British troops, and the proposed membership of Brunei in the Malaysia Federation, which he opposed when oil was discovered in Brunei. Sultan Omar Ali Saifuddin III also introduced the first written constitution in 1959 and was instrumental in transferring the internal administration from British to Brunei hands.

Today, Brunei is ruled by Sultan Hassanal Bolkiah, the 29th Sultan in hereditary succession, popularly referred to as HH. He is a graduate of the British military academy of Sandhurst, and, since 1984, is also in charge of the Ministry of Defence in Brunei. As the Supreme Executive Authority, his Majesty is assisted by the Religious Council, the Privy Council, cabinet ministers, the Legislative Council and the Council of Succession. The cabinet is made up of a blend of royalty, energetic youth and experienced technocrats, aimed at filling the vacuum left by his father's death in 1987. Although interested in the modernization of the state and tolerant of a mild dose of democracy, the Sultan remains a traditional, feudal potentate.

## Society and culture

Brunei is sometimes referred to as a modern Utopia because its people are, by and large, not plagued by poverty or political instability. Instead, they obtain many benefits, including free education and health care. Many Bruneians' aim upon leaving school is to join the government where careers offer exceptional lifelong benefits, as well as substantial salaries. The government, for example, gives low interest loans, provides non-contributory pension plans for the old and disabled and pays for its employees to go on a pilgrimage to Mecca. In a country where there is no personal income tax, where the purchase of a car is subsidized and a gallon of petrol costs less than one US dollar, a family which owns several cars is not exceptional. The possibility of driving, however, is limited; the longest road runs for about 120 kilometres and the entire road network consists of only 600 kilometres. In the capital city of Bandar Seri Begawan, one-third of the 55,000 residents still live in settlements over the Brunei River, known locally as 'Kampong Ayer'. Although the houses, built on stilts, are not very different from those which existed 400 years ago, electricity, running water, refrigerators and colour television sets inside these houses are unmistakable signs that modern conveniences have also come to the traditional water village. Most families living in Kampong Ayer are quite content with their accommodation and have no desire to resettle despite the government's efforts to move them to more modern apartments on land.

Brunei has a small population which, according to the latest census in 1981, was 192,862 people; it reached an estimated 225,000 in 1986 and is expected to be over a quarter of a million by 1990. The major urban centre and capital, Bandar Seri Begawan (previously called Brunei Town), is located in the most populated district of Brunei-Muara, only 9 miles from the coast. The next largest towns are Seria and Kuala Belait, which are both associated with the oil industry, located some 65 miles from the capital. Other principal towns are Tutong and Bandar, in the more sparsely settled districts of Tutong and Temburong. In general, the population in Brunei tends to be concentrated in the coastal zone, away from the relatively rugged and forested interior.

Early in its history, the arrival of Islam and the foundation of the Brunei empire produced a fundamental split in local society – Muslims versus non-Muslims, or Brunei rulers versus the subject population. By the 19th century, all ethnic groups within the Brunei domain were subject to the state's regulations and control. The ruling ethnic Bruneians were a Muslim, Malay-speaking people who claimed to be superior because of their own heroic deeds and their prestigious relationships with Malaya, Java and China. Their society was highly stratified between the nobility and the non-nobles on the basis of how closely they were descended from officials. Nobles (*pengiran* or *raja*) were all patrilineal descendants of a sultan and constituted only 10 per cent of the upper classes. At the head of the nobility were those individuals descended from a current or recent sultan while descendants from earlier sultans formed the lower ranks of the nobility. Those ranking highest in the non-noble classes were the aristocrats (*awang*) who claimed descent from non-Bornean nobility in the ancient past. Beneath the aristocrats were the rank and file Bruneians (*rakyat*), differentiated mainly by their place of residence and occupation. At the bottom of the Brunei status scale was a class of slaves and servants, all chiefly pagan by birth. Historically then, Bruneian society, by the 19th century, was technically plural, with the indigenous Bruneians as overall rulers. Under the British régime and in independent Brunei today, the various subject groups have shown significant signs of coalescing into a population with an identical culture. At the same time, the Malay Muslims have grown by accretion from subject groups and immigrants from Malay and Indonesian areas.

In present-day Brunei, the most important ethnic groups are Malay (65 per cent of the population), including the Bruneians (ethnic Bruneians, who are not to be confused with all residents or citizens of the State of Brunei), the Kedayans and others from Sarawak, Sabah and the Malay Peninsula. The Kedayans are a Malay-speaking group whose agricultural pursuits complemented the trade and maritime activities of the Bruneians. Despite their economic symbiosis, common language and religion, however, the Kedayans have always been a subject population, closer in status to the pagan groups of Borneo. The non-Malay-speaking ethnic groups live mainly in the interior of Brunei; these include the Dusun (8.8 per cent), the Iban or Sea Dayaks (4.2 per cent) and the Muruts (0.9 per cent), amongst others. Most of them are either shifting cultivators, collect various jungle products, or have settled permanently as subsistence farmers. The Iban are relatively recent arrivals to Brunei and continue to be attracted largely as contract workers in the oilfields. With changes brought about in this century through improvements in communication and education, however, the number of ethnic groups is on the decline as the minorities merge with the majority and become classified as Malays.

Economically, there is still a gap between the wealthy and the disadvantaged in Brunei society. Some 60 per cent of the labour force (mostly ethnic Bruneians) are employed in government services and managerial occupations in the private sector, enjoying a higher standard of living than the rest of the population. Malay workers outside the urban areas, unskilled Chinese and indigenous workers employed in the service industry, and immigrant workers doing menial tasks, constitute the underprivileged class. Within this context, the continued extravagance of the royal family could, in the future, generate social discontent among those who are not able to share in the national wealth.

Among the non-Bornean groups in Brunei are the Chinese (21 per cent), some Indians and a few Europeans, mostly British. Nearly all Indians arrived via Labuan Island when it was a British colony. Today, they are associated with commerce and the oil industry. Europeans have never been numerically significant in Brunei, in stark contrast to their influence on the modern history of the country, particularly with regard to material and technical progress. Similarly, the political and economic importance of the Chinese cannot be underestimated. With the arrival of the British, the Chinese found ready protection and ample opportunity for commercial and agricultural development. They quickly replaced the Malays in almost every trade and decisively moved into the import–export business. Politically, they are an element to be reckoned with, despite their reluctance to form political parties. Unofficial estimates place the Chinese population at 65,000 compared to some 150,000 Malays; yet only ten per cent of the Chinese are Brunei citizens. As non-citizens, they do not receive free education or medical care, they are discouraged from owning land and their representation in government is minimal. To become a citizen of Brunei one is required to pass an examination in Malay, the national language, and to have been in continuous residence in the country for at least 25 years. These regulations make it difficult for the Chinese and other minorities to obtain a passport. Clearly, the post-independent status of non-Malays is a potential problem, and while the Sultan is reluctant to make any changes at this time, he acknowledges the fact that certain minorities are disadvantaged in Brunei. Nonetheless, it is also worth noting that relations among various ethnic groups in Brunei are much more tolerant than in other Southeast Asian countries.

Islam is a way of life in Brunei; its manifestations and stature owe much to the country's history and the Sultan's vision of how his people should live. Thus, for the Brunei Malay, loyalty to the Sultan, their country and Islam are one and the same. The Muslims in Brunei are, by tradition, united under the guidance of various religious scholars, prayer leaders and other mosque officials. Nobody dares to challenge the decisions of the Department of Religion or the implementation of new Islamic principles, thus discouraging religious factionalism. As everybody knows everyone else in the community, social pressure ensures conformity and proper behaviour, but, at the same time, provides little opportunity for individual expression. Significantly, the intelligentsia is very much of the same mind, due to a common education and Alma Mater. Virtually all Islamic officials have attended the Sultan Hassanal Bolkiah Institute and, subsequently, the al-Azhar University in Cairo. This effective network of religious officials ensures that the same Islamic philosophy is adhered to and passed down from generation to generation. Unlike other Muslim countries, where many forms of Islam encourage debate about its true interpretation and practice, in Brunei Islam binds rather than separates. Not even under strict Muslim faith (*santri*), however, can society remain totally impervious to outside influences. In the long run, pressures are bound to increase, whether from Islamic fundamentalists who are dissatisfied with Brunei's modern life style, or from non-Malays demanding a greater voice in public affairs.

## The economy

According to the World Bank, Brunei ranks third in the world in per capita income (US $22,000 in 1986). The *Guinness Book of Records* states that the Sultan is the richest man in the world. Indeed, Brunei faces few of the economic problems often experienced by newly independent nations. The investment of accumulated surplus abroad and a favourable balance of payments enable Brunei to finance a development programme entirely from its own budgetary resources. This condition is largely a function of the royalties, taxes, rent and dividends received from the oil and gas industry. The foreign exchange reserves already built up from oil exports are a closely guarded secret, but financial experts estimate that they may exceed US $20 billion, and the investment earnings have already surpassed oil and gas revenues, which are approximately $3 to 5 billion per year.

Oil was first struck in Brunei in 1929 at the onshore site of Seria, but exports did not begin until 1932, when market conditions became more favourable. The development of the Seria oilfields was slow but steady until 1940, when World War II and the Japanese occupation temporarily disrupted production. From 1945 onward, crude oil output increased sharply; it reached its peak production of nearly 44 million barrels in 1956, then slowly declined. This gave rise to concern over the future of Brunei's only source of revenue, until new hydrocarbon resources were discovered on the continental shelf. In 1963, following the introduction of the Petroleum Mining Enactment, new offshore concessions were made available covering some 3,000 square miles of territorial waters up to 600 feet in depth. Today, there are five offshore oilfields in operation, listed here in chronological order of discovery – Southwest Ampa (1963), Fairley (1971), Champion and Fairley-Baram (1973) and Magpie (1975). The giant Champion-7 complex, the largest of its kind in Southeast Asia, was completed in 1983 at a cost of US $360 million. The combined production from these sites peaked at 91 million barrels in 1979, but, since then, has fallen to about 50 to 60 million barrels in the early 1980s.

Natural gas is invariably associated with the exploration of petroleum, and Brunei has become the world's fourth largest producer of liquid natural gas (LNG). With the downturn in crude oil, LNG production, now under a single 20-year contract with Japan, is as important as oil. The discovery of major gas reserves has led to the construction of the world's largest liquefaction plant at Lumpur in 1973 and, in 1984, the opening of a new $100 million refinery. The development of oil and gas is administered by the Brunei Shell Petroleum Group of Companies, consisting of Brunei Shell Petroleum (BSP), Brunei LNG, Brunei Coldgas and the Brunei Shell Marketing Company. The Lumpur LNG plant is jointly owned by BSP, the government and the Mitsubishi Corporation, while oil production is allocated on an equal share basis between Brunei Shell Petroleum and the Brunei government. In recent years, the government has attempted to reduce the dominance of BSP still further by leasing offshore concessions to smaller US companies and by enacting new legislation designed to improve its position in future ventures with foreign oil companies.

This dependent relationship with a major transnational oil corporation is not without certain security benefits to the Brunei government. The British, who maintain a substantial stake in Royal Dutch Shell, have agreed to keep their battalion of Gurkhas in Brunei strictly for the protection of the oilfields, not to maintain internal public order as was the case in 1962. The government is also conscious of the need to develop the country's infrastructure for the days when the oil reserves run out. The largest single item in the national budget is approximately US $150 million for defence; the second largest expenditure is devoted to education and investment in public facilities. Intense building activity in recent years has focused on roads, housing programmes, a new university and a massive hospital complex. In

the 1970s, communication which reflected the external orienta-
tion of the economy was substantially improved by developments
such as a deep-water port (1973), an international airport (1974),
a national airline (1975) and an earth satellite station with links to
Singapore and Britain (1979). The building boom continued into
the 1980s with the construction of the Supreme Court, the
Ministry of Foreign Affairs, and the Nurul Iman Palace, in
preparation for independence. These developmental achievements, which have been accomplished in a relatively short
timespan and with limited technical and administrative experience, cannot be understated.

There is, however, another side to this prosperity and success,
because the domination of the economy by the mining and
service industries, has created a shortage in skilled labour for
other sectors. Almost half of the local labour force works for the
government and another 7 per cent is employed by Brunei Shell.
Both employers provide higher wages and fringe benefits than
elsewhere, making it difficult for other economic activities to
attract workers from an already limited pool of labour.
Immigrant workers are widely used to fill less desirable posts,
although, more recently, the government is restricting their
recruitment fearing that social problems could arise in the future.
Foreign workers currently range from 25,000 to 30,000 in number
(35 per cent of the present labour force). The government is
aware of its labour problems and is encouraging students to go
abroad or to take free tuition at the Institute of Technology, in
order to acquire professional skills or vocational training. As a
consequence of this shortage of skilled labour, little is manufactured locally and most commodities are imported, including
80 per cent of all food requirements.

One of Brunei's priorities in the 1980s, therefore, is to expand
the employment base through economic diversification. Indeed,
this is precisely the theme of the Fifth National Development
Plan (1986-90), released at the end of 1985. The plan takes note
of the negative economic growth during 1985, a result of falling
oil prices and cutbacks in production aimed at extending reserves
into the next century. Since the unfavourable conditions in the oil
market are likely to continue, the plan urges for 'immediate
action' to provide an alternative revenue base. The ambitious
five-year plan calls for: (a) an increased level of agricultural self-
sufficiency and marine fishery in the newly extended 200-mile
fishing zone; (b) a review of existing land-use codes for the siting
of new industrial facilities; (c) a development bank to help fund

private investments; and (d) an industrial policy aimed at reducing imports and boosting export-oriented commodities. Finally, the plan recognizes the need for human resource development through a comprehensive national training scheme in the fields of commerce and industry.

It is difficult to ascertain just how much headway has been made toward implementing the plan's objectives to date. While undoubtedly some success has been achieved, the economy is still overwhelmingly dependent on the petroleum industry. It is possible that, in the long term, the potential exists for developing a high-technology, capital-intensive, low-labour-using industry in Brunei. In principle, this resource-rich state is able to follow such a course since it has the capital available to invest and has no shortage of foreign labour. Success in that direction is, nevertheless, critically dependent upon a locally available, highly skilled and educated labour force which, undoubtedly, will take some time to establish.

## Prospects

Like other small, yet wealthy, nations, Brunei faces the prospect of adapting its traditional Islamic way of life to the necessities of the contemporary world. Modernization will increasingly engender new expectations – internal stability, national security, and relations with neighbours – which will require accommodation. Politically, one of the most frequently asked questions, particularly by the Western media, is: 'How long can the Sultan sustain an absolute monarchy in this modern world?'. It is clear that Brunei's governmental structure is different from other Southeast Asian states; there are neither political parties nor an elected parliament and power is concentrated in the royal family. The present modernizing autocracy, after a recent Cabinet reshuffle, however, appears to be remarkably appropriate for governing the country today. The political system can tolerate wide social and economic change and adapt well to the establishment of a bureaucracy. It cannot, however, cope easily with new political groups demanding change in the system, or transform itself into a representative government.

Economically, Brunei's heterogeneous population, traditional restraints, lack of skilled labour and lack of an internal market, create difficulties in promoting industrialization and agricultural development. The limitation of manpower has also imposed major constraints on the 'Bruneization' of employment, which has been a source of considerable resentment among non-Malay workers. While there is presently no need to fear racial or economic conflict among various sectors of the population, the Sultan is attempting to institute policies aimed at giving the Brunei Malays greater participation in economic activities.

Socially, a cause for concern may be the existence of the present welfare system which tends to perpetuate the *status quo* and, passively, reinforce the simple, unsophisticated *kampong* life. The wealth of a nation may be derived from its natural resources, but, in the end, it is the people who are responsible for maintaining that wealth and determining a country's future. Widespread indifference, even if it only reflects contentment, can become a liability in times of international crises. Priority must be given to upgrade the expertise of Bruneians, partly because of necessity, but more importantly, because an educated and actively involved society is more able to adapt to possible political or economic instability.

Another issue faced by the nascent state is that of internal security. Because of its extreme vulnerability, the maintenance of good relations with its more powerful neighbours is a cardinal aim of Brunei's foreign policy-makers. Its links with ASEAN and the UN, which Brunei joined during the same year it became independent, provide the country with additional insurance, even though neither organization is a defence alliance. Should diplomacy fail and the only alternative were to defend the country by force of arms, the burden would fall on the Royal Brunei Armed Forces (RBAF), numbering about 4,000 persons, with the assistance of friendly nations, such as Malaysia, Singapore and Great Britain. Meanwhile, Brunei's military strategists continue to search for solutions to expand their armed forces; the problem being the lack of citizens, rather than money. There is a natural and immutable law which says that a country with a small territory and population will remain permanently weak, both politically and militarily, no matter how large its foreign reserves may be.

Finally, the Sultan and his advisors must grapple with the problem of integrating Brunei into the regional community. Brunei's foreign policy, despite the British defence link, will be shaped by its relations with its ASEAN neighbours. The Sultan currently has good relations with the Philippines and Thailand. Part of the Philippines, which was once part of Brunei's empire, has been pulled into a different colonial orbit through the interference of the Spanish, and later, the United States. Distant Thailand is linked to Brunei by its provision of about 90 per cent of Brunei's rice consumption. Malaysia and Indonesia, Brunei's nearest neighbours, are more closely tied to the Sultanate through traditional links of a common language, religion and cultural origin. The role played by the two countries during the 1962 rebellion against the Sultanate, however, is still not forgotten. Brunei's refusal to join the Malaysian Federation in 1963 and Singapore's breaking away from the Federation in 1965 have given these two countries a common cause to promote closer relations. As the smallest countries in the region, they are wary of their larger neighbours and, thus, cooperate both militarily and economically. Brunei floats oil and gas, while Singapore has a highly skilled population. The Brunei currency is at par with the Singapore dollar, and Singapore is Brunei's largest ASEAN trading partner. The Brunei government and the royal family also have large investments in Singapore's free-market economy.

Independence has generated great expectations among the people of Brunei, and the Sultan will be called upon to reassert his leadership in both domestic and foreign affairs. In the long term, Brunei must plan and control its development if modernization is to be achieved, and, here, government policies are deeply imbedded in the official faith, Islam. The record has shown, so far, that Brunei has quietly, at its own pace and with much success, made its way into the community of nations.

# Proclamation of Independence Brunei Darussalam

## In the Name of Allah, the Compassionate, the Merciful

PRAISE be to Allah, the Lord of the Universe and may the benediction and peace of Allah be upon Our leader Prophet Muhammad and upon all his Relations and Friends.

WHEREAS the time has now arrived when Brunei Darussalam will resume full international responsibility as a sovereign and independent Nation among the international community of nations;

AND WHEREAS Brunei Darussalam has never been a colony but had since 1847 a special treaty relationship with the United Kingdom of Great Britain and Northern Ireland whereby in 1888 it was agreed that external relations were the responsibility of the Government of Her Majesty the Queen of the United Kingdom of Great Britain and Northern Ireland;

AND WHEREAS a Constitution styled the Constitution of the State of Brunei, 1959 was proclaimed by Our Predecessor Maulana Sultan Sir Muda Omar 'Ali Saifuddien Sa'ddul Khairi Waddien ibni Al-Marhum Sultan Muhammad Jamalul Alam, the twenty-eighth Sultan and Yang Di-Pertuan of Brunei Darussalam in accordance with which the Government of this Nation is regulated and is the supreme law thereof;

AND WHEREAS by the Treaty of Friendship and Co-operation, 1979 made between Us and Her Majesty the Queen of the United Kingdom of Great Britain and Northern Ireland and by the Exchange of Notes between Us and Her Britannic Majesty's Government it was agreed that whatever powers, obligations or responsibility Her Britannic Majesty's Government may have in respect of Brunei Darussalam under all previous treaties, agreements and arrangements between Brunei Darussalam and the United Kingdom which were inconsistent with full international responsibility as a sovereign and independent nation shall terminate on 31 December 1983 and upon such termination all the rights and powers of Our Prerogatives including the responsibility for external relations shall revert to Us as the The Sultan and Yang Di-Pertuan of Brunei Darussalam on the First day of January, Nineteen Hundred and Eighty-Four;

NOW THEREFORE in the name of Allah the Compassionate, the Merciful, We, Sultan Hassanal Bolkiah Mu'izzaddin Waddaulah, The Sultan and Yang Di-Pertuan of Brunei Darussalam and Her Territory and all Her Dependencies, do HEREBY PROCLAIM AND DECLARE in Our name and on Our behalf and for and on behalf of Our Successors and for and on behalf of the people of Brunei Darussalam that as from the First day of January, Nineteen Hundred and Eighty-Four of the Christian era, corresponding to the Twenty-Seventh day of Rabiulawal, of Hijrah of Prophet Muhammad (on Whom be the benediction and

**Proclamation of Independence**

peace of Allah) Fourteen Hundred and Four being the Seventeenth Year of Our reign, Brunei Darussalam is and with the blessing of Allah (to Whom be praise and Whose name be exalted) shall be for ever a sovereign, democratic and independent Malay Muslim Monarchy upon the teachings of Islam according to Ahlis Sunnah Waljamaah and based upon the principle of liberty, trust and justice and ever seeking with the guidance and blessing of Allah (to Whom be praise and Whose name be exalted) the peace and security, welfare and happiness of Our people and the maintenance of friendly relations among nations on the principle of mutual respect for the independence, sovereignty, equality and territorial integrity of all nations free from external interference.

May Allah, to Whom be praise and Whose name be exalted and may the Prophet Muhammad (on Whom be the benediction and peace of Allah) grant his blessing to Brunei Darussalam, for ever and ever. Amen! O Lord of the Universe!

HIS MAJESTY
THE SULTAN AND YANG DI-PERTUAN
BRUNEI DARUSSALAM

Proclaimed at Bandar Seri Begawan this First day of January, One Thousand Nine Hundred and Eighty-Four of the Christian era, corresponding to the Twenty-Seventh day of Rabiulawal, the Hijrah of the Prophet (on Whom be the benediction and peace of Allah) Fourteen Hundred and Four being the Seventeenth Year of Our reign.

The above English translation of the Proclamation of Independence is published with the kind permission of the government of Brunei Darussalam.

# Glossary

| | |
|---|---|
| ASCOPE | ASEAN Council on Petroleum |
| ASEAN | Association of South East Asian Nations |
| *adat* | native customary law, including the rules of proper procedure and conduct |
| BMJ | Brunei Museum Journal |
| BSP | Brunei Shell Petroleum |
| *bangsa* | people, race, ethnic group |
| *batu tarsilah* | genealogical tablet |
| Brunei Darussalam | 'Abode of Peace' |
| Dewan Bahasa dan Pustaka | Language and Literature Bureau |
| *dukun* | term used for a doctor (medicine man) who is often both an herbalist and magician |
| EEZ | Exclusive Economic Zone |
| HRAF | Human Relations Area File |
| *haji* | designation for one who has made the pilgrimage to Mecca |
| Istana nuruı Iman | 'Palace of religious light', Sultan's residence |
| *jawi* | Malay language written in a modified Arabic script |
| JMBRAS | Journal of the Malayan/Malaysian Branch of the Royal Asiatic Society |

## Glossary

| | |
|---|---|
| JSBRAS | Journal of the Straits Branch of the Royal Asiatic Society |
| *kampong [kampung]* | village, compound of houses |
| *Kampong Ayer [Kampung Ayer, Kampung Air]* | water village |
| *ketua* | headman |
| *Merdeka* | Independence, Freedom |
| OPEC | Organization of Petroleum Exporting Countries |
| *padian* | women vendors in small boats |
| Partai Ra'ayat Brunei (PRB) | People's Party of Brunei |
| *pengiran [pangeran]* | title for princes and nobles |
| *pusaka* | heirloom |
| SMJ | Sarawak Museum Journal |
| *shaer* | poetry |

# Chronology

| | |
|---|---|
| **ca. 518** | Brunei, known as Po-'ni or Bun-Lai, first mentioned in Chinese chronicles. |
| **ca. 977** | The King of Brunei sent the first emissary with tribute to China. |
| **1365** | Javanese records made first mention of a kingdom called Buruneng (Brunei). |
| **1408** | The Raja of Brunei, Maharaja Kala, visited China and died there. |
| **1405-15(?)** | The reign of Sultan Muhammad, the first ruler of Brunei to embrace Islam. |
| **1473-1521(?)** | Sultan Bolkiah's reign during Brunei's 'golden age'. |
| **1521** | The first official visit of a Westerner to Brunei, Antonio Pigafetta, the historian of Magellan's first circumnavigation around the world. |
| **1526** | Gorge de Mendezes, a Portuguese Admiral, reached Brunei and signed the first commercial treaty. |
| **1578** | A Spanish fleet attacked Brunei during the Battle of Kastela. |
| **1839** | James Brooke arrived in Sarawak. |
| **1841** | Brunei ceded Sarawak to James Brooke. |
| **1846** | Brunei ceded Labuan to Britain. |
| **1847** | Britain and Brunei signed a treaty to promote commercial relations and the mutual suppression of piracy. |

| | |
|---|---|
| **1848** | Brunei ceded its northern portion of the empire to a British commercial syndicate. |
| **1863** | James Brooke handed over the administration of Sarawak to his nephew, Charles Brooke. |
| **1888** | Brunei became a British Protectorate. |
| **1890** | Brunei ceded the Limbang District to Charles Brooke. |
| **1906** | Brunei received the first British Resident. |
| **1912** | The first Malay school opened in Brunei Town. |
| **1929** | Oil was struck at Seria by Royal Dutch/Shell Oil. |
| **1941** | Japanese landed at Kuala Belait and occupied the Seria oilfields. |
| **1941-45** | Japanese occupation. |
| **1952** | First English medium school was established. |
| **1954** | Brunei annexed its continental shelf by proclamation. |
| **1959** | Brunei was granted its first written constitution. |
| **1950-67** | The reign of Sultan Omar Ali Saifuddin III, the architect of modern Brunei. |
| **1962** | A domestic rebellion occurred, incited by Azahari, the leader of the Brunei's People's Party. |
| **1963** | The first offshore oil concessions were granted to Brunei Shell Petroleum (BSP). |
| **1967** | Brunei issued its own currency. |
| **1968** | The coronation of the 29th Sultan, Hassanal Bolkiah. |
| **1970** | The capital, Brunei Town, was renamed Bandar Seri Begawan in honour of the 28th Sultan, Omar Ali Saifuddin III. |
| **1973** | The official opening of the world's largest LNG plant. |
| **1975** | The Royal Brunei Airline took to the air. |

| | |
|---|---|
| **1979** | Britain and Brunei signed the Treaty of Friendship and Cooperation. |
| **1982** | The Legislative Council declared an Exclusive Economic Zone (EEZ) extending 200 miles offshore. |
| **1984** | On 1 January, Brunei became an independent state; on 7 January, Brunei joined ASEAN; on 21 September, Brunei became the 159th member of the United Nations. |
| **1985** | The University of Brunei Darussalam was founded, and a bilingual system of education was officially declared. |

# Sultans of Brunei: a genealogy

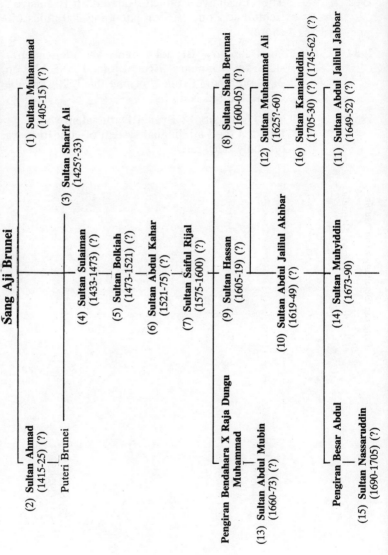

**Pengiran Digadang Shah Mubin**

(17) **Sultan Muhammad Alauddin**
(1730-45) (?)

(18) **Sultan Omar Ali Saifuddin I**
(1762-95)

**Pengiran Shahbandar Abd. Wahab**

(24) **Sultan Abdul Momin**
(1852-85)

(19) **Sultan Muhammad Tajuddin**
(1796-1807)

(20) **Sultan Muhammad Jamalul Alam I**
(1806-07)

(23) **Sultan Omar Ali Saifuddin II**
(1829-52)

(25) **Sultan Hashim Jalilul Alam Aqamaddin**
(1885-1906)

(26) **Sultan Muhammad Jamalul Alam II**
(1906-24)

(28) **Sultan Omar Ali Saifuddin III**
(1950-67)

(29) **Sultan Hassanal Bolkiah**
(1967- .)

(21) **Sultan Muhammad Kanzul Alam**
(1807-29)

(22) **Sultan Muhammad Alam**
(1826-28)

(27) **Sultan Ahamad Tajuddin**
(1924-50)

# The Country and Its People

1 **Background notes: Brunei Darussalam.**
US Department of State, Bureau of Public Affairs. Washington,
DC: US Government Printing Office, 1985. 6p. 2 maps.
A brief introduction to the country providing succinct information about the
people, history, economy, foreign relations, geography and travel.

2 **Borneo: an up-to-the-minute, liberally illustrated report on the British
Borneo territories.**
Kuala Belait: Borneo Bulletin, 1955. 79p. 2 maps.
This pictorial history of North Borneo societies is aimed at the general public.
The volume is divided into three sections: 'Borneo yesterday and today' (p. 8-10),
'Brunei yesterday' (p. 18-20) and 'Brunei today' (p. 54-59).

3 **Borneo scene.**
Ka Foo Wong, with an introduction by Malcolm MacDonald.
Kuching, Sarawak: Anna Photo Co., 1979. 192p. map.
A pictorial ethnography which describes the diversity of racial groups in Sarawak,
Sabah and Brunei. Professional black-and-white and coloured photographs depict
religious ceremonies, market activities, craftsmen demonstrating their skills,
every-day scenes of people on the river, longhouses, fields, forests, villages and
towns.

4 **Brunei: Borneo's Abode of Peace.**
Joseph Judge. *National Geographic*, vol. 145, no. 2 (Feb. 1974),
p. 207-25. map.
A portrayal of 20th-century changes in the cultural and economic conditions of
Brunei. The narrative focuses on the indigenous tribal population in rural areas

attempting to preserve a vanishing life-style in the face of pressures to modernize. Richly illustrated in the *National Geographic* tradition, this article includes seventeen coloured plates.

### 5  Brunei: paradox or paradise?
Wendy Hutton.  *Silver Kris: the Inflight Magazine of Singapore Airlines*, vol. 4, no. 1 (Jan. 1979), p. 20-25.
A perceptive view of life in Brunei, both past and present. The author presents a popular account of Brunei's 'golden age', the people in Kampong Ayer (water village), the Sultan at that time and a visit to a longhouse in the interior of the country.

### 6  Brunei: working paper.
United Nations Secretariat.  New York: United Nations, 16 August 1983. 19p. 2 maps. (Special Committee on the Situation with Regard to the Implementation of the Declaration on the Granting of Independence to Colonial Countries and Peoples).
This 19-page country report provides a wide variety of information on Brunei from 1960 to the early 1980s. The coverage is divided into four chapters: Constitution and political development; Economic conditions; Social conditions; and Educational conditions. A shorter working paper (5 pages), addressing the same topics, was published in August 1981 by the United Nations.

### 7  Brunei berdaulat. (A sovereign Brunei.)
Brunei Darussalam Government.  Singapore: Federal Publications, 1984. 142p.
This illustrated, oversized book was published to commemorate independence. After an association with Great Britain which lasted 96 years, Brunei became independent in 1984 and was formally accepted as the sixth ASEAN (Association of South East Asian Nations) member. This work contains short articles on the country's historical background, the dawning of a new era, the economy, and the land and its people. Many coloured photographs are included.

### 8  Brunei Darus Salam: gambar2 menunjokkan negeri dan pendudoknya. A pictorial review of the land and people.
[Bandar Seri Begawan]: Brunei Shell Petroleum, 1968. 116p. map.
A bilingual portrayal (in Malay and English) of the different life-styles which existed in Brunei in the late 1960s, from the daily activities of the people to the elaborate ceremonies of the royal family. The text is accompanied by many coloured photographs.

### 9  Brunei Darussalam: facts and figures 1986.
State of Brunei.  Bandar Seri Begawan: Prime Minister's Office, [1986]. 6p. map.
An information pamphlet which summarizes the state of the economy, the governmental structure, the national crest, social services, communication and the Fifth National Development Plan (1986-90).

**10  Brunei Darussalam, post report.**
Washington, DC: US Department of State, 1986. 12p. map. bibliog.
Although this official post report was actually prepared for US government
employees planning to be stationed at the American Embassy in Brunei, much of
the information is also of use to business people, researchers, and other official
visitors. The first section describes Brunei's geography, economy, population,
government, transportation and medical facilities. The second part deals with the
living conditions Americans can expect to find while stationed in Brunei. Topics
covered include housing, food, clothing, services, education, entertainment and
the administration of the embassy. Finally, the last part, entitled 'Notes for
travelers' gives information on customs, currency, banking, taxes, local holidays
and also provides a short reading list.

**11  The Brunei Darussalam State Chamber of Commerce review.**
Brunei Darussalam: Abas. Williams Associates, 1985-86. 111p.
map.
This annual publication of the Chamber of Commerce is aimed at providing both
the visitor and the prospective investor with a concise and relevant guide to
Brunei. Much of the information is provided by the Ministries of Finance, Home
Affairs, Foreign Affairs, Culture, Youth and Sports, Brunei Shell and Royal
Brunei Airlines. It comprises a collection of readings on history, geography,
government, economy, agriculture and fisheries, communication, health and
education, customs, places of interest and restaurants. Also included are the
Sultan's acceptance speech on the occasion of the admission of Brunei to the
United Nations and interviews with the Commissioner of Labour, the Managing
Director of Brunei Shell Petroleum and the Director of the Information Section
concerning the background to, and meaning of, independence. Of particular
relevance to the private sector is a chapter on 'Doing business in Brunei', which
lists foreign embassies in Brunei as well as Brunei embassies overseas.

**12  Brunei in pictures. Gambar2 peristiwa di Brunei.**
Bandar Seri Begawan: Pejabat Penerangan Perajaan Brunei, 1961.
44p.
A general overview of the geography of Brunei; constitutional progress; His
Highness the Sultan; development; the gas and oil industry; forest conservation;
population and towns; health services and religion.

**13  Labuan story: memoirs of a small island.**
Maxwell Hall.  Kota Kinabalu, North Borneo: Chung Nam, 1958.
270p. 3 maps.
A popular account of the Malay, Chinese, British and Japanese occupations of
the island of Labuan, located some 40 miles offshore from Brunei. The
association of Brunei and Labuan (meaning anchorage) has, historically, been in
the form of a shelter for Bruneian prahus, and, later, foreign merchant and naval
vessels. In fact, the personal records left by Captain Belcher, Admiral Mundy,
Admiral Keppel and Captain Ross feature prominently in this book; for example,
the intense negotiations between Mundy and Sultan Omar Ali Saifuddin II,
which resulted in the cession of Labuan to the British in 1846, are documented in
some detail. The first governor, James Brooke, and his official, Hugh Low, chose

3

it as the site for Victoria, started mining coal there and introduced a modern system of land tenure. Labuan was central to the efforts of suppressing piracy in that region because it was within easy reach of their northern strongholds. In spite of some rivalry between American, Australian and Labuan trading and mining companies, the island never fulfilled its commercial potential. Some importance, however, must be credited to Labuan for its role as a British naval station against the Japanese in World War II. When Queen Victoria unwillingly received the island from the Sultan of Brunei, it was virtually uninhabited, but by the 1950s more than 10,000 people (Bruneians, Kedayans, Chinese and others) had permanently settled there.

14 **Memperingati penukaran nama Bandar Brunei menjadi Bandar Seri Begawan.** (Commemorating the name change from Bandar Brunei to Bandar Seri Begawan.)
Awang Mahmud Haji Bakyr. Bandar Seri Begawan: Dewan Bahasa dan Pustaka Brunei, 1970. 34p.

This booklet celebrates the change of the name of Brunei's capital to Bandar Seri Begawan, in honour of the Sultan's father.

15 **North Borneo, Brunei, Sarawak (British Borneo).**
George Lawrence Harris. New Haven, Connecticut: Human Relations Area Files (HRAF), 1956. 287p. 17 maps. bibliog. (Country Survey Series, no. 2).

Using the best interdisciplinary and international resources available, the three territories which make up British Borneo are covered in this work up to 1955. All aspects of life are dealt with, including history, geography, religion, trade, welfare, labour, agriculture and social organizations. In all chapters the territories are treated as one region; few major distinctions are made between the colonies of Sarawak and North Borneo (Sabah) and the protectorate of Brunei. The reader is advised that within the context of 'British Borneo', which had once been colonial and still is plural in its socio-economic structure, the information requires careful interpretation. A special warfare issue, for official use only, entitled *Area handbook for British Borneo* (1956. 278p.), prepared by HRAF and the American University in Washington, DC, operating under contract with the Department of the Army, is also available. (See also *Area handbook on British Borneo* (q.v.)).

16 **Petroleum di Brunei.** (Petroleum in Brunei.)
Bandar Seri Begawan: Public Affairs Department, Brunei Shell Group of Companies, 19?-. quarterly.

This very attractive magazine, intended for the general reader, includes articles on the oil industry and a variety of popular topics relating to contemporary society and Brunei's past. It is written both in Malay and English and serves as a public relations vehicle for Brunei Shell.

17  **Sarawak, Brunei and North Borneo.**
    Nigel Heyward.   Singapore: D. Moore for Eastern Universities
    Press Ltd., 1963. 120p. 6 maps.
    The three territories are treated collectively with regards to general geography,
    population composition, economic conditions, history, customs, the arts and
    government organization. This book is part of a series which includes works on
    other Southeast Asian countries.

18  **Wijaya (=victory) Merdeheka (=independence) Brunei.**
    **(Commemorative issue on Brunei's independence).**
    Indian Community in Negara Brunei Darussalam.   Bandar Seri
    Begawan: Star Trading and Printing Co., 1984. 173p.
    A dedication from the Indian community in Brunei to the country's government
    and people, published to commemorate independence in 1984. A multitude of
    coloured plates are included in this work.

**Brunei, the land and its people.**
*See* item no. 40.

*Sunday Times* **spotlight: dawning of a new era: independent and
sovereign Brunei.**
*See* item no. 245.

**The Sultan of Brunei.**
*See* item no. 258.

**Pameran sejarah perkembangan Islam di Brunei.** (Diffusion and
development of Islam in Brunei.)
*See* item no. 532.

**Area handbook on British Borneo.**
*See* item no. 537.

**Selamat Datang. Welcome.**
*See* item no. 588.

**The Malay world of Southeast Asia: a select cultural bibliography.**
*See* item no. 650.

# Brunei in General Works on Southeast Asia

19   **Australasia. Vol. II: Malaysia and the Pacific archipelagoes.**
     Francis Henry Hill Guillemard.   London: E. Stanford, 1894. 574p.
     16 maps. (Stanford's Compendium of Geography and Travel [New
     Issue]).
This second volume of a two-volume set is an edited and greatly expanded version
of A. R. Wallace's *Australasia*. It concentrates on Malaya, Indonesia, Borneo,
the Philippines and the South Pacific islands. Each of the fifteen chapters is
accompanied by a fold-out map, showing topography, settlements, rivers and
boundaries. Chapter seven, entitled 'Borneo' (p. 213-74), provides a survey of the
island's geology, climate, vegetation, native people and agriculture. The
remaining pages deal with the British North Borneo Chartered Company, the
sultans of Brunei, the British occupation of Labuan Island, the Brookes of
Sarawak and the Dutch in the remaining areas of Borneo.

20   **Barbara Hansen's taste of Southeast Asia: Brunei, Indonesia,**
     **Malaysia, the Philippines, Thailand and Vietnam.**
     Barbara V. Hansen.   Tucson, Arizona: HP Books, 1987. 176p.
     map.
A very handsome cookery book containing over 200 recipes of regional
specialities, and enhanced by several coloured photographs. The recipes are
arranged by such categories as seafood, poultry, desserts, sauces and beverages.
A brief synopsis of each country and various menus precede each section of
recipes. An explanation of ingredients and equipment, and a list of mail order
sources for the ingredients is a helpful feature which is seldom found in cookery
books. The author's field-work took her to each country where her sources
included restaurant chefs, cooks at home and street vendors. About a dozen of
the recipes are specifically from Brunei.

6

21 **Borneo jungle: an account of the Oxford expedition to Sarawak.**
   Edited by Thomas H. Harrisson.   London: Lindsay Drummond,
   1938. 254p. map. bibliog.

A collection of personal observations compiled by six members of the Oxford
Exploration Club. Each contribution symbolizes the way in which different
personalities have experienced from, and lived through, the expedition of the
Limbang River area. A bibliography is included which lists the publications
containing the scientific findings of this 1932 expedition.

22 **The cruise of the *Marchesa* to Kamchatka and New Guinea. With
   notices of Formosa, Liu-Kiu, and various islands of the Malay
   Archipelago**
   Francis Henry Hill Guillemard.   London: J. Murray, 1899. 2nd ed.
   455p. 14 maps.

This work contains the observations of a three-year-long voyage to East and
Southeast Asia which was undertaken for the purpose of collecting objects of
natural history. In March 1883, the *Marchesa* spent several weeks in northern
Borneo and the Sulu Archipelago. Chapter XVI, 'Labuan and Brunei' (p. 261-
70), describes the history of the occupation of Labuan by the English during
Rajah Brooke's lifetime. The crew also spent some time in Brunei documenting
life on the river, local customs and a meeting with the Sultan.

23 **Coastal zone protection in Southeast Asia.**
   H. M. F. Howarth.   *International Defense Review*, vol. 16, no. 12
   (Dec. 1983), p. 1,749-53. map.

Maritime tradition runs deep among the non-aligned nations bordering the South
China Sea. In recent years, as a result of the Exclusive Economic Zone (EEZ),
security matters have become more significant and the ASEAN countries and
Brunei have been forced to review their priorities and capabilities. In this article,
the author examines maritime security for six Southeast Asian nations. Coastal
protection requirements for Brunei are, of course, heavily influenced by the need
to protect offshore oil developments, a task carried out by the Royal Brunei
Malay Regiment Flotilla and the Marine Police.

24 **A concise history of Southeast Asia.**
   Nicholas Tarling.   New York; Washington DC; London: F. A.
   Praeger, 1967. 334p. 5 maps. bibliog.

This work is divided into three parts. The first part deals with the geography and
resources of the region, preceded by an examination of its history up to the 18th
century. The second part comprises a review of the long period of substantial
change which also affected Borneo and the Sulu Archipelago (p. 126-29). The
concluding section attempts to deal with the contemporary phase of Southeast
Asian history, with some discussion on British Borneo (p. 189-93; 284-86).

25   **The demography of Malaysia, Singapore, and Brunei: a
     bibliography.**
     Saw Swee Hock.   Hong Kong: Oxford University Press, 1970. 39p.
     (Centre of Asian Studies Bibliographies, no. 1).

A collection of 328 entries, both in the form of statistical surveys and research
publications written in the English language. Less than 15 entries deal specifically
with Brunei.

26   **Essays on Borneo societies.**
     Victor T. King.   Oxford: Oxford University Press, 1978. 256p.
     map. bibliog. (Hull Monographs on Southeast Asia, no. 7).

This book represents one of the first collections of comparative ethnography and
includes contributions by ten established social anthropologists who had recently
completed field research in Borneo. The societies described in this collection
include the Dayak, Kayan, Kenyah, Dusun, Bajau Laut and the Maloh. Although
this work is mainly concerned with the description of significant social features, it
also considers certain theoretical problems in an analysis of cognitive societies in
Borneo. Lastly, the editor also indicates some possible future directions for
comparative sociological inquiry in Borneo.

27   **Ethnic groups of insular Southeast Asia. Vol. 1: Indonesia, Andaman
     Islands, and Madagascar.**
     Edited and compiled by Frank M. Lebar.   New Haven,
     Connecticut: HRAF Press, 1972. 226p. 10 maps. bibliog.

In this work, Lebar attempts to present a systematic survey of people and cultures
of insular Southeast Asia. For every group a series of descriptive ethnographic
summaries with accompanying bibliographies, terminological indexes and ethno-
linguistic maps are provided. For the island of Borneo (p. 147-97), the major
ethnic groups (Dusun, Murut, Bisaya, Melanau, Kenyah, Kedayan, Punan and
Dayak) are analysed in terms of social organization, settlement patterns, religion,
economy, marriage and the family.

28   **The expedition to Borneo of H. M. S. *Dido* for the suppression of
     piracy.**
     Sir Henry Keppel.   London: Chapman & Hall, 1847. 2nd ed.
     2 vols. map.

This narrative, written by the captain of the *Dido*, recounts the events relating to
the elimination of piracy and reveals excerpts from the journal of James Brooke
of Sarawak. At this time James Brooke was Her Majesty's Commissioner as well
as Consul-General to the Sultan and independent chiefs of Borneo. Brunei is
dealt with specifically in volume II (p. 237-66). The author recounts particulars of
the massacre, the destruction of batteries on the Brunei River, the flight of the
Sultan, operations against the Illanun pirates and the formal occupation of
Labuan. The appendix gives full details of the treaty signed in 1824 between
England and the Netherlands, respecting territories and commerce in the East
Indies.

29 **Fiscal system and economic development: the ASEAN case.**
Mukul G. Asher. *Bulletin for International Fiscal Documentation*,
vol. 39 (May 1985), p. 195-208. bibliog.

A broad evaluation of the fiscal policies of the ASEAN countries is attempted in
this article. Some salient features of the revenue and expenditure systems are
presented, after which the author focuses on the effects of these systems on
economic growth, equity and stabilization. The analysis suggests that from the
mid-1960s to 1980, the fiscal system did not hinder macro-economic performance,
but various internal and external factors could create complex fiscal problems for
policy-makers into the late 1980s.

30 **Die Insel Borneo in Forschung und Schrifttum.** (The island of
Borneo in research and literature.)
Karl M. Helbig. Hamburg, GFR: Geographische Gesellschaft in
Hamburg, 1955. 395p. 4 maps. bibliog. (Mitteilungen der
Geographischen Gesellschaft in Hamburg. Sonderdruck. Band 52).

Although written some years ago, this impressive, well-documented treatise (in
German) on the status of research and published literature on all aspects of
Borneo remains a standard work. The first part of the book provides a critical
analysis of the history of exploration, travel and surveys, including the author's
own crossing of the island in 1937. The section concludes with an evaluation of
the results of these activities and their contribution to geology, geography,
history, biology, anthropology, economics and other disciplines. The second part
of the book consists of perhaps one of the most extensive bibliographies on
Borneo, totalling 2,410 entries. These are occasionally annotated and have been
assembled, primarily, from German, Dutch and English libraries and museums.
The entries are grouped under twenty-five subject headings, including: bibliographies, anthropology, geology, biology, history, economy, administration,
and the Chinese in Borneo. An author index is provided.

31 **Introducing the Eastern dependencies.**
British Colonial Office. London: HM Stationery Office, British
Information Service. 1952. 80p. 4 maps

This booklet was designed to give a general introduction to the Federation of
Malaya, Singapore, Hong Kong, North Borneo, Brunei and Sarawak. The
illustrated text focuses on the diversity of the people, and their social and
economic problems, within the context of British rule and guidance.

32 **Malaya, Indonesia, Borneo and the Philippines: a geographical,
economic, and political description of Malaysia, the East Indies and
the Philippines.**
Charles Robequain, translated by E. D. Laborde. London:
Longmans, 1964. 466p. 2 maps. bibliog.

This volume, translated from the French, contains a comprehensive analysis of
the natural environment in the Malay world, its economics, cultural development
and the political systems. Chapter 10, 'Borneo' (p. 215-26), provides summaries
of the geological setting, a demographic profile and the exploration history of the
island.

9

33  **Multinational corporations and industrialization in Southeast and East Asia.**
Basu Sharma.  *Contemporary Southeast Asia*, vol. 6, no. 2 (1984), p. 159-71. bibliog.

Examines the nature of the interplay of multinational corporations (MNCs) and their host governments, with specific reference to the industrialization process of selected Southeast Asian countries. The discussion is divided into four main sections: the magnitude of MNC activities; country policies on foreign direct investment (FDI); industrialization and appraisal of the economics of the countries involved; and lastly a look at the future of international economic relations. The conclusion suggests implications of this study for public policy.

34  **Natural man: a record from Borneo.**
Charles Hose.  London: Macmillan, 1926. 284p. fold-out map.

This book documents the customs and beliefs of indigenous people living under the rule of the third Rajah Brooke of Sarawak. The text is divided into several parts: the early people of Borneo, tribal and village life, arts and crafts, creed and superstition, and morals and mentality. Particular attention is paid to the Punan, Kayan, Kenyah and Iban tribes. The author was a member of the Sarawak State Advisory Council, and is a well-known biologist and photographer. The authentic photographs of the people, their decorative art, personal possessions and living conditions represent the epitome of an earlier civilization.

35  **A short history of Malaysia, Singapore and Brunei.**
C. Mary Turnbull.  Singapore: Graham Brash, 1981. 320p. 11 maps. bibliog; Stanmore, New South Wales: Cassell Australia, 1980. 320 p.

Since the national boundaries of modern Southeast Asia are a comparatively new creation, the history of Malaysia poses special problems. Although Brunei is specifically mentioned in chapters 6 and 18 only, the entire text is of the utmost importance to the study of Brunei, as the description of the land and people, the history, conquests, and so on are all intertwined throughout the region. Turnbull provides a colourful introduction to the history of the region from the first occupation 50,000 years ago to the present. She begins with a description of the geography, people and economy of the area. This is followed by a discussion of the rise of Malacca as an important trade centre, and the complex political and social inter-relationships within the region, the impact of European colonization, expanding British influence and the major issues that shape Malaysia, Singapore and Brunei today. A glossary of important Malay terms is included, together with an eight-page bibliography, divided under several headings, such as Early history, 16th and 18th centuries, and the British colonial period. Selected pages are devoted to the impacts of maritime activities and trading companies on Brunei's early mercantile history as well as the events which led to political independence in 1984. This excellent introductory source to the region also contains many photographs.

36   **Southeast Asian research tools: Malaysia, Singapore, Brunei.**
     William R. Roff, with the assistance of Margaret L. Koch.
     Honolulu, Hawaii: University of Hawaii, Southeast Asian Studies,
     Asian Studies Program, 1979. 61p. (Southeast Asia Paper, no. 16,
     part 4).
This bibliographical survey of existing reference tools is divided into two parts:
(i) reference tools by form, i.e. guides, bibliographies, dictionaries and atlases;
(ii) reference tools by subject, i.e. business, education and geography. Comments
on scope, usefulness and comprehensiveness are provided for each entry.

37   **Tropical rainforests of the Far East.**
     Timothy Charles Whitmore.   Oxford: Clarendon Press, 1984.
     2nd ed. 352p. 23 maps. bibliog.
An authoritative and comprehensive work on the forest botany of Southeast Asia.
Much of Brunei is still covered with tropical evergreen rainforest which is
analysed here with regard to its structure and composition, ecological relations
and the impact made by man. The chapters dealing with man and the tropical
rainforest are particularly relevant in view of the recent explosive rate of
exploitation of the dipterocarp forest in the Bornean highlands. An extensive
bibliography is included.

**Ports and economic development in Borneo.**
*See* item no. 44.

**Islam and development in the nations of ASEAN.**
*See* item no. 525.

**The natives of Sarawak and British North Borneo.**
*See* item no. 550.

**Quer durch Borneo; Ergebnisse seiner Reisen in den Jahren 1894, 1896-
97 und 1898-1900.** (Across Borneo; travel experiences during the years
1894, 1896-97 and 1898-1900.)
*See* item no. 556.

**The Malay world of Southeast Asia: a select cultural bibliography.**
*See* item no. 650.

# Geography

## General

**38  Annotated bibliography on the climate of British Borneo (including Brunei, Labuan Island, North Borneo and Sarawak).**
Simon J. Roman.  Washington, DC: Weather Bureau,
US Department of Commerce, 1962. 21p. 3 maps.

Provides a regional coverage of relevant research reports on meteorological conditions, climatological observations and data summaries.

**39  Brunei in transition: aspects of its human geography in the sixties.**
Khoo Soo Hock.  Kuala Lumpur: University of Malaya,
Department of Geography, 1976. 260p. 28 maps. bibliog. (ITS Occasional Papers, no. 2).

A geographical treatment of settlement patterns, land use and economic activities with an emphasis on the rural sector. Twenty-eight maps and ten diagrams of statistical data, based on field-work and government census reports of the 1940s, 1950s and 1960s, are included.

**40  Brunei, the land and its people.**
Seria, Brunei: Brunei Shell Petroleum Co. Ltd., 1978. 136p.
2 maps.

This short history and geography of Brunei was written to commemorate the first ten years of the reign of the country's twenty-ninth ruler. The book is richly illustrated with good quality colour photographs and drawings.

41  **The geography of the State of Brunei with special reference to agriculture and agricultural systems.**
Bernard Robert Hewitt.  Master's thesis, University of Hull, England, 1975. 373p. 27 maps. bibliog.

This geographical analysis concentrates on subsistence and commercial agriculture, and compares the potential contributions of other primary activities, such as mining, forestry and fishing. To put the economic situation of Brunei into perspective the traditional and contemporary systems of government are examined. The presence of an ancient ruling caste is seen as a major factor in the dichotomy which favours the urban centres rather than the rural sector. The development of agriculture, however, is still regarded as the key to a more balanced economy and greater internal unity within the nation.

42  **Life in the forests of the Far East.**
Spenser St. John, with an introduction by Thomas H. Harrisson. Kuala Lumpur: Oxford University Press, 1974. 2 vols. 3 maps. (Oxford in Asia Historical Reprints).

Few corners of the world have attracted a richer literature than the rainforests of Borneo, particularly such as this, written by a man who pioneered the exploration of the interior in the mid-19th century. The title of this work may be somewhat misleading. Geographically, the description concentrates only on eastern Malaysia and Brunei. Several chapters provide accounts of indigenous people, the Brooke years, the Chinese insurrection of 1857 and missionary activities. The two volumes, however, originally published in 1862 (London: Smith, Elder) and 1863 (2nd ed.), also recount the ascent of the author to Mount Kinabalu and an expedition along the entire Limbang River. The Kingdom of Borneo proper (meaning the Sultanate of Brunei) is the subject of Chapter ten (p. 244-79) in volume two. It briefly covers the system of justice, resource distribution and local government, all of which were in a state of disarray and a source of mistrust at the time. Other topics include the treatment of women and concubines, crime, the method of collecting camphor, the use of coinage and the coalfields on Labuan Island, among others. While St. John spent thirteen years in northwestern Borneo, of less value are his descriptions of the natural environment. As Thomas Harrisson notes, 'on the whole [the author] seems surprisingly insensitive to one of the world's richest and most varied faunas'; yet he learned much about plants, especially the pitcher plant, from Hugh Low and others. Five appendixes on native vocabulary and language are included.

43  **The population geography of the Chinese communities in Malaysia, Singapore and Brunei.**
Niew Shong Tong.  PhD thesis, University of London, 1969. 613 leaves. 35 maps. bibliog.

A study of the migration, growth and distribution of Chinese communities in three Southeast Asian countries, including Brunei. Economic and socio-political aspects of the Chinese overseas population are also analysed.

Geography. General

44 **Ports and economic development in Borneo.**
   J. O. M. Broek.   Minneapolis, Minnesota: Department of
   Geography, University of Minnesota, 1959. 24p. 5 maps.

Borneo has always been on the margin of empires, impossible to be ignored, but
equally impossible to be controlled. Its resources were valuable enough to attract
outsiders, but not large enough to warrant extensive political and economic
investment. This mimeographed report is concerned with Borneo's resources and
the role of ports in future development. The economic situation is evaluated in
terms of the opportunities and obstacles for the island as a whole, the significant
regional characteristics, and a map analysis of trade patterns up to 1953.

45 **Summary of synoptic meteorological observations: Chinese-**
   **Philippine coastal marine areas.**
   National Climatic Center.   Washington, DC: US Naval Weather
   Service Command, 1973. vol. 5. 632p. maps.

Volume 5 comprises four areas: Area 17 – Mindanao W., Area 18 – Balabac
Straits, Area 19 – Brunei NW, and Area 20 – Saigon 300 SE. It contains maps
and tables on percentage frequency occurrence of precipitation, thunderstorms,
fog, wind speed, wind direction, cloud cover, visibility, relative humidity, air
temperature, air-sea temperature differences, sea heights, wave heights, wave
periods and sea-level pressure.

**Brunei berdaulat. (A sovereign Brunei.)**
See item no. 7.

**Brunei in pictures. Gambar2 peristiwa di Brunei.**
See item no. 12.

**North Borneo, Brunei, Sarawak (British Borneo).**
See item no. 15.

**A historic journey across Temburong.**
See item no. 79.

**Brunei, the structure and history of a Bornean Malay Sultanate.**
See item no. 150.

**Area handbook on British Borneo.**
See item no. 537.

**Annual Report.**
See item no. 589.

# Maps, mapping and atlases

46 **Atlas of Southeast Asia.**
   With an introduction by D. G. E. Hall.   London: Macmillan; New
   York: St. Martin's Press, 1964. 84p. 130 maps.
Contains 64 pages of cartographic information with a total of 130 coloured maps.
The introductory pages deal with the region as a whole and are followed by a
section which covers individual countries. In general, the thematic maps
emphasize both physical and cultural features and for every country the
distribution of climate, vegetation, land use, industry, minerals, communication
and population is shown. Furthermore, plans for 6 metropolitan areas are
included, showing public buildings, roads and land-use pattern. Borneo appears
on several pages; however, the most detailed representation is shown at a scale of
1:5,500,000 (p. 24) with an inset for Brunei at a scale of 1:1,000,000.

47 **Bandar Seri Begawan.**
   Bandar Seri Begawan: Brunei Government Printing Department,
   1981. Scale 1:6, 250. Map size: 35 × 30 cm.
This map shows built-up areas, roads, major public and private structures and
*kampongs* of the capital city.

48 **Borneo on maps of the 16th and 17th centuries.**
   Jan O. M. Broek.   *Sarawak Museum Journal*, vol. 11 (1964),
   p. 649-54. bibliog.
An attempt to reconstruct the geographical image of Borneo as it evolved from
the vague ideas put forward in Pigafetta's accounts, to Berthelot's more refined
mapping efforts. For this study the author examined the map collections in
Western Europe and the United States. Maps from the early 16th century onward
are used to trace the authenticity of place-names. By the 1700s the general shape
of Borneo was fairly well established, hydrological surveys provided more exact
information in the 1800s but the interior remained virtually unknown until the
19th century.

49 **Borneo – principal towns (outline map).**
   Washington, DC: US Office of Strategic Services, Research and
   Analysis Branch, 1945. Scale 1:4,750,000. Map size: 31 × 27 cm.
This map shows international boundaries, boundaries of British dependencies and
major towns.

50 **British Borneo geology.**
   British Territories in Borneo.   Geologic Survey Department, 1959.
   Scale 1:1,000,000.
A complete coverage of surficial geology and classification of sedimentary and
igneous rocks. Elevation in contours and selected depth isolines are provided.

51 **Brunei and adjacent territories.**
Bandar Seri Begawan: Survey Department, Government of Brunei,
1937. Scale 1:250,000.
A useful base map which shows primary and secondary survey stations, roads,
rivers, settlements, state and district boundaries, and selected contours.

52 **Brunei – oil and gas: petroleum mining agreement in respect of
onshore state lands.**
[s.1.], 1965. Scale 1:10,000 (2 sheets).
This black-and-white map shows oil facilities of Seria and Belait, forest reserves,
government reserves and lands occupied as of 1963.

53 **'Brunei surveys' 1934-38.**
Ivan C. Booth. *Brunei Museum Journal*, vol. 4, no. 4 (1980),
p. 119-31.
The objective of this article was to elaborate on and personalize the records of an
official report, entitled 'Triangulation of Brunei', published by the Surveyor
General in 1938. The observations in the records include data on base-lines,
topographical mapping and the partial delimitation of the Brunei–Sarawak
boundary.

54 **Decisions on names in Brunei, North Borneo, and Sarawak.
(Cumulative decision list no. 5207).**
US Board on Geographic Names. Washington, DC: Department
of the Interior, 1952. 103p.
This compilation gives 1,885 geographical locations (by coordinates) in the three
territories, as of June 1952. The majority of these names are now officially used
by the US government.

55 **Grand atlas, South East Asia, South Pacific Ocean [Grand atlas
Hensan Inkai).**
Tokyo: Toyoshuppan, 1975. 85p. 96 maps. bibliog.
The island of Borneo is featured in a map on the scale of 1:3,385,000 (p.17).
Scales of the other maps vary.

56 **Ilmu alam ringkas Brunei.** (Geography of Brunei.)
Ali Haji Hasan. Bandar Seri Begawan: Dewan Bahasa dan
Pustaka, 1979. 51p. 23 maps.
This atlas, aimed at the general public, includes maps, mostly in colour, on
climate, population, topography, political divisions, resources and transportation.

57 **Kuala Belait.**
[Bandar Seri Begawan]: Surveyor General of Brunei, 1972. Scale
1:6,250.
This coloured map, showing the built-up area, includes roads, public buildings,
temples, cemeteries, etc.

58 **Language atlas of the Pacific area. Part II: Japan area, Taiwan
(Formosa), Philippines, mainland and insular Southeast Asia.**
Stephen A. Wurm, Shiro Hattori.    Canberra: Australian Academy
of the Humanities in collaboration with the Japan Academy, 1983.
2 vols. 47 maps.
Pertinent to Brunei is the coloured map, no. 41, which shows the major languages
and sub-groups of the northern part of Borneo. The most important languages
include the Malay, Rejang-Baram and Kayan-Kenyah groups.

59 **Malaysia and Brunei.**
US Central Intelligence Agency (CIA).    Washington, DC: CIA,
1978. Scale 1:3,600,000. Map size: 27 × 67 cm.
A coloured map which shows relief shading and spot heights. Lambert conformal
conic projection and standard parallels of 6 degrees and 30 degrees are also given.
A map featured in the margin shows: agriculture and land use; industry and
mining; ethnic groups and population.

60 **Maps and the history of Brunei.**
D. E. Brown.    *Brunei Museum Journal*, vol. 3, no. 1 (1973),
p. 88-90. 3 maps.
One of the most prominent geo-political features of the State of Brunei is the
irregularity of its boundaries which separate it from neighbouring Sarawak. These
boundaries reflect the outcome of partitioning which began around 1840 and
ended in 1905. The most significant event occurred when Sir Charles Brooke,
Rajah of Sarawak, forcibly occupied the Limbang watershed in 1890. In this
article the author attempts to show the role of cartographical evidence in the
Limbang affair. Partitioning halted when Great Britain and Brunei signed an
agreement and established a British Resident in the country.

61 **Maps, plans and charts of Southeast Asia in the Public Record
Office.**
N. Blakiston.    *Southeast Asian Archives: the Journal of the
Southeast Asian Regional Branch, International Council on
Archives*, vol. 2 (July 1969), p. 21-64.
The cartographic material housed in the Public Record Office (PRO) in London and
described in this catalogue amounts to more than 350 maps, charts and plans. This
material appears as a printed list and card-index in the libraries of the Colonial
Office and the PRO, respectively. Thus, two sets of records for various
geographical regions exist. The first set gives the title, description, scale, author
and date of 30 maps and charts of the northwestern coast of Borneo, Labuan,

**Geography.** Maps, mapping and atlases

Brunei and the Sulu Archipelago. Also included in this set are maps of the East Indian Archipelago, the Straits Settlements and Peninsular Malaya. The second set describes 7 maps of Labuan (1848 to 1894) and 16 of North Borneo (1842 to 1938), in addition to other parts of Southeast Asia which are available from the PRO card-index of maps.

62   **The mediaeval cartographer of Borneo.**
      Robert Nicholl. *Brunei Museum Journal*, vol. 4, no. 4 (1980),
      p. 180-237. 14 maps. bibliog.

Nicholl surveys 300 years of cartographical contributions to the discovery and territorial conflicts of Borneo and, specifically, Brunei. Individual maps and atlases are examined in terms of their usefulness in explaining historical events and changes in geography.

63   **Muara, Brunei.**
      Bandar Seri Begawan: Survey Department, Government of
      Brunei, 1969. Scale 1:12,500.

Topographical series showing contours (10 feet intervals), vegetation cover (mangroves and swamps), recreational areas, cultivated areas, buildings and roads. Some details of Muara harbour facilities and the recently constructed navigational channel are also provided.

64   **Negara Brunei Darussalam: tourist map.**
      Surveyor General, Brunei.   Bandar Seri Begawan: Surveyor
      General, 1983. map.

Side 1 of this two-sided coloured map is a country map (scale 1:250,000) which shows rivers, roads, settlements and points of interest. Side 2 gives major cities: Bandar Seri Begawan, Seria and Bangar (scale 1:5,000), Tutong (scale 1:10,000), Kuala Belait and Muara (scale 1:12,500). Street patterns, public buildings, banks, post offices, information centres and hotels are shown for the named cities.

65   **Northeastern Borneo.**
      Washington, DC: US Office of Strategic Services, Research and
      Analysis Branch, 1946. Scale 1:4,750,000.

Shows coastal towns, villages and major roads. Relief and topography are represented by hashures (a shading method).

66   **Philip's regional wall map of Northern Borneo: Sabah, Sarawak and Brunei.**
      Philip (George) and Son, Ltd.   London: London Geographical
      Institute, 1968. Scale 1:1,000,000. Map size: 77 × 111 cm.

A coloured map which shows relief by contours, spot heights and gradient tints. Other features include rivers, roads and boundaries.

67   **Place names in 16th and 17th century Borneo.**
Jan O. M. Broek. *Imago Mundi*, vol. 16 (1962), p. 129-48.
16 maps. bibliog.
An in-depth investigation of the location and identification of place-names around
the coast of Borneo. A variety of sources ranging from 16th-century small-scale
world maps to the most recent large-scale topographical sheets were examined.
The main collections consulted were those of the Library of Congress in
Washington, DC; the New York Public Library; the American Geographical
Society, New York; and also collections in the British Museum; the Royal
Geographical Society in London; and various locations in the Netherlands, such
as the Maritime Museum in Rotterdam. While this study revealed significant time
lags between the 'known and shown' due to the fact that geographical knowledge
was treated almost as secret intelligence, it also pointed to the spatial division of
Borneo by European commercial interests in the 16th and 17th centuries.

68   **Sarawak and Brunei.**
[Kuching, Sarawak]: Land and Survey Department, 1963. 3rd ed.
Scale 1:1,000,000. (Sarawak Series, no. 7).
Shows altitude, rivers (tinted), mountain peak elevations, roads, boundaries and
coastal towns.

69   **The sixteenth century cartography of Borneo.**
Robert Nicholl.   *Brunei Museum Journal*, vol. 3, no. 4 (1976),
p. 96-126. 18 maps. bibliog.
Ten early maps showing the basic outline of the island of Borneo are identified in
this paper. Due to their poor reproduction each original map is accompanied by
an enlarged tracing with modern script. Most of these maps concentrate on the
northern coast of Borneo and were obtained from documents such as Magellan's
*Voyage* and *Portugaliae Monumenta Cartographica*. For many years after
Pigafetta drew his sketch map of Brunei Bay, great expanses of the Borneo coast
remained uncharted. Only in the 17th century, when the Portuguese lost their
possessions to the Dutch, were the exploration and mapping of the southern coast
carried out.

# Geology and
# Minerals

70  **Bruneica clypea N. Gen. N. Sp., a recent remaneicid
    (Foraminiferida: trochamminacea) from brackish waters of Brunei,
    northwest Borneo.**
    Paul Bronnimann, A. J. Kew, Louisette Zaninetti. *Revue de
    Paleobiologie*, vol. 2, no. 1 (May 1983), p. 35-41.
Describes the morphology of a foraminifera, Brunei clypea, recently found in
shallow down-stream deposits of the Brunei River. Details of the specimen are
shown in 26 photographs.

71  **The effects of late tertiary and quaternary tectonic movements on the
    geomorphological evolution of Brunei and adjacent parts of Sarawak.**
    G. E. Wilford. *Journal of Tropical Geography*, vol. 24 (1967),
    p. 50-56. 5 maps. bibliog.
The geomorphological evolution of Brunei and adjacent parts of Sarawak is
discussed in terms of the tectonic uplifting and tilting that have influenced the
process of erosion and deposition. Three cycles of erosion during the Pliocene and
Pleistocene periods have resulted in widespread peneplanation. Hinterland uplift
coupled with coastal subsidence appear to have been a common feature in this
part of Borneo during Neogene times.

72  **Geology and hydrocarbon potential of the South China Sea.
    Possibilities and examples of joint research and development:
    workshop report.**
    C. Y. Li, Mark J. Valencia. Honolulu, Hawaii: East-West Center,
    1980. 37p. 9 maps.
The results of a meeting of fifty leading authorities drawn from government
agencies, oil companies and academic institutions from twelve countries,

20

discussing the exploitation of hydrocarbon in the South China Sea. Some twenty-two papers were presented in three sections: offshore-oil production in countries bordering the South China Sea; geology and hydrocarbon potential of the South China Sea; and the technological, economic, legal and environmental aspects. This publication contains a summary of these papers, recommendations regarding research efforts, environmental guidelines and joint arrangements for exploration.

73  **The geology and hydrocarbon resources of Negara Brunei Darussalam.**
Edited by D. M. D. James.    Bandar Seri Begawan: Muzium Brunei, 1984. 169p. 71 maps.

A high-quality publication based on the geological investigations of hydrocarbon explorations by Brunei Shell and the Geologic Survey Department. This work represents the first detailed analysis of the onshore and offshore geology of Brunei, with an emphasis on sedimentology, palaeontology and geological structure.

74  **The geology and mineral resources of Brunei and adjacent parts of Sarawak with descriptions of Seria and Miri oilfields.**
G. E. Wilford.    Kuala Belait, Brunei: Government Printing Office, 1961. 319p. 68 maps. bibliog. (Brunei Geological Survey Department, Memoir, no. 10).

A comprehensive geological survey designed to assist the first five-year Development Plan. The eight principal chapters deal with geography, stratigraphy, geomorphology, geological history, engineering geology and various mineral resources. Many illustrations are included.

75  **The geology and mineral resources of the Labuan and Padas Valley area, Sabah, Malaysia.**
Robert Angus Munroe Wilson, with contributions by N. P. Y. Wong.    Kuching, Sarwak: Government Printing Office, 1964. 150p. 13 maps. (Geological Survey, Borneo Region, Malaysia, Memoir no. 17).

A complete scientific analysis of major rock formations, geological history and economic potential of the Labuan Island, Padas Valley and Brunei Bay area.

76  **Geology of Sarawak, Brunei and the western part of North Borneo.**
P. Liechti, in association with F. W. Roe, N. S. Haile, H. J. C. Kirk.    Kuching, Sarawak: Government Printing Office, 1960. 2 vols. 12 maps. bibliog.

This two-volume publication provides the first detailed account of the geology of 58,000 square miles of Sarawak, Brunei and Western Sabah. The reports make available to the general public geological information which has been collected over a fifty-year period of scientific exploration by the Royal Dutch Shell group of oil companies whose activities started in 1910 with the discovery of the Miri oilfields on the Sarawak–Brunei border. The first volume deals with regional

21

geology, stratigraphy, igneous rocks, tectonics, morphology and geological history. This 360-page text includes 12 maps, 18 geological diagrams and 73 black-and-white photographs. The second volume is a portfolio of maps which contains 4 sheets showing the surface geology at a scale of 1:500,000. Other sheets include rock stratigraphy, columnar sections (scale 1:25,000) and tectonic cross-sections (scale 1:1,000,000).

77 **Geosynclinical theory and the organizational pattern of the north-west Borneo geosyncline.**
Neville Seymour Haile. *Quarterly Journal of the Geological Society of London*, vol. 124, no. 494, part 2 (March 1969), p. 171-94. 4 maps. bibliog.

The north-west Borneo geosyncline occupies most of Sarawak, Brunei and western Sabah, extending over a distance of 800 kilometres. This paper outlines the geology and geotectonic aspects of the geosyncline. The very thick strata deposited in the geosyncline varies in age from late Cretaceous to late Cainozoic and are defined by four rock groups: the Rajang, Baram, Plateau and Brunei Groups.

78 **Gravel in Temburong District and its suitability as concrete aggregate.**
R. B. Tate. Kuala Belait, Brunei: Geological Survey Department, Government of Brunei, 1968. 28 leaves. 3 maps. (ITS Technical Report, no. 1).

In 1967 prospecting began in the Temburong District to locate adequate gravel deposits for the future construction of roads and an airport. It was estimated that a total of 26 million tons of gravel existed as reserves in the district. The report presents the geology, petrography, and the economic and engineering characteristics of the gravel material. The results of these investigations show that the material is quite suitable for most construction purposes.

79 **A historic journey across Temburong.**
G. C. Harper. *Brunei Museum Journal*, vol. 3, no. 3 (1975), p. 131-45. map.

This is an account of the trials and tribulations of two explorers, Mr. Morgan, a Shell geologist, and Mr. Stiff, an administrator of Shell Oil as they travelled through Temburong District to reach the 6,000-foot range of Pagon Peak. The objective was to carry out a geological survey of the Temburong District which had never before been traversed by Europeans. Excerpts from the diaries of both explorers give a detailed picture of the hardships encountered while rafting on the Temburong River and its tributaries.

80 **Longshore drift and its effect on the new Muara Port.**
R. B. Tate. *Brunei Museum Journal*, vol. 2, no. 1 (1970), p. 238-52. 2 maps.

Long monotonous stretches of sandbars and beach deposits fringe the coastline near the Muara harbour area. Consequently, the linear sediments and shallow waters have reduced the feasibility for the development of a deep-water port. After site surveys and model tests the Brunei government decided to construct an artificial deep-water canal through the sandbars with a velocity strong enough to prevent deposition of sediments. This not only provided access to the open sea but also created a sheltered area behind the sandbars suitable for the development of the Muara Port. However, recent evidence indicates that waves and storm conditions have transported sand into the deep-water basin at Muara, making continuous dredging necessary. The development of Muara Port, the author states, is yet another example where natural forces are made to act differently and it provides an opportunity to study the effects of man's interference with his environment.

81 **Malaysia und Brunei.**
Lothar Lahner. Hannover, GFR: Bundesanstalt für Geowissenschaften und Rohstoffe; Stuttgart, GFR: In Kommission, E. Schweizerbartsche Verlagsbuchhandlung, 1982. 108p. 24 maps. bibliog. (Rohstoffwirtschaftliche Länderberichte, no. 26.
[Country Reports of Economically Strategic Raw Materials, no. 26])
A regional analysis (in German) of mineral geology for the whole of Malaysia and Brunei. Chapter one concentrates on the general distribution and trade patterns of important mineral resources. Other chapters are devoted to a more detailed interpretation of the geological structure and its relationship to such minerals as petroleum, natural gas, bauxite, tin, copper and coal deposits.

82 **Method of analyzing performance of gravel-pack completions in Seria field, Brunei.**
R. E. Jones, G. Thorp. *Journal of Petroleum Technology*, vol. 32, no. 3 (1980), p. 496-504.
The majority of wells in the Seria field require sand control during their production lifetime, and over the years many gravel packs have been placed. The productivity achieved by various gravel-pack repair techniques has been difficult to analyse due to the lack of reliable data points and a wide range of values. This paper presents a method of evaluating gravel-pack completions which allows the use of small samples of observed data to be checked against theoretically derived values. The results provide an insight into the mechanics of impairment and lend support to previously suspected causes of impairment.

83 **The northwestern oil basin of Borneo.**
H. P. Schaub, A. Jackson. In: *Habitat of oil: a symposium conducted by the American Association of Petroleum Geologists, including papers presented at the 40th annual meeting of the association at New York, March 28-31, 1955.* Edited by Lewis G. Weeks. Tulsa, Oklahoma: American Association of Petroleum Geologists, 1958. p. 1,330-36. map.
Describes the oil basin which covers Sarawak, Sabah and Brunei with respect to its structural geology, the tectonics of the basin, and the occurrence of oil.

# Geology and Minerals

84 **Notes on Brunei coal (1830-1924).**
Matassim Haji Jibah. *Brunei Museum Journal*, vol. 4, no. 4
(1980), p. 104-18. map. bibliog.
Presents a history of coal mining and production in the Muara Town area of
Brunei. Prior to 1925 the coal industry was an important contributor to state
revenues. As oil production increased in the 1930s and 1940s, the interest in coal
disappeared and, today, the mines remain as something of an historic monument.
Photographs are included.

85 **Offshore exploration in Brunei**
Abdul Kani Haji Mohd. Salleh. *Energy* (Oxford), vol. 10, nos. 3/4
(1985), p. 487-91. 2 maps.
Brunei's concession system was amended in 1982 to allow the Brunei government
to participate in up to 50 per cent of all offshore oil ventures. Concessionaires
include Brunei Shell Petroleum and Jasra Jackson. This paper traces the history
of offshore exploration and the petroleum laws, as they apply to offshore acreage.
1982 was also the year the government submitted to the Legislative Council a bill
declaring an exclusive economic zone extending 200 nautical miles offshore.

86 **Paleo-environmental studies in Brunei.**
R. B. Tate. *Brunei Museum Journal*, vol. 3, no. 2 (1974),
p. 285-305. bibliog.
Excellent exposures of hydrocarbon-bearing deltaic sediments along the coast of
Brunei provide classic sections where these economically important rocks can be
studied in detail. Palaeo-environmental studies have been pursued by the oil
industry in order to discover stratigraphic oil traps. This paper discusses the
lithological order of deposition, sedimentary structure and biological activity of
the Temburong, Belait, Miri, Seria and Liang formations. Graphical records of
these sections illustrate the sedimentary sequences from which the ancient
sedimentary environments have been deduced.

87 **Palynological study of a Holocene peat and a Miocene coal deposit
from NW Borneo.**
J. A. R. Anderson, Jan Muller. *Review of Palaeobotany and
Palynology*, vol. 19, no. 4 (1975), p. 291-51. 2 maps. bibliog.
The development of peat deposits near Marudi (Sarawak) and coal deposits near
Berakas (Brunei) are studied pollen-analytically and stratigraphically by comparison with present-day swamp vegetation along the Bornean coast. A total of 76
pollen and spore types were recognized and are briefly diagnosed in this paper.
The floristic composition in both bogs, separated in age by about seven million
years, is closely comparable. Minor differences can be attributed to size,
ecological conditions and accessibility from mainland reservoirs. The coastal peat
swamps of Sarawak and Brunei cover 12.5 per cent of the land surface (15,700
square kilometres) and represent a valuable resource for the northwestern forests
of Borneo.

88 A palynological study of Pliocene sediments from the Liang
formation, Brunei.
Wendy Gillian Taylor.   MS thesis, University of Hull, England,
1984. 103 leaves. 2 maps. bibliog.

This study presents a palynological analysis of 13 samples from the Liang
formation and its Lumut member, collected from Penanjong Beach and the
Lumut Hills of Brunei. The Liang formation is dominated by pollen from the
coast and upland basin, whereas the Lumut member was deposited under esturine
and freshwater peat swamp conditions. The palynomorphs are described and
combined with other microfossil evidence to reconstruct floral communities,
palaeo-environments and palaeogeographic changes in the profile. A Middle to
Lower Pliocene age is proposed from the palynological evidence for both the
Liang formation and its Lumut member.

89 Planktonic foraminifera and time-stratigraphy in well ampa-2.
H. R. Eckert.   *Brunei Museum Journal*, vol. 2, no. 1 (1970),
p. 320-27. map.

Foraminifera are single-celled animals whose shells are preserved as fossils in
many geological formations. Petroleum geologists have long recognized the value
of planktonic foraminifera as indicators of age. This study deals with foraminifera
occurring in sediments obtained from a test drill 18 miles north of Seria in the
oilfields off the coast of Brunei. The data confirmed that during the Tertiary
period this foraminifera (Globorotalia) formed the basis for a worldwide
stratigraphic correlation.

90 Scanning electron microscope studies of selected foraminifera from
the Seria formation, Penanjong, Brunei.
D. N. P. Mahmood.   *Brunei Museum Journal*, vol. 3, no. 2 (1974),
p. 271-84.

Foraminifera have been analysed using a scanning electron microscope. With this
technique twenty genera of the Seria oil formation have been identified in this
article. Seven genera are further analysed using micro-photography.

91 Structural framework of the Sunda Shelf and vicinity.
Zvi Ben-Avraham.   PhD thesis, Massachusetts Institute of
Technology and Woods Hole Marine Biological Laboratory,
Cambridge, Massachusetts, 1973. 269p. 18 maps. bibliog.
(Unpublished manuscript).

The Sunda Shelf is one of the most extensive and coherent shelves in the world.
Of particular interest is the northern province which consists of two large
sedimentary basins: the Brunei and the Gulf of Thailand. A geo-physical survey
and structural studies of the sea floor surrounding the shelf were combined to
develop an evolutionary scheme of the Sunda Shelf and adjacent deep seas.
Water depth, sedimentary thickness and the gravity and magnetic fields were

continuously measured. These data and earlier studies of the northern shelf provide a comprehensive picture of the geological framework of the entire Sunda Shelf.

92　**The structure of development of the peat swamps of Sarawak and Brunei.**
　　J. A. R. Anderson.　*Journal of Tropical Geography*, vol. 18 (1964), p. 7-16. map. bibliog.

In Brunei peat swamps cover 380 square miles, representing 22.6 per cent of the state's territory. The study outlines the phases in the evolution of peat swamps based on a series of profiles which detail the nature of subsoil underneath the peat. This information provides additional clues for the interpretation of the post-glacial history of the Sarawak–Brunei coastline.

93　**Volcanic control of structures in north and west Borneo.**
　　J. McManus, R. B. Tate.　*Southeast Asia Petroleum Exploration Society. Offshore Southeast Asia Conference* (Singapore), 17-18 Feb. 1976), p. 1-13. 2 maps. bibliog.

This review of the geology of north and west Borneo is presented to illustrate the interrelationship between a fracture pattern, volcanic activity and sedimentation. It is speculated that conventional source rocks could be deposited between zones of volcanic activity. In providing rich soil, clastic particles and vertical movement, the effects of volcanic activities shed new, and somewhat unexpected, light on the understanding of a traditional geosyncline. Although such volcanic province would normally not attract petroleum geologists, it is possible for coarse epiclastic rocks to become reservoirs. If these are transported into marine embankments, they might become a source rock for oil deposits.

**Rajah Charles Brooke and mining concessions in Brunei 1888-1924.**
*See* item no. 218.

# Flora and Fauna

94  **An annotated checklist of Brunei butterflies, including a new species
of the genus Catapaecilma (Lycaenidae).**
Alan C. Cassidy.  *Brunei Museum Journal*, vol. 5, no. 2 (1982),
p. 202-72. map.
During the period 1978 to 1981 several expeditions were mounted in Brunei with
the aim to study the country's moths and butterflies. The sites where insects were
captured ranged in altitude from sea-level to 5,500 feet up on the Pagon Ridge.
This paper includes an identification list of all butterflies collected during the
expeditions, those available in the Brunei Museum collection and some species
collected by other individuals in Brunei.

95  **An annotated checklist of the birds of Borneo.**
Bertram E. Smythies.  *Sarawak Museum Journal*, new series,
vol. 7, no. 9 (1957), p. 523-818. map. bibliog.
This issue of the *Sarawak Museum Journal*, entirely devoted to the subject of
Bornean birds, comprises a large body of information derived from a series of
expeditions and from literature. This considerable undertaking was supported by
the governments of all three territories – North Borneo, Brunei and Sarawak.
The annotated checklist starts with a survey of the literature and a list of museums
housing important collections of Bornean birds. The annotations of each species
include scientific identification, geographical distribution, the location of the
specimen and references to the literature.

96  **The application of quantitative methods of vegetation survey. III: a
re-examination of rain forest data from Brunei.**
M. P. Austin, P. S. Ashton, P. Greig-Smith.  *Journal of Ecology*,
vol. 60 (1972), p. 305-24. bibliog.
Vegetation and soil data from two rainforest sites in Brunei have been subjected
to principal component analysis and optimal agglomeration analysis using single

27

cycle fusions. The results confirm that variation within this rainforest is more related to soil gradient than to chance or opportunity in the establishment of species.

97   **The birds of Borneo.**
      Bertram E. Smythies.   Edinburgh, London: Oliver & Boyd, 1968.
      2nd ed. 593p. map. bibliog.
An authoritative reference work on 549 species of Bornean birds, many of which can be found throughout Brunei. The first part of this work is devoted to man and his relationship with birds. In the words of the author 'there is probably no other part of the world where birds and men are more intimately intermixed than in Borneo'. The author's discussion mentions the obvious connections, such as: decorative feathers; the Imperial Pigeon; the use of the nest of the swiftlets as food; the use of the Rhinoceros Hornbill in woodcarving; body tattoo themes; and birds as pets. More significantly, however, birds are interwoven into the whole texture of thought and belief. They play a large part in mythology, such as in the cults of birdmen and shamans. One chapter is devoted to augural birds of the Iban. The second half of this book concentrates on the identification of birds by their distribution, ecology, habitat and behaviour, race and sub-species, food requirements and voice. The inclusion of 51 colourplates and 50 black-and-white photographs have added both to the value and usefulness of this volume.

98   **Conservation in Brunei.**
      Russell A. Mittermeier.   *Brunei Museum Journal*, vol. 4, no. 4
      (1980), p. 251-61. 2 maps.
Although Brunei does not, as yet, have any national parks or sanctuaries, an important Wild Life Protection Enactment was passed in 1978. This Act empowers the Sultan to establish wildlife sanctuaries by decree and to publish a list of protected species that cannot be hunted or exported. Other conditions for successful conservation are discussed in this article, such as the prohibition of guns since 1962, the fact that the Muslim population does not hunt or consume monkeys or wild pigs, and a lack of large-scale timber exploitation which would destroy wildlife habitats. Several potential sites for national parks are recommended and a list of species officially protected since 1978 is included.

99   **Distribution of recent benthonic foraminifera in the 'inner' Brunei
      Bay.**
      Ho Kiam Fui.   *Brunei Museum Journal*, vol. 2, no. 3 (1971),
      p. 124-37. 6 maps.
The benthonic foraminifera represent a group of Protozoans found on the sea floor. This study is part of a project carried out by Brunei Shell to investigate recent deposition in the coastal and offshore areas of Brunei. It establishes the distribution of recent benthonic foraminifera in the 'inner' Brunei Bay area, and their relationship with the environments in which they occur.

100 **Ecological studies in the Kerangas forests of Sarawak and Brunei.**
E. F. Brunig.   Kuching, Sarawak: Borneo Literature Bureau for
Sarawak Forest Departments, 1974. 237p. 6 maps. bibliog.

This study of lowland tropical forests contains: an inventory of the Kerangas flora;
a survey of soil conditions, and the composition and structure of the forest; and
an investigation of their ecology in relation to other forest communities.
'Kerangas' is a word in the Iban language; it describes dryland sites in the lowland
and submontane zones which, due to their soil condition, are unsuitable for
growing rice. This work includes numerous illustrations and tables, together with
an extensive bibliography.

101 **Ecological studies in the mixed Dipterocarp forests of Brunei State.**
P. S. Ashton.   Oxford: Clarendon Press, 1964. 74p. 25 maps.
bibliog. (Oxford Forestry Memoirs, no. 25).

The Dipterocarpaceae, or Kaum Damar, are the principal family of timber trees
in Brunei. In view of the important implications for forest management and
exploitation, quantitative studies into floristic and structural variation in mixed
Dipterocarp forests have been carried out. This report describes the methods and
results of these investigations. The first chapter outlines the variations in climate,
soil and geology. Later chapters discuss the vegetation in relation to these
environmental variations. Numerous photographs and a lengthy (unpaginated)
appendix are included.

102 **An enlarged checklist of Brunei butterflies (Lepidoptera: rhopa-
locera) including descriptions of one new species and two new
subspecies.**
Alan C. Cassidy.   *Brunei Museum Journal*, vol. 6, no. 1 (1985),
p. 135-68. bibliog.

This checklist of butterflies in Brunei is an expanded and updated version of one
produced by the author in 1982 (see *BMJ*, vol. 5, no. 2, p. 202-72). Additional
new taxa from recent captures are analysed, including *Halpe clara*, *Amathusia
utana aglaza* and *Deramas jasoda herdji*. The aim of this list, like his previous
one, is to provide a taxonomic baseline for the ecological study of Brunei's
butterfly fauna.

103 **An expedition to Mt. Batu Lawi, an hitherto unexplored mountain
in northern Sarawak.**
J. C. Moulton.   *Journal of the Straits Branch of the Royal Asiatic
Society*, vol. 63 (1912), p. 1-104. map.

A daily notebook (from 2 May to 17 June 1911) of an arduous expedition into the
interior of what is today essentially Brunei territory. The journey consisted of a
loop starting at the Limbang River and returning via the Baram River. Nine
appendixes provide information on plants, birds and insects. Examples of native
vocabulary were also collected during the expedition, primarily from the Tabun,
Murut and Kalabit tribes. Frequent references are made to Spenser Buckingham
St. John who made a similar journey which is recorded in *Life in the forests of the
Far East* (q.v.).

## Flora and Fauna

104 **Hand-list of the birds of Borneo**
J. C. Moulton. *Journal of the Straits Branch of the Royal Asiatic Society*, vol. 67 (1914), p. 125-91. bibliog.

This compilation of Bornean birds consists of (a) the evolution of nomenclature and record-keeping of birds in the region, (b) a list of 555 species compiled from those of 43 different authors, and (c) bibliographical references to all papers devoted to Bornean avifauna. Each record contains the name of the sub-specie, the person who first collected each sub-specie with the date of capture, the author who first recorded it from Borneo and the date of the published record.

105 **Mammals from Borneo.**
Edward Banks. *Brunei Museum Journal*, vol. 4, no. 2 (1978), p. 165-241.

A general treatment of mammals which inhabit the tropical rainforest of Borneo. The first nine pages describe the rainforest environment for monkeys, cats, deer, squirrels and tree-shrews. The remaining section of the paper consists of a descriptive list of forty-five mammals. A coloured drawing of every animal is included.

106 **Manual of Dipterocarp trees of Brunei State.**
P. S. Ashton. London: Oxford University Press, 1964. 242p. map. bibliog.

Brunei's forests are potentially her most permanent natural asset. In order to develop a plan for efficient exploitation and regeneration, however, an inventory of the forest must first be completed. This book provides an answer to this need. The author describes 154 different trees in the Dipterocarp (Kaum Damar) family, that are found in Brunei, how to recognize them, their abundance and where they grow. This manual is the result of 3 years of field-work (1957-60), and contains many excellent photographs and line-drawings of plant details. A glossary to botanical terms is included for the benefit of foresters.

107 **Notes on the order Mantodea with reference to Brunei.**
Erika Birkenmeier. *Brunei Museum Journal*, vol. 1, no. 1 (1969), p. 225-33.

Provides a great deal of background information on the Mantodea (large, elongated, rather slow-moving insects that are striking in appearance due to their peculiarly modified front legs) in general, such as its global distribution, morphological structure and ecological requirements. A preliminary appraisal of the order Mantodea in Brunei, based on several available collections in Borneo, concludes this article.

108 **Notes on the vegetation at a variety of habitats in Brunei.**
B. C. St. G. Allen. *Brunei Museum Journal*, vol. 5, no. 3 (1983), p. 200-21. bibliog.

In this article, the author presents a broad classification of forest types, ranging from the coast to the highlands of Brunei, based on field observations. Differences in the environmental processes in lowland heath, hill Dipterocarp and montane forests clearly emerge when these habitats are related to each other. The effects of differences in altitude are particularly apparent in the weathering and leaching of the soil. Increased accumulation of organic matter and the occurrence of moss species are examples of this pattern.

109   **Observations of birds in Brunei.**
Anthony P. Smith.   *Sarawak Museum Journal*, new series, vol. 25, no. 46 (1977), p. 235-69.

A list of birds compiled from individual records kept by several people from 1970 to 1975. It is, however, not as comprehensive as that of Bertram E. Smythies, *The birds of Borneo* (q.v.), because no extensive visits into the jungle were made. The information mentioned in this list includes reference numbers from *Birds of Borneo*, English and Latin names, size, common habitat and sighting details.

110   **Observations on *Amantis reticulata* (Haan) in Brunei (Dictyoptera-Mantidae).**
Erika Birkenmeier.   *Brunei Museum Journal*, vol. 2, no. 3 (1971), p. 147-59.

The *Amantis reticulata* is a very active and certainly one of the smallest types of mantid in Brunei. Over a period of 4 years, 100 specimens (larvae and adult insects) have been used for collecting data on colouration, measurements, larval growth, annual distribution and behaviour. A number of enlarged drawings are included.

111   **Observations on the habit of the Proboscis monkey, *Nasalis larvatus* (Wurmb), made in the Brunei Bay area, Borneo.**
James A. Kern.   *Zoologica*, vol. 46, no. 11 (1964), p. 183-92. map. bibliog.

The habitat, population, density, movement, feeding behaviour and other activities of the Proboscis monkey are described. In all of Borneo, except Brunei, the species is legally protected.

112   **Potential tree species for Negara Brunei Darussalam.**
Brunei Ministry of Development.   Bandar Seri Begawan: Ministry of Development, Town and Country Planning Department, 1985. 65p.

A report of forty tree species which focuses on the botanical origin, the habit of growth and the economic value of each plant. Botanical and common names for each species are included, together with numerous colour illustrations.

113   **A preliminary survey of the Ophioninae (Hymenoptera, Ichneumonidae) of Brunei.**
Ian D. Gauld.   *Brunei Museum Journal*, vol. 6, no. 1 (1985), p. 169-88. bibliog.

The Ophioninae (nocturnal winged insects) known to occur in Brunei are identified and discussed in relation to Bornean fauna in general. A total of 44

31

**Flora and Fauna**

Ophioninae species are believed to exist in Brunei. The affinities between these and other Ophioninae fauna on other Southeast Asian islands are briefly discussed. Notes are included on apparent seasonal and altitudinal faunal variations and differences in the sex ratio of species at different altitudes. Five new species of *Enicospilus* are described and placed within the currently recognized taxonomic framework.

114   **The recording of bird song in Brunei.**
       T. C. White, J. R. Neighbour.   *Brunei Museum Journal*, vol. 5,
       no. 1 (1981), p. 127-46. bibliog.
The results of a recording expedition of bird-songs and calls in the lowland forest areas of Brunei. The author discusses the equipment and techniques used and some of the problems faced in recording the language of twenty-six different birds. A list of known recordings of birds from Bernard E. Smythies' *Birds of Borneo* (1960 ed.) is appended.

115   **Settlement and growth of the oyster '*Saccostrea cucullata*' in Brunei waters.**
       David J. Currie.   *Brunei Museum Journal*, vol. 4, no. 3 (1979),
       p. 182-98.
Investigations into the establishment of an oyster culture were carried out in 1977-78 as part of a programme to assess the potential for marine aquaculture in Brunei. Research included collecting information on methods of oyster-growing from different regions in the world, gathering local meteorological data, testing different kinds of collectors, selecting suitable areas for the settlement of oysters in Brunei Bay, and recording growth rates from spat that had settled on collectors at different times over the one-year test period.

116   **Some freshwater aquarium fish of Brunei.**
       Sharon Eden.   *Brunei Museum Journal*, vol. 5, no. 4 (1984),
       p. 181-202.
A great variety of small aquarium fish may be found in the rivers and streams of Brunei. The fish described and illustrated in this article were collected in the Labi, Anduki and Kuala Belait areas. This represents a useful guide to tropical fish for aquarists around the world. Twenty-two colour plates are included.

117   **Some notes on the birds of Brunei.**
       Eric Kidd.   *Brunei Museum Journal*, vol. 4, no. 2 (1978),
       p. 115-64. bibliog.
The purpose of this paper is to record the occurrence of Brunei birds (78 species) and attempt to put this information in the context of what is currently known about their status in Borneo as a whole. The emphasis is on birds of prey and those species which could be easily observed by car and boat. Birds of the interior forest environments are excluded. An annotated list of species seen by the author during his two and a half years of work in Brunei is included in the appendix.

118  A study of lowland rainforest birds in Brunei.
     Eric Kidd, Richard Beales.  *Brunei Museum Journal*, vol. 4, no. 1
     (1977), p. 197-225. map. bibliog.
Presents the results of field observations on birds in a forest area which is 18 miles
from Bandar Seri Begawan. The study was carried out from December 1975 to
December 1976 and resulted in the production of an annotated list of 113
identified species. The difficulties encountered in doing field-work in a forest
habitat are also described.

119  The Ulu Temburong expedition of 1978.
     M. G. Allen.  *Brunei Museum Journal*, vol. 4, no. 3 (1979),
     p. 107-81.
The Temburong region in Brunei is an area of largely untouched primary forest
ranging from the 6,000 feet Bukit Pagon Ridge to mangrove swamps along the
coast. A wide range of fauna and flora can be found in this region which has never
been studied in any detail, making it a most suitable environment for scientific
exploration. In 1978 a fully integrated expedition was launched involving the
Muzium Brunei (the Brunei Museum), British scientists from Harewood and the
Tenth Gurkha Rifles Company. The military not only used the expedition as a
training exercise for soldiers, but also provided life support for the base camp.
During this four-week expedition scientists in their chosen fields made observations which were published as the following papers: S. L. Sutton, 'The climate of
the Ulu Temburong' (p. 109-12); Tony Harman, 'Bukit Retak camp. 1450 meters'
(p. 113-18); John Patchett, 'Exploring the Pagon Ridge' (p. 119-21); Tony
Harman, 'Catching, preserving and transporting Lepidoptera in tropical rain
forests' (p. 122-31); Peter Brown, 'Observations of birds during the expedition
period, 29 September-4 November, 1978' (p. 132-55); S. L. Sutton, 'A portable
light trap for studying insects of the upper canopy' (p. 156-60); S. L. Sutton, 'The
vertical distribution of flying insects in the lowland rain forest of Brunei: preliminary report' (p. 161-70); Peter Brown, 'Mammals observed in Brunei' (p. 174-79);
and C. A. Ussher, 'Brunei's largest snake' (p. 180-81).

120  The vertical distribution of flying insects in lowland rain-forests of
     Panama, Papua New Guinea and Brunei.
     S. L. Sutton, C. P. J. Ash, A. Grundy.  *Zoological Journal of the
     Linnean Society*, vol. 78, (1983), p. 287-97. bibliog.
Ultraviolet light traps were set up at four vertical levels to monitor the
distribution of insects in the rainforests of three countries, including two sites in
Brunei. The forest comprised undisturbed mixed Dipterocarp in the Ulu
Temburong region of Brunei. The sampling method and the analysis used is
described by toxonomic order. The authors conclude that flying insects in tropical
forests are not always concentrated in the upper canopy, although there is a
tendency for this to occur where a simple topography and forest structure exist.

## Flora and Fauna

121 **Wanderings in the great forests of Borneo.**
Odoardo Beccari. Singapore, Oxford, New York: Oxford
University Press, 1986. 423p. bibliog. (Oxford in Asia Hardback
Reprints).
Beccari offers an intriguing picture of the natural and human conditions of
Sarawak, Labuan, Brunei and North Borneo at the close of the James Brooke
era. Seen through the eyes of a dedicated botanist, the observations made on the
land and the people are closely linked to the philosophy of environmental
determinism. Chapter 17, for example, reports on how the offshore islands, the
bay and the river shape Malay-Brunei values and existence in the mid-1800s
(p. 242-55). Above all, the book stands out as a vivid record of the diverse
tropical fauna and flora of the area, and is considered today to be of enduring
biological value. The work was translated from the Italian edition, entitled *Nelle
foreste di Borneo* and it is reprinted here from the 1904 English translation,
published by Archibald Constable & Co., London.

**Tropical rainforests of the Far East.**
*See* item no. 37.

**Forest trees of Sarawak and Brunei and their products.**
*See* item no. 434.

# Archaeology and Prehistory

122 **Ancient glass beads from Brunei and Sarawak excavations (compared).**
Thomas H. Harrisson. *Brunei Museum Journal*, vol. 3, no. 1 (1973), p. 118-26. bibliog.
Glass beads are among the few durable products of prehistoric human activity which can survive in tropical conditions as markers of the past. However, because of the small size of these beads, the limited use of pattern, standardization in bead-making, and similarity in style and decoration, identification has become a difficult task to perform. Consequently, the comparison and classification of beads in this study are primarily based on colour. The occurrence of both blue beads and white beads is conspicuously strong at two Brunei sites. Although one type covers a greater time-span, the other, which covers a relatively short period, is of a later date. The extent to which these apparent differences reflect variations in regional taste or trade routes remains to be confirmed and, moreover, scientifically tested.

123 **Archaeological excavations in protohistoric Brunei.**
Matussin bin Omar. Bandar Seri Begawan: Muzium Brunei, 1981. 116p. maps. bibliog. (Penerbitan Khas, Muzium Brunei, bil. 15 [Brunei Museum, Special Publication, no. 15]).
Discusses the results of excavations at two sites approximately three miles outside the capital, Bandar Seri Begawan. The emphasis is on locally produced earthenware pottery and ceramics imported from the 10th to the 17th centuries. A hypothesis is presented which advocates contact through trade with China and Thailand. The artefacts found during the field excavations remain in the Brunei Museum.

124 **Borneo.**
Wilhelm G. Solheim, II. *Asian Perspectives*, vol. 1, nos. 1-2
(summer 1957), p. 93-100. bibliog.

An overview of archaeological work carried out in Sarawak and Brunei during the
period 1949 to 1957, with an accompanying four-page bibliography. All
information included in this article was provided by Thomas H. Harrisson, who
directed the field-work and who has since published extensively on this subject
area. This article is, therefore, principally of historical interest.

125 **Brown spouted jars, a facet of ceramic history, in [sic] Brunei view.**
Barbara V. Harrisson. *Brunei Museum Journal,* vol. 3, no. 3 (1975),
p. 186-200. bibliog.

The only other ceramic collection comparable in composition and variety, though
not in quality, to that of Sarawak, is now housed in the Brunei Museum. This
study attempts to interpret a large collection of artefacts, with special emphasis on
seven specimens of spouted jars. Judging from the quantity of imported ceramics
now available from archaeological sites and from native possessions, the value of
ceramic trade between the Asian mainland and Brunei Bay must have constituted
a significant source of income for the Sultanate when it assumed early heights in
prosperity and power.

126 **Brunei, Sarawak and the Kota Batu lands 1903-1917.**
A. V. M. Horton. *Brunei Museum Journal*, vol. 6, no. 1 (1985),
p. 62-74. bibliog.

In 1903 Sir Charles Brooke, second Rajah of Sarawak (1868-1917), acquired an
estate of 3,500 acres at Kota Batu, stretching from the old consulate site of Brunei
Town for some three miles down the left bank of the Brunei River. This
acquisition was followed by a stormy controversy between Brunei and Sarawak
and is the subject of this paper. The land was returned to Brunei after the
departure of the British Consul Hewett. Kota Batu has remained of importance to
the Brunei people because it is the site of the tombs of early sultans, including
that of Sultan Bolkiah I. These leaders symbolically represent the 16th-century
'golden age' of the Bruneian empire. In the 1950s moreover, archaeologists
uncovered evidence which suggests that Kota Batu may have been the site of
Brunei's ancient capital. By 1970 the Brunei government had bought 36 acres at
Kota Batu for the purpose of preparing the site for the Brunei Museum. See also
Thomas Harrisson's 'First radio-carbon dates from Kota Batu, Brunei and
associated dating problems in Borneo' (q.v.).

127 **A classification of archaeological trade ceramics from Kota Batu,
Brunei.**
Barbara V. Harrisson. *Brunei Museum Journal*, vol. 2, no. 1
(1970), p. 114-88. bibliog.

Identifies the Kota Batu site and summarizes its historical significance. The author
states that, 'Kota Batu existed for roughly 1000 years, from the 7th century of the
early T'ang Dynasty . . . to the middle of the 17th century when Asian trade links
were disrupted through the arrival of the Europeans in the area who brought in
their wake political instability, bloody wars and eventual decline.' Of the 6,230

sherds (broken pieces of an earthen vessel) excavated, no complete vessel was found and only a few could be reconstructed to their full outline. The sherds are classified into seven basic types and a detailed description of each is given. Many plates are included.

128  **Deep level carbon dates from Kota Batu, Brunei (95 BC to 1300 AD).**
Thomas H. Harrisson.  *Brunei Museum Journal*, vol. 2, no. 3 (1971), p. 96-107. bibliog.
Harrisson presents findings made in 1970 from artefacts which were submitted to the Geochrom Laboratories in Cambridge, Massachusetts for dating. Since these samples were taken from relatively undisturbed sites at depths ranging from thirty to ninety feet, dates go as far back as 95 BC. Kota Batu is seen as unique in Southeast Asia, in terms of having a cultural continuity covering a period of no less than seven centuries. Many other significant Iron-Age sites cover a span of two to three centuries only, according to the author. Eight tables are included.

129  **Distributions of Chinese and Siamese ceramics in Brunei.**
Metussin Omar, P. M. Shariffuddin.  *Brunei Museum Journal*, vol. 4, no. 2 (1978), p. 59-66. bibliog.
Historical and archaeological evidence suggest that direct trading contact between Brunei and China began during the Sung period (AD 960-1279) and was well established by the 13th century. Chinese traders also made contact with Siamese (Thai) merchants and, consequently, Siamese ceramics reached Brunei indirectly. This paper describes several archaeological sites which contain Chinese and Siamese ceramics in central and eastern Brunei to show the extent of economic relations between Brunei, China and Thailand.

130  **European trade ceramics in the Brunei Museum.**
Barbara V. Harrisson.  *Brunei Museum Journal*, vol. 3, no. 1 (1973), p. 66-87. bibliog.
The ceramic collection in the Brunei Museum consists of tableware used and traded in Borneo from the early centuries of the Christian era to the present. The 127 pieces were acquired between 1963 and 1971, exclusively from Brunei owners. The description in this article focuses on the origin by country, chronological history and forms of each piece. Several pages are devoted to the identification of trademarks and decorations using available literature on the subject. The museum also has a collection from the oriental classical period which is described in one of the guides to the museum's ceramic gallery (see item no. 608).

131  **First radio-carbon dates from Kota Batu, Brunei and associated dating problems in Borneo.**
Thomas H. Harrisson.  *Brunei Museum Journal*, vol. 2, no. 1 (1970), p. 188-97. bibliog.
This paper reports on a set of dates determined by the radio-carbon (c-14) method on charcoal remains found in 1953 at 25-feet depths at Kota Batu, a former capital of Brunei. The dates range from 1300 to 1815.

132   **Kota Batu in Brunei (introductory report).**
Barbara V. Harrisson, Thomas H. Harrisson.   *Sarawak Museum Journal*, new series, vol. 7, no. 8 (1956), p. 283-319. map.

This report describes a small fraction of the planned full-scale excavation of the Kota Batu site. Part I provides a background of Kota Batu based on folklore and preliminary excavations. Part II analyses the materials found so far at the site – coins, glass, metal, pottery, charcoal and bones.

133   **Marks on Chinese ceramics excavated in Brunei and Sarawak.**
John Pope.   *Sarawak Museum Journal*, new series, vol. 8, no. 11 (1958), p. 267-72.

Provides an analysis of fragments of Chinese porcelain bowls. Pope states that marks found on four ceramic Ming pieces excavated in Brunei show Chinese characters corresponding to the words Kota Batu.

134   **The Ming Gap and Kota Batu, Brunei (with an appeal for help).**
Thomas H. Harrison.   *Sarawak Museum Journal*, new series, vol. 8, no. 11 (1958), p. 273-77.

The Ming Gap refers to the total absence of objects from the Ming Dynasty along the entire coast of Sarawak. Kota Batu is probably the only and richest Ming site north of Sarawak, on Brunei Bay. The author presents several explanations for this situation using the evidence gathered up to the late 1950s.

135   **The Minutti collection of bronzes in Brunei.**
Thomas H. Harrisson.   Bandar Seri Begawan: Muzium Brunei, 1973. 34p.

Describes a rare collection of twenty-six antique bronze vessels from China's Chou, Han, T'ang and Ming dynasties. The collector Mr. R. Minutti, presented all twenty-six pieces as a gift to the Brunei Museum, where they are permanently displayed. Each piece is illustrated here with black-and-white photographs.

136   **A note on the stone wall and earthen causeway at Kota Batu.**
Metussin Omar.   *Brunei Museum Journal*, vol. 5, no. 3 (1983), p. 27-50. map. bibliog.

Much archaeological research has been carried out in Brunei since the early 1950s in an attempt to locate the probable site of the ancient town of Kota Batu. This paper provides a preliminary record of a stone wall at Kota Batu, in an effort to reconstruct the landscape of Brunei's 16th-century capital, Brunei Town. Other evidence, such as pottery remains, is mentioned in connection with these excavations.

137 **Palaeolithic (Stone Age) studies in Borneo and adjacent islands.**
Thomas H. Harrisson. *Brunei Museum Journal*, vol. 3, no. 2
(1974), p. 235-52. bibliog.
After 20 years of field-work Harrisson has surveyed prehistoric evidence for the
whole of the island of Borneo, recognizing the existence of inter-island and
mainland relationships at some point in the past. The sources used are Dutch and
Asian publications, various collections of stone tools and bones from Sarawak and
Sabah, and fossil teeth and tektites from Brunei. Yet, according to the author, for
Borneo and to some degree other islands, archaeologically accepted data is
meagre in quantity and generally poor in quality prior to about 400,000 years BC.

138 **Prehistoric glass analyses for Brunei.**
Thomas H. Harrisson. *Brunei Museum Journal*, vol. 3, no. 2
(1974), p. 232-34.
In 1967 a selected series of glass beads, bangles and vessels excavated during the
past twenty years in Sarawak and Brunei were submitted to the Corning Glass
Museum, in New York, for analysis. The objective of this exercise was to measure
the extent to which Brunei glass from the site of Kota Batu was the same or
different from that of other sites. The results have demonstrated that most of the
glass imported to Brunei arrived at least 1,000 years ago and did not originate in
China. Yet, the porcelain stoneware found side-by-side with the glass at the same
excavation proved to be Chinese, Indo-Chinese or Thai. This suggests a pattern of
glass trade from somewhere west of India which then merged with the China
trade as it entered Borneo.

139 **The prehistory of Borneo.**
Thomas H. Harrisson. *Asian Perspectives*, vol. 13 (1970),
p. 17-45. bibliog.
A summary report covering the prehistory of all of Borneo, although the coverage
is uneven. It is primarily concerned with Sarawak and Brunei with less data
presented on Sabah and Kalimantan. The first half of the paper presents a history
of archaeological research in Malaysia, Borneo and Brunei, and provides an
explanation of the use of local folklore and genealogies in reconstructing the
prehistory of the area. The second half consists of short descriptions of the major
findings, divided into several archaeological periods: 'early Stone Age', the
'advent of iron', 'Islam and Ming' and 'the European order'.

140 **Prehistory of the Indo-Malaysian Archipelago.**
Peter Bellwood. Sydney; Orlando, Florida: Academic Press,
1985. 370p. 26 maps. bibliog.
Presents a multidisciplinary reconstruction of the prehistory of Indonesia,
Malaysia and Brunei. Since modern boundaries have little meaning in this study
of the remote past the region is referred to as the Indo-Malaysian Archipelago.
Several interlinked aspects of prehistory are reviewed, mainly from data produced
by the discipline of biological anthropology, linguistics and archaeology. The
overall time-span involved runs from two million years ago to approximately

**Archaeology and Prehistory**

AD 1000. In general, the book ceases with the historical civilizations of the first millennium AD, although in some remote regions prehistory continues almost to this day.

141  **A preliminary account of surface finds from Tanjong Batu beach, Muara.**
Metussin Omar.  *Brunei Museum Journal*, vol. 3, no. 3 (1975), p. 158-74. 2 maps. bibliog.

The first report on archaeological discoveries made at Tanjong Batu beach on the coast of Brunei. It describes the rock and soil conditions of the site, the collection of 193 sherds and the significance of Tanjong Batu in relation to other sites. Indications are that Tanjong Batu has a much earlier history than Kota Batu and was part of a trading network with other sites in northern Borneo during the Sung period (AD 1127-1279).

142  **Pusaka, heirloom jars of Borneo.**
Barbara V. Harrisson.  Singapore: Oxford University Press, 1986. 55p. 2 maps. bibliog.

In the past, large ceramic jars have been traded from the Asian mainland in exchange for food and jungle products. In Borneo they have been passed down through generations as traditional heirlooms along with other antiques. This book focuses on three aspects of the Borneo experience with respect to jars, each one concerned with a different time period. In the first part, potters who currently make jars were interviewed and observed at work. This permitted the tracing of their Chinese origin, their production techniques and the verification of their ability to reproduce jars faithfully, a skill which has prevailed on the island since long before 1900. Secondly, the extrinsic aspects of heirloom jars were examined through the literature. Legends, beliefs, and customary law reveal how the social and economic interests of individuals were intertwined with the possession of heirloom jars. The third aspect is provided by a large sample of jar fragments excavated in Brunei which had been an extrepôt in the 15th and 16th centuries. Modern methods of sherd analysis have enabled the identification of types of jars traded in Brunei up until 1578 when the settlement excavated was destroyed. The 55-page text is supplemented by 32 coloured plates and 164 black-and-white drawings and photographs. This work is based on the author's PhD thesis (q.v.).

143  **Pusaka, heirloom jars of Borneo.**
Barbara V. Harrisson.  PhD thesis. Ithaca, New York: Cornell University, 1984. 166 leaves. map.

In this thesis, Harrisson examines Bornean heirloom jars through the literature. Archaeological fragments from a Brunei site, at a time when jars from Thailand were the most common imports, are also mentioned. A diversity of jars, as preserved in Brunei and Sabah collections are described, ranging in date from the 9th to the 20th century. Approximate origins for several classes of jars from China, Vietnam, Thailand and Borneo are also proposed.

144 **Radio carbon ages from quaternary terraces – prehistory in Brunei.**
R. B. Tate. *Brunei Museum Journal*, vol. 2, no. 3 (1971),
p. 108-23. 2 maps. bibliog.
Wood and coal collected from quaternary sediments have been dated by the
radio-carbon method in an attempt to correlate ancient marine terraces near the
Brunei coast. The results are discussed in relation to eustatic changes in sea-level
and crustal movement. The quaternary sediments were discovered during recent
excavations for the construction of Brunei's International Airport.

145 **Recent archaeological discoveries in East Malaysia and Brunei.**
Thomas H. Harrisson. *Journal of the Malaysian Branch of the
Royal Asiatic Society,* vol. 40, part 1 (1967), p. 140-48.
Presents a progress report on archaeological excavations during 1966 at various
cave sites in Sarawak and Sabah. In that year not only had the temporary museum
in Brunei received new important collections, but also site protection had been
granted for archaeological digs in the area.

146 **The Stone Age in Brunei.**
Metussin Omar, P. M. Shariffuddin. *Brunei Museum Journal,*
vol. 3, no. 4 (1976), p. 127-41. map. bibliog.
This analysis details the findings of stone implements at Tanjong Batu beach in
1974, suggesting the presence of Stone-Age people in Brunei. The morphology,
type of rock and function of various Neolithic adzes are described. Now that
evidence of Neolithic Brunei has been discovered the authors hope that evidence
of the preceding periods, namely Palaeolithic and Mesolithic, can be brought to
light in future explorations.

147 **Sungei Lumut: a 15th century burial ground.**
Barbara V. Harrisson, P. M. Shariffuddin. *Brunei Museum
Journal*, vol. 1, no. 1 (1969), p. 24-56. bibliog.
A detailed report on material recovered from a probable 15th-century burial site
at Sungei Lumut, some 50 miles west of Bandar Seri Begawan. The important
wares, totalling 1,477 sherds, were reconstructed into 53 original vessels. Dating
was accomplished on the basis of the presence of Sawankhalok wares and certain
early Ming wares. No human remains have survived at the site. The colour
frequency pattern of beads found at Lumut is very similar to that of Kota Batu,
but distinct from that of older Sarawak sites. The burial assemblage suggests
pagan rather than Moslem practices at Lumut sometime after the nearby capital
of Brunei became a stronghold of Islam. Numerous plates are included.

**Some problems of getting materials for the Brunei Museum.**
*See* item no. 615.

**Archaeology and Prehistory**

**Malaysian studies: archaeology, historiography, geography and bibliography.**
*See* item no. 651.

**Prehistory and archaeology of Malaysia and Brunei: a bibliography.**
*See* item no. 655.

# History

## General

148 **Brunei: a historical relic.**
Leigh R. Wright. *Journal of the Hong Kong Branch of the Royal Asiatic Society*, vol. 17 (1977), p. 12-29. bibliog.
Presents an accurate summary of the history of Brunei. Each period of history is evaluated on its own merit, frequently supported by quotes from the writings of Pigafetta, the Brookes and British government officials. The author brings together many factors which have brought about the political decline of the Sultanate and subsequent territorial acquisition by outsiders. It is argued that two events contributed to the salvation and revitalization of Brunei – the discovery of oil in commercial quantities in 1929 and the appointment, in 1906, of a British resident advisor to help the Sultan manage his affairs.

149 **Brunei: past and present.**
S. J. Fulton. *Asian Affairs* (London), vol. 15 (1984), p. 5-14.
A most readable account which summarizes the economic and political history of Brunei. The essay reflects topics in which this former Commissioner-General of the United Kingdom in Southeast Asia was interested in: pre-European government, succession of the Sultanate, treatise between Great Britain and Brunei, the 1962 revolt, the Gurkhas, and the importance of petroleum. This article is recommended to the unacquainted reader who is interested in a chronological history of the sultanate. See also Srikant Dutt's 'Brunei: the forgotten state of Southeast Asia' (*China Report* (India), vol. 17, no. 6 (1981), p. 33-41).

150  **Brunei, the structure and history of a Bornean Malay sultanate.**
D. E. Brown.  Kota Batu, Brunei: Brunei Museum, 1970. 235p.
maps. bibliog. (Brunei Museum Journal. Monograph Series,
vol. 2, no. 2).

Traces the history of socio-political change in Brunei. The process of social
change and continuity is revealed through ethnic groups, social classes and village
organizations. In addition, Brown takes into account 'units', such as technical
departments, commercial establishments and State Councils, of a Western-style
government. The author concludes that Brunei's social history appears to have
been largely determined by the conflict between the more traditional and the
imported structural units. This monograph represents a substantial contribution to
the social history of Brunei, and a valuable and comprehensive reference source
to students and specialists on the region. This work is based on the author's PhD
thesis, *Socio-political history of Brunei: a Bornean Malay Sultanate* (Cornell
University, Ithaca, New York, 1969).

151  **A gambling style of government: the establishment of Chartered
Company's rule in Sabah, 1878-1915.**
Ian Black.  Kuala Lumpur, New York: Oxford University Press,
1983. 254p. 3 maps. bibliog. (East Asia Historical Monographs).

The author has produced a valuable history of the early years of Company rule in
colonial Sabah. The narrative takes the reader through the Company's forty years
of experience in ruling a territory of multi-ethnic tribes. Accounts are also given
of the origin of the company and the acquisition of land by the US Consul in
Brunei, Charles Moses, and the American Trading Company in 1865. Although
Black only briefly examines the competition between Sabah and Sarawak over the
shrinking territory of Brunei at that time, he is to be commended for his diligent
research of colonial records and his interpretation of the Company's under-
financed and blundering style of administration.

152  **Malaysia, Singapore and Brunei, 1400-1965.**
Joginder Singh Jessy.  Singapore: Longman Malaysia, 1974.
2nd ed. 559p. 37 maps.

This volume completes a set of three books; the other two are entitled *History of
Southeast Asia* (1500-1945) and *From Empire to Commonwealth* (1740-1963). All
three books present a concise history of the Malay world in which Brunei played a
significant role for more than three centuries. Part IV of this volume, 'Under
British rule' (1873-1942) and Part V, 'Nationalism' (1942-1965), are particularly
relevant. Both parts cover the impact of the Brooke's period on Brunei, the origin
of the North Borneo Company and, later, the Brunei revolt of 1962 and the
Indonesian confrontation. These books were written to meet the requirements of
the general reader and for those preparing for the Cambridge Overseas School
Certificate examination.

153   **The postal history of Brunei, 1906-1937.**
      J. S. Lim.   *Brunei Museum Journal*, vol. 4, no. 1 (1977),
      p. 112-27.

Provides a brief history of the postal service in Brunei, covering the period 1906
to 1937. The year 1906 was used as a convenient starting point because it was then
that the British Resident System was introduced and the first Brunei Annual
Report was published. The article covers the following topics: the establishment
of the Post Office in the capital; the services offered by the Post Office; the
transportation of internal and overseas mail; the handling of mail; and the
revenues generated by postal activities. The progress and development of the
postal service during this period was very much influenced by economic growth in
Brunei.

154   **Problems of piracy in the Sultanates of Sulu and Brunei in the
      eighteenth and nineteenth centuries.**
      Zahir Giri Ahmad.   MA thesis, University of Hull, England,
      1978. 88 leaves. 2 maps. bibliog.

An assessment of the political and economic conflicts resulting from the practice
of piracy in the Brunei–Sulu region during the late 18th and early 19th centuries.
Both sultanates were similar in their social and political structure, but insular Sulu
was pressured by the Spaniards and, thus, developed a war-like régime. Coastal
Brunei, on the other hand, was an assembly of rivers controlled by a highly
stratified society. Within this context the thesis develops two themes: the role of
piracy as an institution and a source of revenue for the Sulu Sultanate; and the
role of Sino–Sulu trade, and piracy associated with the prosperity of the Malay
élite in Brunei.

155   **A sketch of the history of Brunei.**
      H. R. Hughes-Hallett.   *Brunei Museum Journal*, vol. 4, no. 1
      (1981), p. 1-18.

A chronological treatment of the history of Brunei from the earliest discoveries by
Asians and the 'golden age' of the Brunei kingdoms, to the arrival of the
Europeans. The rise and fall of successive rulers during the last two centuries is
emphasized. The references are drawn from official and local records of Sarawak
and British North Borneo. A chronological list of twenty-seven sultans of Brunei
is appended. (Reprinted from *Journal of the Malayan Branch of the Royal Asiatic
Society*, vol. 18, part 2 (1940), p. 23-42).

156   **Slave markets and exchange in the Malay world: the Sulu Sultanate
      1770-1878.**
      James F. Warren.   *Journal of Southeast Asian Studies*, vol. 8
      (1977), p. 162-75. 2 maps. bibliog.

The Sulu Sultanate was the centre of extensive raiding and slave trading activities,
concentrated at Jolo Island. This article looks at the internal demand for slaves,
the redistribution network, the principal markets and the factors which
determined the value of individual slaves. For example, if they were female,
young, healthy and Brunei Malay, they were sold without difficulty at higher than

average prices. Long-distance slave raiding became linked to commercial activities in the form of procuring trade commodities which affected not only Sulu but also Brunei, Mindanao and Molucca.

157  **The social structure of nineteenth century Brunei.**
D. E. Brown.  *Brunei Museum Journal*, vol. 1, no. 1 (1969), p. 166-79. bibliog.

Brunei's history goes back perhaps a thousand years and involved territory extending from present-day Sarawak to as far north as Manila. Between then and the 19th century, Brunei's domain was occupied in one way or another by the white rajahs of Sarawak and the British North Borneo Company. Europeans justified their encroachment by claiming that Brunei's government was decayed, intolerably corrupt and even tyrannical. These claims became axioms in descriptions of Brunei and probably prevented any attempt to produce a general and dispassionate account of Brunei's social organization. In this paper, the author makes an attempt to correct that deficiency. Setting theoretical problems aside, the description focuses on the ruling class and their view of the social order of the 19th-century Bornean empire.

158  **Southeast Asia, history and the present day.**
Moscow: 'Social Sciences Today' Editorial Board, USSR Academy of Sciences, 1982. 215p. bibliog. (Oriental Studies in the USSR, no. 6).

Soviet historians have, in the past two decades, written several books on Brunei. Some of the major works on the history and socio-economic development of Brunei are reviewed in the chapter entitled 'Malaysia, Singapore and Brunei' (p. 74-90).

159  **Sultan Mumin's will and related documents.**
D. E. Brown.  *Brunei Museum Journal*, vol. 3, no. 2 (1974), p. 156-70. 3 maps. bibliog.

The documents presented in this paper were brought together in the hope of throwing light on three problems. The first is concerned with the identity and participation of the members who composed the 'Constitution' of Brunei. A second problem is the extent to which Brunei administered its domain as a geographical entity rather than the 'personal' empire of the Sultan. The third problem is concerned with the authority of Sultan Abdul Mumin and a letter he wrote in 1881 in which he stated the disposition of his own property after his death. The letter which is generally called a 'will', is presented in both Jawi and English translations.

160  **The Sultanate of Brunei.**
Peter Bellwood.  *Hemisphere*, vol. 22, no. 11 (Nov. 1978), p. 18-23. map.

Recounts the archaeology, early history and efforts to preserve Brunei's past in the light of the establishment of a national museum at Kota Batu in 1970. Also mentioned are several archaeological sites which provided evidence that the cultural origin of the Brunei people goes back some four centuries before the introduction of the Islamic tradition.

**A concise history of Southeast Asia.**
*See* item no. 24.

**Borneo on maps of the 16th and 17th centuries.**
*See* item no. 48.

**Brunei, Sulu and Sabah: an analysis of rival claims.**
*See* item no. 190.

**The Lanun pirate states of Borneo: their relevance to Southeast Asian history.**
*See* item no. 205.

**Revolt in Borneo.**
*See* item no. 219.

**Silsilah Raja-Raja Berunai.** (Genealogy of Brunei's sultans.)
*See* item no. 257.

**The Chinese in Borneo 1942-1946.**
*See* item no. 264.

**Political history of Brunei.**
*See* item no. 310.

**History of Brunei for lower secondary schools.**
*See* item no. 479.

**Annual Report.**
*See* item no. 589.

# Pre-16th century

161 **Background to Philippine nationalism: the complex impacts of past influences from Brunei Bay and elsewhere.**
Thomas H. Harrisson. *Brunei Museum Journal*, vol. 2, no. 1 (1970), p. 209-37. bibliog.

Harrisson, a scholar resident in Borneo for more than two decades, attempts to establish the evolution of Philippine nationalism using the earliest available writings. He argues that piracy and the slave trade affected the influence of Islam and that Spain, using missionaries, achieved many local successes in spreading Christianity. As a result, Borneo, Sulu and Mindanao became a zone of conflict and rivalry for several centuries. Close association between the Philippines and

# History. Pre-16th century

the Muslim Sultanate of Brunei can be traced back well over a century before the appearance of Pigafetta's chronicles. However, since there is nothing in any of the early Western accounts to match Pigafetta's description of the year 1521, the author relies extensively on Pigafetta's text of Magellan's expedition. The author also admits that, as the quality of past evidence is open to suspicion, there must be some uncertainty regarding the conclusion drawn from these records. He concludes that more indepth research is required.

162 **Berunei in the Boxer Codex.**
John S. Carroll. *Journal of the Malaysian Branch of the Royal Asiatic Society,* vol. 55, part 2 (1982), p. 1-25. map. bibliog.
The Boxer Codex is a Spanish manuscript from the Philippines, of uncertain authorship, dated ca. 1590, which covers much of Asia. The author has translated the section relating to Berunai (Brunei), presenting details on royal customs, manners, crime and punishment, and religious practices. It closes with a commentary (p. 17-21) which attempts to corroborate these descriptions with other writings of Pigafetta, Hugh Low and Chinese records of that period.

163 **Brunei rediscovered: a survey of early times.**
Robert Nicholl. *Journal of Southeast Asian Studies,* vol. 14, no. 1 (March 1983), p. 32-45. bibliog. Also published in: *Brunei Museum Journal,* vol. 4, no. 4 (1980), p. 219-37. bibliog.
A scholarly interpretation of historical documents and travellers' accounts as they relate to the early history of Brunei up to the 16th century. Using sources taken from the archives of Goa, Lisbon, Macao and Seville, the author postulates that the advent of the Portuguese and the conversion of the royal family to Islam constitute the dividing line between mediaeval and modern history in Brunei. The earliest references to Brunei are those made by Arabic scholars in the mid-13th century. Accordingly, the reason for contact with Brunei was to promote the trade in camphor between China, Brunei and other parts of Southeast Asia. Various factors are mentioned which subsequently contributed to Brunei's expansion over neighbouring territories and their controlling of trade among islands in the Philippines. The Great Khan of China is mentioned for his unsuccessful attempt to capture Brunei territory for its abundance of gold and cowries. Towards the end of the 14th century, all of Brunei's former possessions became part of the Majapahit empire and control was reduced to its own heartland around Brunei Bay. In the early 15th century Brunei maharajas once more tried to reassemble their empire by seeking support from the Chinese. With the arrival of the Portuguese in the early 16th century Brunei had entered a third era of ascendency. Of the mediaeval history of Brunei, only fleeting glimpses can be caught, and the author concludes that its full exposition must await research by Chinese and Arabic scholars. This is a slightly revised version of a paper read at the Eighth Conference of the International Association of Historians of Asia at Kuala Lumpur, August 1980.

164 *Maragtas:* **the Datus from Borneo.**
Manuel L. Carreon. *Sarawak Museum Journal*, vol. 8, no. 10
(1957), p. 51-99. bibliog.
The *Maragtas* is a history of the first inhabitants (the Datus) on the island of
Panay in the Philippines. It describes the arrival of the Datus from Borneo, their
culture and settlements on Panay and their expansion to other regions of the
Philippines up to the arrival of the Spaniards. In this issue of the *Sarawak
Museum Journal* the entire text of the *Maragtas* has been translated into English
from the vernacular version written by Pedro A. Monteclaro in 1901. The
*Maragtas*, originally recorded in archaic script on bark, by word of mouth and in
chants, is not to be considered a true account but is, nevertheless, of great
importance as a source of information of great antiquity.

165 **Notes on some controversial issues in Brunei history.**
Robert Nicholl. *Archipel*, vol. 19 (1980), p. 25-41. map.
In his interpretation of old European and Chinese documents, the author
attempts to clarify several important, but unrelated, issues of early Brunei. For
example, he deals with the identification and possible location of P'o-ni (a rival
capital), other cities such as Muara and Kota Batu, and the question of how and
when Brunei embraced Islam. As with all Nicholl's writings, this investigation is
well articulated and researched.

166 **P'o-li in Borneo.**
Ronald Braddell. *Sarawak Museum Journal*, new series, vol. 5,
no. 1 (1949), p. 5-9.
Investigates the toponyms P'o-li and P'o-ni, referring to Borneo or Brunei, based
on early Chinese records. Accordingly, foreign intrusion into Borneo must have
begun, in all probability, at the beginning of the Christian era, if not before then.
The accounts of P'o-li in the histories of various Chinese dynasties are made with
reference to shipping routes throughout the South China sea used by such famous
voyagers as Ch'an Chun and Marco Polo in 1292.

167 **Pre-Western Brunei, Sarawak, and Sabah.**
James P. Ongkili. *Sarawak Museum Journal*, new series, vol. 20,
nos. 40-41 (1972), p. 1-20. bibliog.
Primarily a history of Brunei, the author skillfully traces the events of the pre-
Western period in order that the subsequent era of Western domination can be
placed in a clearer perspective. It is unfortunate that apart from the *Silsilah Raja-
Raja Berunai* (Genealogy of Brunei's sultans) (q.v.), the pre-European period is
conspicuous for the absence of indigenous historical sources, even though Brunei
is one of the oldest sultanates in the Malay world. The author, therefore, has no
other alternative but to look elsewhere for sources of Brunei's forgotten past. As
such, archaeological work from Kota Batu, Pigafetta's accounts and Chinese
sources are used to fill the gap.

168 **Spain and the island of Borneo. Translated by Gerard Lemountain.**
Frederick Blumentritt. *Brunei Museum Journal*, vol. 4, no. 1
(1977), p. 82-96.

Borneo exercised a very important influence on the Philippine Archipelago in the
16th century. Not only were the Muslim princes of Luzon in the Philippines
presumably natives of Borneo but also the Koran was introduced there from
Borneo. Borneo trading vessels called at all ports of the Philippines and thus a
long relationship between Spanish-controlled Manila, various Philippine sultanates and the Sultanate of Burney (Brunei) existed. That relationship is the subject
of this paper including: the conflicts, the domination, the dependency between
foreign powers and the sultanates of the region. These accounts were first
published in 1886 and since then a vast amount of new material has come to light.
This article, however, remains as a valuable source of information on the early
history of Brunei.

169 **Stories of first Brunei conquests on the Sarawak coast.**
A. E. Lawrence. *Sarawak Museum Journal*, vol. 1, no. 1
(Feb. 1911), p. 120-24.

These accounts of Brunei's conquest of the Milano coastal district were gathered
from natives at Mukah in Sarawak. According to these, Brunei's fleets, under the
auspices of Sultan. Alak Betatar, in about 1400, were ordered to raid Milano
settlements on the coast and the Igan River. This action was taken in response to
an attack on Tutong and Belait by Tugau, a powerful ruler of the Igan watershed.
Upon conquest, the chiefs of the region were allowed to rule their people as
dependents of Brunei on the condition that they acknowledge Alak Betatar as
their supreme ruler and pay him annual tribute. Later, when Brunei had become
a Muslim state the native Milano chiefs were replaced by *pengirans* from Brunei
who generally married into families of the chiefs. These stories, which originated
some 500 years ago, have never been recorded, but have been handed down by
word of mouth through the generations. Interwoven with fables and legends
about various heroes in their conquest the historical accuracy of these stories
remains uncertain.

170 **Traces of the origin of the Malay Kingdom of Borneo proper with
notices of its condition when first discovered by Europeans, and at
later periods.**
J. R. Logan. *Journal of the Indian Archipelago and Eastern Asia*,
vol. 2, no. 8 (Aug. 1848), p. 513-27.

A re-evaluation of the process of settlement and the period of the first Malayan
occupation of the portions of Borneo known as the Malay kingdom of Brune. The
author relies heavily on published histories, expeditions and missionaries'
accounts. For instance, the descriptions of the people, the town of Brune and the
commodities for which Brune was noted are all derived from the writings of
Thomas Forrest, Hugh Low, Pigafetta and Sir Stamford Raffles.

171 **Trade patterns and political developments in Brunei and adjacent areas, AD 700-1500.**
P. Bellwood, Matussim bin Omar. *Brunei Museum Journal*, vol. 4, no. 4 (1980), p. 155-79. map. bibliog.
Portuguese and Spanish accounts of the 16th century describe the Islamic Sultanate of Brunei as having developed a centralized trading pattern with China, Sarawak and the Philippines as early as AD 1000. Archaeological evidence of the activities described here comes from the sites of Kota Batu and Kupan in Brunei. Findings at these sites include Chinese ceramics and coins of the T'ang, Sung and Ming dynasties as well as locally made pots found in association with Chinese imports at sites in Malaya, Brunei and, possibly, Hong Kong. Four illustrations are included.

172 **Visit of the 'King of Brunei' to the Emperor Yung Lo of China: contemporary and ancient accounts.**
*Journal of the Malaysian Branch of the Royal Asiatic Society*, vol. 57, part 1, no. 246 (1984), p. 1-4.
An anecdote related to the visit of the King of Brunei (and 150 officials) to the Fukien Province in China in AD 1408. The King, unexpectedly, fell sick, however, and died in China. A royal burial ceremony followed. Several years later the new King of Brunei visited the mausoleum in Nanking to pay homage to the late ruler. This initiated a friendly relationship and a long history of diplomatic relations between China and Brunei. This article was published in the *People's Daily* (Beijin, 25 December 1983) and was translated by Su Cheng Yee, Su Translation Service, Kuala Lumpur.

# The 16th and 17th centuries: the Spanish and the Portuguese

173 **Aganduru Moriz' account of the Magellan expedition at Brunei.**
John S. Carroll. *Brunei Museum Journal*, vol. 6, no. 1 (1985), p. 54-61.
A translation of a narrative by Aganduru Moriz, an Augustinian priest describing Magellan's visit to Brunei in 1521. It is a very different account than that written by Pigafetta, who was a recorder on that expedition, or by Transylvanus, a German who interviewed survivors of the expedition when they returned to Spain.

174 **Antonio Pigafetta's account of Brunei in 1521.**
D. E. Brown. *Brunei Museum Journal*, vol. 3, no. 2 (1974), p. 171-79. bibliog.
Pigafetta was the recorder on Magellan's voyage around the world. Various portions of Pigafetta's eye-witness account of Brunei have been published in a

number of places. This lengthy extract describing a two-day visit with the King of Brunei is taken from the translation which appeared in volumes 33 and 34 of *The Philippine Islands, 1493-1898* (q.v.).

175 **Brunei and the Moro Wars.**
F. Delor Angeles. *Brunei Museum Journal*, vol. 1, no. 1 (1969), p. 119-32. map. bibliog.

In this paper, the author examines the Moro Wars between the Spanish colonial government in the Philippines and the Muslim principalities. They were fought to advance Spain's national interests, not only over the Mindanao Muslims, but also over the Portuguese and the sultanates of Ternate and Brunei. The wars began with a Spanish attack on the capital of the Sulu Sultanate in 1578 and ended with the Spanish withdrawal from the Philippines in 1898.

176 **European sources for the history of the Sultanate of Brunei in the 16th century.**
Edited by Robert Nicholl. Bandar Seri Begawan: Muzium Brunei, 1975. 104p. (Penerbitan Khas, Muzium Brunei, bil. 9 [Brunei Museum, Special Publication, no. 9]).

A unique collection of texts from early Spanish, Portuguese and Dutch sources up to 1615. The 115 items, translated into English and arranged in chronological order, contain accounts of Magellan's expedition, missionary activities, early wars, regional trade and the letters of the King of Portugal to the Sultan. The documents are extraordinary because they so often and so frankly describe the brutal behaviour of the Europeans (the Spanish in particular) toward the indigenous people. The author has, nonetheless, shown ingenuity in obtaining obscure and often inaccessible material. He also draws attention to untapped archival documents at Lisbon, Rome, Seville and Simancas. For a review of this publication by Thomas H. Harrisson see *Journal of the Malaysian Branch of the Royal Asiatic Society* (vol. 49, no. 1 (1976), p. 151-52).

177 **The first voyage round the world by Magellan. Translated from the accounts of Pigafetta, and other contemporary writers. Accompanied by original documents, with notes and an introduction, by Lord Stanley of Alderley.**
Edited and translated by Henry Edward John Stanley. London: Hakluyt Society, 1874. 257p. 2 maps. (Works Issued by the Hakluyt Society, 1st Series, no. 52)

On August of 1519 Magellan left Spain with 230 men in 5 vessels in what was to be the greatest enterprise ever undertaken by any navigator during the Age of Discovery. Twenty-one months later on 15 July 1521, the Spanish fleet arrived in Brunei. Antonio Pigafetta was one of 18 men who succeeded in returning to Spain in the only surviving ship, the *Victoria*. His records were among the most valuable cargo the expedition brought back from the first circumnavigation of the world. In this volume Pigafetta wrote about the daily events at sea, and the people, cultures and places encountered throughout the course of the voyage. The reception by the 'King of Burne' and scenes of the city (Kampong Ayer) described by Pigafetta during their 2-week stay in Brunei (p. 110-18) have been widely quoted by historians.

178 **The Philippine Islands 1493-1898. Vol. 4: 1576-1582: expedition to Borneo, Jolo and Mindanao.**
Edited by Emma Helen Blair, translated by James Alexander Robertson, with historical introduction and additional notes by Edward Gaylord Bourne. Cleveland, Ohio: A. H. Clark, 1903-09 , p. 148-303.

Describes in detail the preparation of the voyage and the reception in Brunei and Jolo experienced by members of a Spanish fleet. The objective of the expedition was to introduce the Sultan to Christianity and to gather information about the customs, laws and lifestyles of the native people. The Spanish were unsuccessful, however, for the Sultan refused them an audience. The expedition lasted from 19 April 1578 to 10 June 1579 and was headed by Francisco de Sande, Governor and Captain-General of the Western Islands (The Philippines). A description of this expedition can also be found in John S. Carroll's 'Francisco de Sande's invasion of Brunei in 1578: an anonymous Spanish account' (*Brunei Museum Journal*, vol. 6, no. 2 (1986), p. 47-71. bibliog.).

179 **The Philippine Islands 1493-1898. Vols. 33 and 34: 1519-1522: first voyage around the world.**
Edited by Emma Helen Blair, translated by James Alexander Robertson, with historical introduction and additional notes by Edward Gaylord Bourne. Cleveland, Ohio: A. H. Clark, 1903-09. 2 vols. 20 maps. bibliog.

Includes an account by Pigafetta, the recorder during Magellan's voyage, of a visit to the 'City of Brunei'. They were received with hospitality and visited the King (Sultan) to offer presents. Here, the grandeurs of an Asian court were spread before them, which Pigafetta briefly describes. The visitors were given permission to take on fresh supplies and to trade at pleasure. This fascinating and rare interpretation of 16th-century Brunei is widely quoted by historians. An unusual amount of references and footnotes related to other published material, mainly by Pigafetta, is also included.

180 **Relations between Brunei and Manila AD 1682-1690.**
Robert Nicholl. *Brunei Museum Journal*, vol. 4, no. 1 (1977), p. 128-76.

Provides a translation (42 pages) of the document *Filipinas Legajos 13 and 14*, housed in the Archivo General de Indias in Seville, and dated 1683-90. The author provides a short introduction to this document in which he tries to reinterpret certain historical events from the new evidence presented in the documents. The original *Filipinas Legajos*, written in a beautiful court hand describes, in detail, a friendship treaty, trade agreement and a visit made by the Spanish Ambassador to Brunei. It also provides some rather biased observations about Sultan Muhammad Ala'uddin and his system of government.

181 **Spanish accounts of their expeditions against Brunei 1578-79.**
D. E. Brown. *Brunei Museum Journal*, vol. 3, no. 2 (1974),
p. 180-221.

In 1578 the Spanish Governor and Captain-General for his Majesty of the
Western Islands (The Philippines) decided to travel with a fleet of galleys to the
island of Borneo, to introduce the natives to Christianity, learn about their
customs and laws and to 'reduce them' to the domain of his Majesty. In order to
prepare for the voyage the Governor interviewed former residents of Borneo and
sent letters to the King of Brunei. Arriving at the Brunei River delta the Spanish
fleet was attacked and a battle ensued, but ultimately the port of Brunei was
captured. This account was extracted from a collection, entitled *The Philippine
Islands 1493-1898. Vol. 4: 1576-1582: expedition to Borneo, Jolo and Mindanao*
(q.v.).

182 **The story of Bendahara Sakam.**
Jamil Al-Sufri. *Brunei Museum Journal*, vol. 3, no. 3 (1975),
p. 109-15.

Raja Bendahara Sakam was a member of the royal family and an outstanding
hero of his time, for he led the campaign against the Spaniards in the 'Castilian
War' of 1580. This account of the conflict is based on memories of the older
generation and correspondence sent between the Spanish Governor in Manila and
Sultan Saiful Rijal between 1576 and 1578. It presents a vivid depiction of the
people's love for their Sultan and their hatred for the Spanish, not only because of
their oppressive administration but because they also forced the people of Brunei
to embrace Christianity.

**Berunei in the Boxer Codex.**
*See* item no. 162.

**Brunei and camphor.**
*See* item no. 373.

# The 18th to 20th centuries: the British and the Brookes

183 **The bloody revolt in Brunei: a brief study on the success and failure
of the Party Ra'ayat of Brunei.**
Ibrahim Ariff. s.l.: [1963]. 27 leaves.

A detailed mimeographed account of the 1962 people's armed rebellion against
the British colonial authorities. The independence movement was immediately
suppressed by the British Army and the People's Party leadership went
underground. Their continued struggle, however, eventually resulted in independence some twenty years later.

184 **Borneo and British intervention in Malaya.**
Nicholas Tarling. *Journal of Southeast Asian Studies*, vol. 5,
no. 2 (Sept. 1974), p. 159-65. bibliog.

Tarling focuses on the controversy that has surrounded the question of British
intervention in Malaya, designed primarily to keep out other major powers. Not
unrelated to this was the British government's move to support James Brooke's
acquisition of Labuan in 1846 and, a year later, to sign a treaty with Brunei. The
fragmentation of the Borneo Territories prompted the idea that Borneo might
follow Malaya's example of adopting a Resident System and, subsequently, create
a federation of states. The success of these measures led some colonial officials to
believe that a similar structure was possible for Borneo. In 1957, however,
Malaya gained its independence. Both Brunei, who jealously guarded its oil, and
the indigenous people, were not interested in a federation. In the years to come
Malaysia emerged and the Borneo Territories developed a loose form of
association, more in keeping with their pre-colonial past.

185 **Borneo and the Indian Archipelago: with drawings of costume and
scenery.**
Frank S. Marryat.   London: Longman, Brown, Green &
Longmans, 1848. 232p. map.

In this work Marryat has provided a narrative of observations made during the
last surveying cruise of the HMS *Samarang* to Southeast Asian, Chinese and
Japanese ports during the year 1843. The vessel spent several weeks calling on
major settlements along the northern coast of Borneo, before it left for Manila.
During this time the *Samarang* was used by Rajah James Brooke and Muda
Hassan to visit Brunei (p. 105-18). The author describes, in vivid detail, the tense
moments in the negotiations between the visiting party and the Sultan. In the end,
the Sultan signed a treaty by which he bound himself to respect the British flag, to
turn over the possession of Labuan to Brooke, to discountenance piracy and to
install Muda Hassan into office with appropriate rank. Upon leaving Brunei the
island of Labuan was surveyed for good anchorage, water supply and potential
coal deposits. This episode provides a rare glimpse into the preparations for, and
the conduct of, an audience with a 19th-century Sultan in Brunei.

186 **British administration in Brunei 1906-1959.**
Anthony Vincent Michael Horton.   *Modern Asian Studies*,
vol. 20, no. 2 (1986), p. 353-74. bibliog.

A well-written coverage of five decades of British administration in Brunei in the
first half of the 20th century. During this period a number of successes and
failures were recorded which are reviewed in this study. By establishing a
Residency, the British government ensured the continued existence of the
Sultanate, it prevented Brooke from further cessions, and brought stability in
public services and government finance. The capital and technical expertise of the
British Malayan Petroleum Company produced the petroleum which provided the
revenues to finance the development of a Welfare State in the 1950s. However,
among the failures of the British presence were the loss of the Limbang territory,
and the inability to defend Brunei in 1941 or to bring about democracy. The
revolt of the People's Party in 1962 prevented any intention to move toward a
democratic system of government.

187   **British policy in the Malay Peninsula and Archipelago, 1824-71.**
      Nicholas Tarling.   Kuala Lumpur, Singapore: Oxford University
      Press, 1969. 236p. 2 maps. (Oxford in Asia Historical Reprints).

This work first appeared as an entire issue of the *Journal of the Malayan Branch of the Royal Asiatic Society* (JMBRAS), 1957. It was originally presented as the author's thesis (Cambridge University, 1956). Tarling attempts to describe and analyse, through to the interpretation of British documentary evidence, the development of British policy in the Malay–Brunei region between 1824 and 1871. One important feature of this book is the discussion of Foreign Office policy in the area, as affected by commercial interests and by strategic considerations. It also presents an interesting history of British policy toward the various political forces in the region, both native and European (Dutch), as conceived by the authorities in Britain, India and the Straits Settlements. According to Tarling, so far the Foreign Office and Colonial Office documents at the Public Record Office and the East India Company, as well as the India Office records at the Commonwealth Relations Office, have never before been used for such a purpose.

188   **British policy in the South China Seas area, with special reference**
      **to Sarawak, Brunei and North Borneo, 1860-1888.**
      Leigh R. Wright.   PhD thesis, University of London, 1963.
      450 leaves. 4 maps. bibliog.

The objective of this thesis is to analyse the development of Britain's foreign policy in the South China Sea during the latter half of the 19th century. In the 1840s and 1850s that policy was hesitant and faltering, but after 1860 it became a definite movement toward regional domination. British activity was increasingly motivated by the fear that another power might acquire a foothold in northern Borneo and, therefore, threaten the trade routes to China. With the granting of naval protection to Sarawak in the 1860s Britain proclaimed a sphere of influence over much of the North Bornean coast. This was, in part, as much a reaction toward the French presence in Indo-China as it was a reflection of the new imperialistic feeling in Britain itself. The suspension of German intentions in the area moved Britain to sponsor the state of North Borneo under rule by a chartered company. By a protocol with Germany and Spain she defined her sphere in Borneo. Finally, Britain granted protectorates over Sarawak, Brunei and North Borneo.

189   **The British Residency in Brunei, 1906-1959.**
      Anthony Vincent Michael Horton.   Hull, England: University of
      Hull, Centre for Southeast Asian Studies, 1984. 95p. 2 maps.

A concise and scholarly account of Brunei's economic and political history during the British Residency system. The author discusses the achievements and failures of the British occupation with reference to oil explorations, defence and independence. The appendixes offer a wide range of annual economic statistics for the period.

## 190 Brunei, Sulu and Sabah: an analysis of rival claims.
Brock K. Short. *Brunei Museum Journal*, vol. 1, no. 1 (1969), p. 133-46.

An exposé of the rivalry over the North Borneo territory involving the Philippines, the Brunei and Sulu sultanates, the British government, Rajah Brooke, Western trading companies and several individual entrepreneurs. The annals of Brunei provide conflicting information about this period but it is evident that by the beginning of the 17th century, Brunei had probably ceased to have any sovereignty over the northeastern portion of Borneo. Several writers claim that by 1763 Sulu had established *de facto* control over the region. It was then that the East India Company negotiated for exclusive trading rights with the Sulu territory. When, in 1805, the company abandoned the cession which Sulu had granted, northeastern Borneo became a 'no-man's land'. In the interim between the appearance of the East India Company and the British North Borneo Company, Illanun and Dayak pirates controlled coastal settlements and traffic in the South China Sea. Conditions had become so chaotic by 1865 that the American Consul and adventurer, C. L. Moses, leased territory on Kimanis Bay, not from Sulu but from Brunei. Subsequently, the bay and adjacent areas were taken over by the Austrian Consul, von Overbeck, the key figure in this dispute from the Philippines' point of view. Finally, in 1881 the Overbeck rights in Sabah were transferred to the British North Borneo Chartered Company. The company secured its peaceful occupation by treaty and was sovereign in the region until after the Second World War. A more recent issue addressed by this article is concerned with the Philippine claim to Sabah.

## 191 The burthen, the risk and the glory: a biography of Sir James Brooke.
Nicholas Tarling. Kuala Lumpur, Oxford, New York, Melbourne: Oxford University Press, 1982. 465p. 2 maps. bibliog.

This impressive treatise of the first white Rajah of Sarawak, although drawing considerably on previously published biographies, presents crucially important data on Brunei's involvement. The format is neatly ordered into chapters covering five phases of James Brooke's career from his birth in 1803 to his death in 1868. Everyone who had a supporting role in the drama of Sarawak–Brunei history of the period covered (including several sultans) is sufficiently mentioned to make this a useful compendium of events and a source of reference for students of Bornean history.

## 192 A centenary: W. H. Treacher and the Limbang revolt, 1884-1885.
Anthony Vincent Michael Horton. *Sarawak Museum Journal*, new series, vol. 34, no. 55 (1985), p. 91-99. bibliog.

In 1884 the Limbang district, inhabited by Muruts, Bisayas and Kedayans, was the most valuable territory remaining in Brunei's shrinking domain. As a consequence of Brunei's misgovernment, a long tradition of discontent existed in Limbang. This article focuses on the first stage (1884-85) of the final uprising which culminated in 1890 with the transfer of Limbang to Sarawak. Mr. W. H. Treacher, Acting British Consul-General in Borneo at the time, served as mediator between the Sultan and the tribal groups in Limbang.

193  **The development of Brunei during the British residential era 1906-1959: a sultanate regenerated.**
Anthony Vincent Michael Horton.  PhD thesis, University of Hull, England, 1985. 681p. 2 maps. bibliog.

The author attempts to demonstrate how the mismanaged and dissonant Brunei Sultanate was regenerated by the introduction of a British Resident in 1906, and the more recent discovery of petroleum, becoming a prosperous modern state by 1959. Initially, the British presence provided for a period of containment and consolidation by eliminating governmental abuses and introducing administrative reform. Brooke's influence was eliminated and, with clearly defined borders, Brunei ceased to be an indeterminate empire. The country's finances were rescued with the exploitation of oil reserves which opened up prospects for substantial development after 1930. The people's standard of living was improved by the introduction of formal education and medical care, the development of roads and plantation agriculture and the eradication of cholera, smallpox and other diseases. Progress towards modernization, however, was briefly disrupted by the Japanese occupation and the subsequent need for reconstruction. Post-war improvements included the extension of electricity and water supplies, the elimination of malaria, the introduction of the old age pension and a sharp reduction in infant mortality. The 1950s witnessed the construction of the airport, highways to the oilfields and the national mosque, as well as mechanization in fisheries, rice and rubber cultivation. In short, a comparison between the conditions of the country in 1906 and 1959 leaves little doubt that Brunei was indeed, a sultanate regenerated.

194  **The ending of Brunei rule in Sabah 1878-1902.**
I. D. Black.  *Journal of the Malaysian Branch of the Royal Asiatic Society*, vol. 41, part 2 (Dec. 1968), p. 176-92. bibliog.

A business transaction in 1877 between Sultan Mumin and a prominent British firm transferred the territories of Sabah from Brunei ownership to British control. A company was set up with a Royal Charter to rule while the cost of administration and profits were derived from taxation and local resources respectively. The author details the pacification of tribal groups and the exploitation of the land. Basically, the company took power in a country where no power existed. As the last European intruder it had simply to gather up and reconstitute some of the fragments of Brunei's decayed government.

195  **Entrepôt at Labuan and the Chinese**
Nicholas Tarling.  In: *Studies in the social history of China and Southeast Asia: essays in memory of Victor Purcell (26 January 1896 – 2 January 1965)*. Edited by Jerome Ch'en, Nicholas Tarling. Cambridge: Cambridge University Press, 1970. p. 355-73.

The British government sought to develop Labuan Island into an entrepôt and coal mining centre worked by imported Chinese labour. Within a decade of becoming a Crown Colony (in 1846), however, the administration considered abandoning their activities on the island. The article expands on several reasons for the economic failure, including mismanagement, the poor quality of coal, and commercial difficulties in the face of Dutch restrictions on British trade in the region. Labuan also played a decisive role in Brooke's initial plans for Brunei. He intended to use the island as a base from which to exterminate piracy, to gain influence in Brunei proper, and to develop new sources of commerce. The author describes the difficulties and obstacles encountered by Brooke while pursuing his goals.

196   **The establishment of a Residency in Brunei: 1895-1905.**
       Colin N. Crisswell.   *Asian Studies*, vol. 10 (1972), p. 95-107.
       bibliog.

Reviews the complex negotiations over the future of the Sultanate in the closing decades of the 19th century. In order to strengthen its position and fend off other colonial powers Britain decided to grant a Royal Charter to the North Borneo Company in 1881 and establish protectorates in the three territories of Sarawak, North Borneo and Brunei in 1887. Under this arrangement British officials considered it desirable that Brunei should ultimately be divided among its neighbours. Sultan Hashim strongly opposed any efforts toward the extinction of the ancient sultanate and became even more determined when, in 1890, Britain accepted Rajah Charles Brooke's annexation of the Limbang River. The negotiations over Brunei's fate continued for several more years between the Foreign Office, the Colonial Office, the North Borneo Company, Charles Brooke and the Sultan. This paper is based on the author's PhD thesis (see the following item).

197   **The establishment of a Residency in Brunei: a study in relations**
       **between Brunei, North Borneo, Sarawak and Britain 1881-1905.**
       Colin N. Crisswell.   PhD thesis, University of Hong Kong, 1971.
       178 leaves. 3 maps. bibliog.

Examines the fascinating political rivalry between the British Colonial Office, the North Borneo Company, Sultan Hashim and Rajah Brooke over the destiny of the frontier territories between Sarawak and Brunei. See also the previous item and A. V. M. Horton's 'Sir Charles Brooke's visit to Brunei: April-May 1906' (*Brunei Museum Journal*, vol. 6, no. 2 (1986), p. 116-27. bibliog.). This article describes the events surrounding a visit made by Rajah Charles Brooke to Brunei when he learned the Foreign Office was about to appoint a Resident in Brunei. From a long-term perspective the events of 1906 represented the last serious attempt by Brooke to swallow up Brunei.

198   **Five years in China: from 1842 to 1847. With an account of the**
       **occupation of the island of Labuan and Borneo by Her Majesty's**
       **forces.**
       Frederick Edwyn Forbes.   London: Richard Bentley, 1848. 405p.
       map. Reprinted: Taipei: Ch'eng Wen Publishers, 1972.

Describes the journeys made by the commander of the HMS *Bonetta* across China observing the customs and culture of the country and its inhabitants. Chapters 17 to 20 (p. 284-323) focus on the Treaty of Labuan, the massacre of Brunei, customs of the Borneo Malays and the search for coal on Labuan. The massacre refers to the conflict between Sultan Omar Ali Saifuddin II (1829-52) and

**History.** The 18th to 20th centuries: the British and the Brookes

Pengiran Muda Hashim who was to become Sultan with the assistance of James Brooke. The plot was aborted, however, and Pengiran Muda Hashim and his family committed suicide.

199   **The Foreign Office and North Borneo.**
Leigh R. Wright. *Journal of Oriental Studies*, vol. 7, no. 1 (Jan. 1969), p. 76-99. bibliog.

In no other age in history is the imprint of personal influence upon institutions more obvious than 19th-century Victorian England, and in no other place can we better see these personalities involved in policy making than the Foreign and Colonial offices of Whitehall. This essay will consider the interrelationship of two phenomena of policy making upon the process of British empire building in northern Borneo in the late 19th century. The first is the role of the permanent staff in the Foreign Office, and the second is the relationship between permanent staff and retired Asian hands, usually occupied with obtaining commercial influence for the British empire.

200   **Historical notes on the North Borneo dispute.**
Leigh R. Wright. *Journal of Asian Studies*, vol. 25, no. 3 (May 1966), p. 471-84. bibliog.

A thorough examination of the international rivalry which led up to the demarcation of North Borneo between Spain and Britain, with Germany as an interested party in the background. Furthermore, the granting of territory to international businessmen, Alfred Dent and Baron Gustav von Overbeck, by the Sultan of Sulu is the basis of the Philippine claim to North Borneo. However, the story really begins with the Sultan of Brunei who was sovereign over all of northern Borneo, the Sulu Archipelago and part of the Philippines. With the decline of Brunei, Sulu achieved independence and established its rule over parts of northern Borneo. Effective rule came to the area only with control by the North Borneo Chartered Company in the 18th century. With the success of British diplomacy in the 19th century, North Borneo became British.

201   **A history of Sarawak under its two white rajahs.**
Sabine Baring-Gould, C. A. Bampfylde.   London: H. Sotheran, 1909. 464p. map.

According to the preface, written by Charles Brooke, this work should be regarded as his biography, although the contents more closely reflect the book's title. However, in contrast to James Brooke's biography, *The burthen, the risk and the glory: a biography of Sir James Brooke* by Nicholas Tarling (q.v.), this study covers far more extensively the influence of Brunei on Sarawak's history and that of northern Borneo in general. Of the seventeen chapters at least four are partly or wholly devoted to topics such as the first European contacts with Bruni (chapter two), Bruni and its court (chapter three), and the first British treaty with Bruni and its relation to piracy (chapter four). Clearly, the most relevant section of the book, entitled 'Bruni', (chapter eight, p. 326-72), is primarily concerned with the oppression and misgovernment of the working class, the Rajah's policies toward the Baram and Limbang river territories and Britain's occupation of Labuan. In short, the book should be seen as an absorbing history of Charles' early adventures in Borneo and his lengthy disputations with British colonial officers and the rulers of Brunei in the late 19th century.

## 202   Hugh Low on the history of Brunei.
D. E. Brown.   *Brunei Museum Journal*, vol. 1, no. 1 (1969), p. 147-56. bibliog.

In 1880 Hugh Low published accounts of the history of Brunei which were largely derived from *Selesilah (Book of Descent)* and appeared in the *Journal of the Straits Branch of the Royal Asiatic Society* (vol. 5 (1880), p. 1-35). Since that time very little similar material derived from Brunei sources has been published. For this reason the author feels justified by adding yet another, heretofore, unpublished account of Brunei's past from the pen of Hugh Low. A colonial officer on Labuan, Sir Hugh Low sent reports to England on historical events that shaped the internal affairs of Brunei up to 1875 and also clarified the dispute between Brunei and Sulu over control of northern Borneo. This paper comprises relevant extracts from that report.

## 203   James Brooke and Asian government.
Graham Saunders.   *Brunei Museum Journal*, vol. 3, no. 1 (1973), p. 105-17. bibliog.

Presents a revealing account of James Brooke's opinion of Asians and their system of government based largely on his personal journal and correspondence to friends and family. His decision in 1841 to accept the government of Sarawak and to reform the government of Brunei cannot be fully understood without reference to his changing attitude and opinions prompted by the travels on his own schooner, the *Royalist*, to Celebes, Singapore, Brunei and Sarawak. Several writers quoted by Saunders generally agree that Brooke considered all Asians with whom he had contact to be inferior and only fit to govern themselves under European guidance.

## 204   James Brooke's visit to Brunei in 1844: a reappraisal.
Graham Saunders.   *Sarawak Museum Journal*, new series, vol. 17, nos. 34-35 (1969), p. 294-314. bibliog.

The purpose of this article is to re-evaluate the cause and effect of Brooke's visit to Brunei in 1844. Since no Malay version is available, most historians tend to accept Brooke's own interpretation of the events. The author urges that 'the Brooke era needs to be considered from the viewpoint of the people whose life they so greatly affected.' Undoubtedly, very different conclusions may yet be drawn.

## 205   The Lanun pirate states of Borneo: their relevance to Southeast Asian history.
Leigh R. Wright.   *Sabah Society Journal*, vol. 7, no. 4 (1979-80), p. 207-17. bibliog.

During the intervening period between the decline of the Sultanate of Brunei in the 18th century and the emergence of the European empires in the late 19th century, pirates states generally ruled the region. They had well established centres of control along the coast of northern Borneo and the islands in the Sulu Sea. This article re-examines the Lanun 'states' of Borneo and the slave trade with Tungku, Brunei Town and Jolo. Lunan cruisers were very active in Tempasuk, Pandasan and Marudu Bay, conducting business with some of the sultans of Brunei. When Rajah Brooke and the British Navy declared war against the Malay and Lanun pirates, the coastal communities settled down to more peaceful pursuits on the shores of Marudu and Brunei Bay.

206 **The life of Sir James Brooke, Rajah of Sarawak: from his personal papers and correspondence.**
Spenser St. John. Edinburgh, London: William Blackwood & Sons, 1879. 406p. map.

Presents a biography of James Brooke based on much of his unpublished correspondence, documents and journals. Chapters five (p. 99-122) and thirteen (p. 247-60), are specifically pertinent to Brunei although other chapters are also occasionally relevant. Subjects covered in these chapters include: 'Events in Brunei and on the north-west coast', 'Murder of Muda Hassim and his family', 'Capture of Brunei' and 'Return to Borneo'.

207 **Piracy and politics in the Malay world: a study of British imperialism in nineteenth-century South-East Asia.**
Nicholas Tarling. Melbourne: F. W. Cheshire, 1963. 273p. 2 maps.

A study of 19th-century British policy in the Malay Archipelago with particular emphasis on the suppression of piracy in Bornean waters. Chapter three, entitled 'The Bugis, the Brunei Malays, and the Dayaks' (p. 112-45), is most relevant to the political history of Brunei. Here, the author discusses the Bugis' efforts to retain a commercial monopoly on the east coast of Borneo and the control of Dayak trade by local Malay officials. Most significantly, however, this chapter provides an exposé of Brooke's early attempts to foster commercial enterprise in Brunei by destroying piracy and extortion.

208 **Nineteenth century Borneo: a study in diplomatic rivalry.**
Graham Irwin. Singapore: Donald Moore Books, 1955. 337p. 4 maps. bibliog.

Deals primarily with the consequences of Dutch and British policy upon the arrival of James Brooke. Fearing that other powers, namely Germany and Holland, would gain a foothold on Borneo, the British established three protectorates: Brunei, Sabah and Sarawak. This authoritative study of the 1809-88 period is based on extensive research into English and Dutch colonial records. Of special interest to the Brunei scholar is chapter 10, entitled 'The partition of Borneo' (p. 191-217) detailing the events by which Brunei dwindled to its present size.

209   **North Borneo.**
      Lord Brassey.   *Nineteenth Century*, vol. 22 (July-Dec. 1887),
      p. 248-56.
A traveller's account by an English passenger on the *Sunbeam* in 1887, detailing
his observations of Kuching, Brunei, Labuan and various parts of North Borneo.
The subject matter relates primarily to the resources, labour and trade, which
these areas were able to supply to British commercial interests.

210   **Observations on the Brunei political system 1883-85.**
      Peter Leys, with notes by Robert M. Pringle.   *Journal of the
      Malaysian Branch of the Royal Asiatic Society*, vol. 41, part 2,
      (Dec. 1968), p. 117-30. bibliog.
The observations mentioned in the title consist of two memoranda sent to the
Foreign Office in London between 1883 and 1885 by Peter Leys, the British
Administrator of Labuan. Leys devoted these memoranda to matters of taxation,
tenure and political rights over the outlying districts in the Sultanate of Brunei.
The author describes a system of rights over people and revenues in outlying river
areas as exercised by officers and nobles (*pengiran*). They involved judging
criminal offences, levying taxes and controlling trade.

211   **The origins of British Borneo.**
      Leigh Richard Wright.   Hong Kong: Hong Kong University
      Press, 1970. 237p. 3 maps. bibliog.
The culmination of fifty years of involvement in Southeast Asia gave Britain
secure control over northern Borneo and the eastern part of the South China Sea
in 1890. This book is a study of Britain's progressive involvement in Borneo from
1860 to 1888 and shows how it reflects the development of foreign policy in
London. Two basic factors in Britain's Far Eastern policy were involved: one was
the need to maintain and protect the trade route to East Asia; the other factor
was the changeover from primarily a commercially to a politically based imperial
policy. Chapter IV, entitled 'Britain and Brunei 1868-1878' (p. 84-125), focuses
on Britain's policy as based on the Brunei treaty of 1847. That treaty was
designed to prevent Rajah Brooke of Sarawak from further annexing more
Brunei territory. The chapter concentrates on two questions: the territorial
possessions of the Baram River and Labuan Island, and the issue of succession to
the throne of Brunei, intended to strengthen the Sultan's government against
Brooke and improve Britain's position. Also included is the protectorate
agreement with the Sultan of Brunei, dated 17 September 1888 (p. 213-15). This
work is based on the author's PhD thesis, *British policy in the South China Seas
area . . .* (q.v.).

212   **Origins of the Limbang claim.**
      Colin N. Crisswell.   *Journal of Southeast Asian Studies*, vol. 2,
      no. 2 (1971), p. 218-28. map. bibliog.
The dispute over the claim for the Limbang River has its origin in the 1880s when
North Borneo and Sarawak were conspiring against each other to gain possession
of Brunei's shrinking territory. Since that time the problem has been continually

smouldering, every now and then breaking out into verbal conflict between Brunei and Malaysia. The issue is a complex one and this account provides a detailed scholarly analysis of the background to the Limbang claim. In 1906 Britain considered returning the river to Brunei several times but no action was taken. The claim was advanced again recently by the present Sultan, but, a century after the claim was originally made, the descendants of the Limbang rebels may well wonder if their economic interests would be better served by a return to oil-rich Brunei.

213 **The partition of Brunei.**
Leigh R. Wright. *Asian Studies*, vol. 5, no. 2 (1967), p. 282-302.
The political map of Brunei and the demarcation of territories were largely the result of international rivalries and imperialist interest with marginal considerations toward the indigenous state. By the second half of the 19th century Brunei was in the later stages of decline, her Sultan and ministers competing with each other for the wealth to be made from territorial cessions. Rajah Brooke of Sarawak had ambitions to rule all of northern Borneo. Under the energetic administration of W. H. Treacher, however, the North Borneo Chartered Company decided to oppose Brooke's advance and, itself, developed an absorption policy toward Brunei. Britain's objectives were to prevent the intervention of other foreign powers in northern Borneo and to secure her own dominant position there as an imperial power. This involved stabilizing the political situation by settling the rival claims of Sarawak to the south and the Chartered Company to the north of Brunei. The delineation of the three states, Sarawak, North Borneo and Brunei, and the establishment of normal relations between each state and Britain were eventually achieved by forming political protectorates. Nonetheless, the evidence presented in this article makes it quite clear that Britain fully expected Brunei to be completely absorbed by her neighbours, since nothing in the protectorate agreement stood in the way. Thus, the present small enclave of Brunei resulted from a continued rivalry over the Limbang and Lawas River districts along the borders of that country.

214 **The partitioning of Brunei.**
K. G. Tregonning. *Malayan Journal of Tropical Geography*, vol. 11 (1958), p. 84-89. map.
This account of the partitioning of Brunei carefully follows a chronological sequence of events in tracing the political geography of the Sultanate during the 19th century. The position and objective of each party: James Brooke, the Sultan, the British North Borneo Company and the British government are clearly defined. As the oil resources provided Brunei with new economic strength, it was able to 'speak for itself'. In fact, the author speculates that Brunei Bay and Labuan could again become a political and economic unit, given the increased scope in development capability and oil wealth Brunei has since acquired.

215 **Pengiran Indera Mahkota Shahbandar Mohammad Salleh and James Brooke in the history of Brunei.**
Matassim Haji Jibah. *Brunei Museum Journal*, vol. 4, no. 3 (1979), p. 38-51. bibliog.
An intriguing episode of local history which recalls the early encounters between James Brooke and Mahkota, the, then, Governor of Sarawak. A conflict arose between the two when Brooke attempted to extend his territory into Brunei and Mahkota, the Sultan's principal adviser, warned of a Western 'take-over'.

216 **Pg. Anak Hashim's role in Brunei affairs prior to his accession to the throne in 1885.**
Colin N. Crisswell. *Sarawak Museum Journal*, vol. 25, no. 46 (1977), p. 41-54. bibliog.
When Anak Hashim, the second son of Sultan Omar Ali Saifuddin II (1818-52), became Sultan in 1885, Rajah Charles Brooke hoped this would lead to the cession of the Limbang area to Sarawak. At this time, Anak Hashim was seen as a man of outstanding ability and character. When Brooke's hopes were dashed, however, the Sultan was branded to be cruel, inefficient, and only interested in money, yet resisting Sarawak's offer to take over the rest of the Sultanate. By concentrating on an examination of the actions of Anak Hashim prior to his accession, the author hopes to gain a more balanced picture of this key figure in 19th-century Brunei history. Moreover, his career is a good illustration of the struggle within the royal family that lasted throughout that century and was an important, contributing factor to Brunei's inability to resist European incursions.

217 **Public Officers Agreement between the Government of the United Kingdom of Great Britain and Northern Ireland and the Government of the State of Brunei.**
British Parliamentary Papers. London: Her Majesty's Stationery Office, 1973. 13p.
Defines and clarifies nine articles pertinent to the conditions of public service for British Civil Service personnel in the State of Brunei. The articles address the eligibility for retirement and pension, termination of service and payment of pension. The agreement is made and expressed in both the English and Malay languages.

218 **Rajah Charles Brooke and mining concessions in Brunei 1888-1924.**
Anthony Vincent Michael Horton. *Journal of the Malaysian Branch of the Royal Asiatic Society*, vol. 59, part 1 (1986), p. 49-72. bibliog.
The existence of coal in Brunei was discovered as early as 1837. Mr. W. C. Cowie, a steamship operator, obtained the first concession to work the coal deposits near Muara. This paper details the circumstances under which three concessions (1882, 1884 and 1887) were negotiated to mine and export coal from the Muara Kuala Brunei district. In 1888 the Muara mining rights were sold to Sir Charles Brooke whose ultimate ambition was to incorporate all of Brunei with Sarawak. The Rajah's mining operations, financed by the Sarawak government, were unprofit-

able ventures, however, and with the arrival of a British Resident in 1906, the land rights were signed back to Brunei in 1932. Today, little evidence remains where Brooketon, the mining town named after Brooke, once stood.

219   **Revolt in Borneo.**
      Edgar O'Ballance.   *Army Quarterly and Defence Journal*, vol. 87
      (Oct. 1963-Jan. 1964), p. 91-98.

The unrest in Brunei in 1962 can be traced to the proposal to form the Federation of Malaysia, consisting of Malaya, Singapore, Sarawak, Brunei and North Borneo. The opposition did not come from the Sultan, but rather from the People's Party (Partai Ra'ayat) led by Azahari, a Brunei Malay with a left-wing background. The rebels achieved a successful initial take-over swiftly and the Sultan, with his police force, was forced to withdraw. In response, the Sultan appealed to the British for help and, within days, several thousand British and Gurkha troops were airlifted from Singapore to Labuan Island. Generally, the rebels were no match to the British invasion and by mid-1963 the revolt was finally crushed. As to the external reaction to this affair, the Philippines found much satisfaction in the revolt and still insist that North Borneo is theirs. Indonesia openly supported the rebels and suggested that the territory should be given the right of self-determination. China sympathized with those rebelling against the British colonial system. A curfew is still in place today for fear that the core of rebels still at large could present a potential danger and may break out again as soon as conditions are ripe.

220   **The 'Sarawak Gazette' and the British Residency in Brunei, 1906-**
      **1924.**
      A. V. M. Horton.   *Sarawak Gazette*, vol. 109, no. 1485
      (Oct. 1985), p. 27-32.

The purpose of this article was to illustrate the transformation of official Sarawak attitudes toward Brunei during the reign of Sultan Sir Muhammad Jemal-ul Alam (1906-24), as revealed in the pages of the *Sarawak Gazette*. This journal, first published in 1870, was edited by a member of the Rajah's Civil Service and, therefore, reflected official thinking on major issues. Some of the issues of the *Gazette* featured articles designed to show that the Rajah was more popular in Brunei than the British Resident. After the death of Rajah Charles in 1917 the *Gazette* softened its approach toward the British administration in Brunei.

221   **Sarawak's relations with Britain, 1858-1870.**
      Leigh R. Wright.   *Sarawak Museum Journal*, new series, vol. 11,
      nos. 23-24 (1964), p. 628-48. bibliog.

This study primarily deals with those aspects of Sarawak's 19th-century history which shed light on her relations with Britain, and which led to the protectorate agreement in 1888. From almost total abandonment in the 1850s, Britain was brought to admit her interest in Sarawak by 1869.' The author clearly illustrates that an unstable situation existed in Sarawak as a result of native plots, the Mukah River incident with Brunei subjects, the status of Sarawak *vis-à-vis* Brunei, and the existence of other European powers in the area. Thus, Britain's policy of support and protection (as in the case of Brunei) developed slowly and with each step it went only so far as was absolutely necessary and acceptable to Parliament in London.

222  **Sir James Brooke and Brunei.**
Nicholas Tarling. *Sarawak Museum Journal*, new series, vol. 11, nos. 21-22 (1963), p. 1-12. bibliog.

Although much has been written about James Brooke, the nature of his policies and their impact have rarely been analysed. This paper discusses these topics with particular reference to the 1840s and 1850s. Brooke's intentions were to suppress piracy, to deal with the problem of traditional commerce and to acquire Labuan as an entrepôt and coaling station. His policy was one of regulating the commercial practices of the Brunei chiefs by piecemeal pressure in favour of visiting Chinese traders from Labuan.

223  **The status of Sarawak under Rajah James Brooke and British recognition.**
Leigh R. Wright. In: *International Conference on Asian History, University of Hong Kong (Aug. 30-Sept. 5, 1964)*, 13p. bibliog.

This essay traces the history of Sarawak from the time when it was a province of Brunei through the Brooke era and Britain's involvement to 1888 when a formal protectorate was declared. The author pays particular attention to the evolution of British defence policy designed to protect Sarawak and Brunei against the threat of piracy.

224  **Steps in the acquisition of North Borneo.**
K. G. P. Tregonning. *Historical Studies: Australia and New Zealand*, vol. 5, no. 19 (Nov. 1952), p. 234-43. bibliog.

Describes the efforts made by several business-minded individuals, such as the American Consul, Claude Lee Moses, and American merchant, J. W. Torrey, the British trading house 'Dent Brothers', the Scotsman, W. C. Cowie and others to set up commercial ventures in Brunei and North Borneo. What began as an obscure American venture became the territory of the North Borneo Chartered Company.

225  **Treaties and engagements affecting the Malay States and Borneo.**
Sir William George Maxwell, William Sumner Gibson. London: Jas. Truscott, 1924. 276p.

Part four (p. 143-53) deals specifically with Brunei treaties of the 1840s through to the 1920s. These include the cession of the island of Labuan, the agreement for British protection and the agreement for the appointment of a Resident.

226 **Two colonial office memoranda on the history of Brunei.**
Sir Reginald Edward Stubbs, edited and annotated by
D. E. Brown.   *Journal of the Malaysian Branch of the Royal
Asiatic Society*, vol. 41, part 2 (Dec. 1968), p. 83-116. map.

The two memoranda were written by Sir Reginald Edward Stubbs in 1905 and
1911, respectively, during his career in the Colonial Office. The first memorandum, entitled 'Brunei and the Limbang' was written and printed for the use of
the Colonial Office and focuses on the events in the 1880s and 1890s when
Sarawak seized the Limbang district from Brunei. The second memorandum,
according to Brown, describes the final events, decisions and negotiations which
were to secure Brunei's boundaries through a Protectorate Agreement placing a
Resident in Brunei. It also documents the first five years of the Brunei Residency.

227 **The undeclared war: the story of the Indonesian confrontation 1962-
1966.**
Harold James, Denis Sheil-Small.   London: Leo Cooper, 1971.
201p. 5 maps; Kuala Lumpur: University of Malaya Co-op
Bookshop, 1979. 201p.

Describes how British, Gurkha and Commonwealth troops guarded a thousand-
mile long frontier against Indonesian guerrillas attempting to destroy Malaysia
and create a pan-Indonesian empire. Part one, entitled 'The Brunei revolt', is a
narrative of how a dissident faction within Brunei almost succeeded in a take-over
and supported the Indonesian cause. British interference, however, undermined
that revolt.

228 **The white rajahs. A history of Sarawak from 1841 to 1946.**
Steven Runciman.   Cambridge: Cambridge University Press,
1960. 320p. 3 maps. bibliog.

A modern history of Sarawak based on an objective attempt by the author to
interpret the evidence available. The official history of Sarawak, however, was
written by Baring-Gould and Bampfylde in 1909. The theme of Runciman's work
is to trace nearly 100 years of economic and political development in Sarawak
under the leadership of the Brooke family – Rajah James, Rajah Charles and
Rajah Vyner. It also provides a good introduction to the island of Borneo, its
people and the arrival of the Europeans. Of particular importance is the chapter
entitled 'Great Britain and Brunei' (Book III, Chapter II, p. 174-201), which
focuses on the relationship between Rajah Charles, the British Foreign Office, the
North Borneo Company, Sultan Munim and, later, Sultan Hashim over the
border territories and political future of Brunei. To save Brunei from Sarawak's
aggression a British Residency was established there but Charles Brooke always
believed that it was his duty to rescue the 'native tribes' from a suppressive and
chaotic Sultanate. An author and subject index is included, together with a
glossary of terms and titles.

229 **The white rajahs of Sarawak.**
Alastair Morrison. *Hemisphere*, vol. 28, no. 1 (July-Aug. 1983),
p. 20-26. map.
The story of an unusual adventurer, a 'cultivated Englishman', who, with his
successors, was to rule the State of Sarawak and former Brunei territory for a
century. It also covers the final demise of Dayak rebels who opposed Brooke's
administration and territorial cessions.

**Maps and the history of Brunei.**
*See* item no. 60.

**A gambling style of government: the establishment of Chartered
Company's rule in Sabah, 1878-1915.**
*See* item no. 151.

**Malaysia, Singapore and Brunei, 1400-1965.**
*See* item no. 152.

**Brunei and the Moro Wars.**
*See* item no. 175.

**Brunei kearah kemerdekaan.** (Brunei towards independence.)
*See* item no. 232.

**Brunei 1839-1983: the problems of political survival.**
*See* item no. 293.

**Report on Brunei in 1904.**
*See* item no. 313.

**Agreement between Her Majesty the Queen of the United Kingdom of
Great Britain and Northern Ireland and His Highness the Sultan of
Brunei amending the Agreement of 29 September 1959.**
*See* item no. 317.

**The United States Consul and the Yankee Raja.**
*See* item no. 347.

**The Iban of Sarawak under Brooke rule, 1841-1941.**
*See* item no. 543.

# Independence to the present

230 **Brunei Darussalam: the fruits of independence?**
Michael Leigh. *Ilmu Masyarakat* (Malaysian Social Science
Association Publication), no. 9 (April-Sept. 1985), p. 65-72.
bibliog.
A useful survey of contemporary Brunei summarizing its economic prosperity,
internal defence issues, the minority problem and membership of ASEAN. The
author also poses the question: 'how long can the Sultan maintain an autocratic
system of rule?' A scenario is presented in the event of another revolt.

231 **Brunei in transition.**
A. J. Crosbie. *Southeast Asian Affairs* (1981), p. 75-92.
The signing of the Treaty of Friendship and Cooperation between Britain and
Brunei in 1979 marked the beginning of a five-year period of transition leading to
full independence in 1984. After many years of maintaining a *status quo*, Brunei is
now being transformed into a sovereign nation with all the responsibilities
inherent in that role. The author looks at several internal constraints and external
pressures, including: size of the population, shortage of trained manpower, an
imbalanced age structure, a centralized form of government, the dependency on
oil, the need to diversify the economy, taking a position on regional issues and
coping with external criticism.

232 **Brunei kearah kemerdekaan.** (Brunei towards independence.)
Zaini Haji Ahmad. Selangor, Malaysia: Haji Zaini bin Haji
Ahmad, 1984. 97p.
A richly illustrated political history of the events and developments in the early
1940s which led to the expansion of Malay nationalism in Brunei. The first
political organization of Brunei, the People's Party, launched an armed revolution
against British colonialism in December 1962.

233 **Brunei on the morrow of independence.**
Donald E. Brown. *Asian Survey*, vol. 24, no. 2 (Feb. 1984),
p. 201-08.
Aside from the usual treatment of Brunei's past, the author presents some current
problems which Brunei is facing, together with predictions for the near future.
These include the dependency on petroleum, the nature of the post-independent
government, the lifestyle of the royal family and the provision of employment for
qualified Bruneians. As to the future, westernization is likely to continue and will
almost certainly clash at times with those who promote Islam. The economy,
however, will continue to thrive as long as the oil and gas industry remains viable.

234 **Brunei: the new independent state.**
Sabiha Hasan. *Pakistan Horizon*, vol. 37, no. 2 (1984), p. 72-82.
bibliog.

A useful review article which covers the 'golden age' of Brunei, foreign occupation and self-determination. Despite its affluence, Brunei still faces certain problems. Some of the internal problems include the widening gap between the urban rich and the rural poor, the degree of power concentration in the royal family, the lack of national security and the acute labour shortage, which is also blamed for the difficulties encountered in diversifying the economy. In relation to Brunei's foreign policy, the author reviews the government's position with ASEAN, the neighbouring states and the Islamic block.

235 **Brunei: what changes will independence bring?**
Chris Lim. *Asian Business Quarterly*, vol. 4, no. 4 (1980), p. 25-28. map.

A special feature article which examines the preconditions for Brunei's independence and the possible implications, particularly in the areas of national security and economic development. In earlier times, Brunei's wealth and small size were often cited as grounds for doubt about its security in a volatile region. Furthermore, Brunei's strained relations with its neighbours stem from the events which occurred during the 1962 rebellion. With the passage of time, however, many of these fears have dissipated. Other possible areas of contention mentioned in this article are the sharing of wealth between Shell Petroleum and the government, the ability to maintain a monarchical constitution, and the importance of diversifying the economy.

236 **Commemorative booklet on the admission of Brunei Darussalam into ASEAN (Association of South East Asian Nations).**
ASEAN Secretariat. Jakarta, Indonesia: Public Information Office, ASEAN Secretariat, 1984. 40p. map.

Includes the opening messages of the foreign ministers of all six ASEAN countries and outlines main areas of cooperation between them in political, economic, social, cultural, scientific and technological developments. Coloured illustrations are also provided.

237 **Illuminating the path to independence: political themes in *Pelita Brunei* in 1983.**
Roger Kershaw. *Southeast Asian Affairs*, (1984), p. 67-85.

The government's weekly bulletin, *Pelita Brunei*, is a valuable source for the official viewpoint and also, by inference, for the problems which the administration might be facing at any particular time. This article analyses the political themes of *Pelita Brunei* throughout 1983, when the country was preparing for independence. The final section reviews the reporting of Brunei in the British press for the same period, focusing primarily on security and defence issues. The purpose of the paper is to let Brunei's government 'speak for itself' through the medium of English translations and summaries. The message is an appealing one and deserves to be more widely heard.

238 **Independence. Problems of a brave new Brunei.**
Clare Hollingworth. *Sunday Telegraph Magazine*, (Feb. 1984),
p. 16-21.
A well-illustrated news report on the country's geography, history and diverse
population. More significantly, however, the article takes a close look at the
deteriorating relations between Britain and the Sultanate, the rights of women,
expatriate labourers and local Chinese, as well as the lavish lifestyle of the royal
family. The author concludes: 'how long the state can continue to deny personal
freedom after independence must depend on a complacent community and the
absence of external interference.'

239 **Internationalization of the Brunei question and its implications.**
Mustafa bin Nasar. BA thesis, University of Singapore, 1980.
151 leaves. bibliog.
This thesis examines the dynamics involved in Brunei's march toward full
independence, particularly following the debate of the Brunei question by the
United Nations. A view of Brunei's future viability as an independent state is also
provided.

240 **Kesultanan Brunei Darussalam akan masuk manjadi anggota
ASEAN ke-6.** (The Sultanate of Brunei Darussalam will be the
sixth member of ASEAN.)
*Sinar Harapan*, vol. 12 (1 Jan. 1984), p. 1-6.
This Indonesian newspaper article comments on Brunei's entrance into ASEAN
(Association of South East Asian Nations).

241 **Merdeka! Freedom at midnight for Asia's newest nation – a special
report.**
*Asiaweek*, vol. 10, no. 1 (6 Jan. 1984), p. 17-45. map.
This leading Asian news magazine looks at the political events, key personalities
and socio-economic issues which shaped the destiny of Brunei up to its
independence. Special sections are devoted to discussions about the people,
defence and the economy. Personal interviews with Sultan Hassanal Bolkiah and
Azahari, the rebel chief of the 1962 revolt, are included. The Brunei-based
correspondent, Anthony Paul, summarizes the action and personalities of several
Englishmen who played a major role in Brunei's domestic affairs over a period of
nearly 150 years.

242 **Negara Brunei Darussalam: a new nation but an ancient country.**
Sharon Siddique. *Southeast Asian Affairs*, (1985), p. 97-108.
map.
Evaluates Brunei's first full year of independence. The account opens with
descriptions of the Proclamation of Independence and the official ten-day
celebration. During 1984 the Sultan revealed his new cabinet and the government
joined the Organization of Islamic Conferences, the United Nations and ASEAN.
Siddique states that repeated references were made at this time to Islam's role as
the official state religion. In defence, the Brunei armed forces (some 4,000 strong)

held their first joint exercise with troops from Singapore. The agreement with the
Gurkha Batallion of the British Army continued essentially unaltered. The
economy is examined in terms of how Brunei spends its petro dollars in
agriculture, fisheries, construction and social services. Increased efforts in
education are designed to train the workforce and to improve the educational
opportunities for the older generation. Lastly, although world attention focused
on Brunei in 1984, the government appeared to react negatively toward Western
media coverage.

243  **Nervously into the world.**
     Rodney Tasker.  *Far Eastern Economic Review*, vol. 115, no. 11
     (12 March 1982), p. 22-28. map.
A very informative account of the prospects and problems which Tasker thought
Brunei would encounter as it joined the family of independent nations. The
author has included many interesting insights concerning the negotiations and
events leading up to Brunei's independence from Britain in 1984. There was much
speculation at that time as to how the government might be restructured and how
the Sultan planned to maintain internal stability. As to the state of the economy,
heavy reliance on oil and gas is predicted to continue whilst for every other
sector, apart from construction, the future appeared bleak.

244  **Protected state or new nation? Brunei: a case study in political
     geography.**
     Peter C. N. Hardstone.  *Tijdschrift voor Economie en Sociale
     Geografie*, vol. 69, no. 3 (1978), p. 165-71. map. bibliog.
An examination of Brunei's geo-political history and nation-building during the
1970s. The characteristics necessary for a state to exist, such as delimited
boundaries, an economic structure, a system of communication and sovereignty in
external relations are all related to the case of Brunei. In terms of future political
development the paper examines three alternatives: maintain a *status quo* with
regards to a British presence, merge Brunei with Malaysia, or establish a
completely independent state followed by the development of a distinct Brunei
nationalism. In 1984 Brunei actually chose the third alternative, and with the
emergence of Brunei as a new nation, the chapter of European imperialism in
Southeast Asia was finally brought to a close.

245  *Sunday Times* **spotlight: dawning of a new era: independent and
     sovereign Brunei.**
     *Sunday Times* (Singapore), (1 Jan. 1984), p. 1-12.
To celebrate independence, various correspondents cover such topics as: the
nature of government; economic outlook; 'one country – many faces'; moments
in history; life-styles; and 'into the future'.

**Brunei berdaulat.** (A sovereign Brunei.)
*See* item no. 7.

**Wijaya** (=victory) **Merdeheka** (=independence) **Brunei. (Commemorative
issue on Brunei's independence).**
*See* item no. 18.

# The Sultans

**246 Brunei.**
  G. E. Cator. *Asian Review*, vol. 33, no. 124 (1939), p. 736-44.
The author, who served as British Resident in Brunei, begins this article with a review of the decline and fall of Brunei, as told in the Official Records, which formed the prelude to the Annual Report of the British Resident in 1906. More importantly, however, this account provides a rare opportunity to gauge the depth of the people's loyalty to their Sultan and the past glory of Brunei as embodied in the ceremony of 'The Blooming'. This event is known locally as *puspa*, a Sanskrit word referring to the blooming of the lotus flower, and is celebrated when a Sultan has ascended to the throne as a minor, comes of age, and subsequently assumes full and undivided control. This process of assuming full sovereignty is preceded by long and serious conferences which are meticulously recorded in this article. The atmosphere of this occasion is revealed, in particular, in the statement that: 'it was impossible for even the most stolid Englishman not to be moved by the passion of loyalty evoked, and among the people of Brunei it was evident that tension was strung to its highest pitch' (p. 742). The author regrets not having kept a more detailed record of this local custom, since not only was it the first time that a European had participated in such a ceremony, but, also, there has been no subsequent repetition.

**247 Brunei forms of address, titles and government officials.**
  Bandar Seri Begawan: s.n., 1984. 56 leaves.
Provides a list of substitutions for the first, second and third person as used by the Sultan, the *wazirs* (the five highest noble officials), the *cheterias* (ranking below the *wazirs*), and the common nobles. These speech forms are used before the name or title of the person spoken of. The use of these forms (which are euphonious kin terms) is in accordance with the relative standing in the royal family between the person spoken to and the person spoken of.

248 **The coronation of Sultan Muhammad Jamalul Alam, 1918.**
   D. E. Brown.   *Brunei Museum Journal*, vol. 2, no. 3 (1971),
   p. 74-80.
Compares two eye-witness accounts of the Sultan's coronation: the first by Haji
Abdul Ghaffar bin Abdul Mumin (as retold by Amin Sweeney) and the second by
M. S. H. McArthur. In general each account is written from a different point of
view. The principal contrast is between Haji Abdul Ghaffar's sociological
sensitivity and McArthur's more psychologically slanted comments. In their
treatment of personages, however, both differed profoundly; Haji Abdul Ghaffar
was somewhat more precise in his reporting of chronology, which could also be
attributed to the narrower range of events reported and the greater length of his
account.

249 **The genealogical tablet (Batu Tarsilah) of the sultans of Brunei.**
   P. M. Shariffuddin, Abdul Latif bin Hj. Ibrahim.   *Brunei
   Museum Journal*, vol. 3, no. 2 (1974), p. 253-64. bibliog.
The purpose of this article is to revise Hugh Low's transcription of the
genealogical tablet which is located at the tomb of Sultan Mohammad Jamalul
Alam. The emphasis is not so much on the transcription or errors in spelling,
however, as on the date which was fixed by Low. By using a new method, the
authors were able to read the tablet more clearly. It is unfortunate that this error
in the date has been accepted by various authors over time, together with that
given for the Brunei Annual Reports.

250 **In the grandest tradition, the new Istana is today's Versailles.**
   Xavier Marshall, photographs by Akio Kawasumi.   *Connoisseur*,
   vol. 214 (Sept. 1984), p. 113-17. map.
Although this paper includes an historical introduction to Brunei, it is largely
devoted to a discussion of the architectural features and interior design of the
Istana Nurul Iman (the Palace of Religious Light). During an interview, the
architect Leandro V. Locsin of Manila and the interior designers, Dale and Pat
Keller of New York revealed many facts and figures about the nature and
quantities of building materials used, and the origin and value of the palace's
interior decoration. In terms of architectural composition, the central element is
the boat-shaped double roof flanked by two mosques, each capped with a dome
and plated with twenty-two carat gold. One of the challenges for the interior
designers was to humanize the gigantic spaces available and, yet, maintain the
necessary palatial grandeur. No expense was spared to create an aura of
sumptuousness. The palace may look slightly ostentatious to Westerners, but
certainly not to Bruneians. As they see it, it is the focus of national pride, a
triumph in technology, and a symbol of political and religious stability.

251 **Memperingati ulang tahun ke-10 perpuspaan. (Commemorating the
   10th anniversary of the coronation 1968-1978).**
   Bandar Seri Begawan: Muzium Brunei, 1978. 42p.
In a very colourful pictorial display (with text in both English and Malay), this
book presents the life history of His Highness the Sultan, Sir Muda Hassanal
Bolkiah, including his coronation ceremony and the country's progress between
1968 and 1978.

252 **A modern Xanadu: the new Royal Palace of Brunei by architect Leandro Locsin with interiors by Dale Keller Associates.**
Martin Filler, with photographs by Oberto Gili. *House and Garden*, vol. 156, no. 10 (Oct. 1984), p. 154-63, 236-46.

To coincide with the commemoration of independence in January 1984, the Sultan built a new royal palace, the Istana Nurul Iman, at an estimated cost of nearly $500 million. Located on a 350-acre site overlooking the Brunei River, the palace boasts close to 1,800 rooms, 22 carat gold-plated domes, a roof-top heliport and underground parking for 800 cars. In addition to a detailed description of the multitude of rooms and their functions, the author also describes the dazzling Independence Day banquet. The article is accompanied by several marvellous, full-sized, coloured photographs of the interior, which give the reader a true feeling of living in royal splendour.

253 **Power behind the throne.**
Suhaini Aznam. *Far Eastern Economic Review*, vol. 133, no. 38 (18 Sept. 1986), p. 30.

An obituary of the twenty-eighth Sultan of Brunei, Muda Omar Ali Saifuddin III, more familiarly know as 'the Seri Begawan', who died at the age of seventy-one on 7 September 1986. His seventeen-year reign was punctuated by two major events: the abortive civil rebellion led by the Brunei People's Party in 1962 and the cooling of relations with Malaysia after 1963, when Brunei opted to stay out of the Federation. Despite having independence as his goal, his relations with Britain were always friendly. He was knighted in 1953.

254 **The royal wedding.**
P. M. Shariffuddin. *Brunei Museum Journal*, vol. 1, no. 1 (1969), p. 1-4.

The royal wedding of the present Sultan, Hassanal Bolkiah, the twenty-ninth Mohammedan ruler of Brunei, on 29 July 1965, was conducted in accordance with modern procedures. Only very few people can remember the old traditional practices at royal weddings, since the last one so celebrated occurred in 1934. An eye-witness of this rare event was interviewed by the author, thus giving the reader a unique opportunity to find out how royal weddings were celebrated in times past.

255 **Sejarah rengkas: panji2 negeri Brunei. Brunei state crest: a short sketch.**
Abdul Latif Haji Ibrahim. Kota Batu, Brunei: Muzium Brunei, 1972. 25p. (Penerbitan Khas, bil 2; Special Publication, no. 2)

The original royal emblem was introduced to Brunei during the reign of the third Sultan, in the early 15th century, perhaps from the Middle East. Many modifications in design occurred through time as its use changed from a royal emblem to a state crest; however, its original status has always been maintained. The present state crest was superimposed on the state flag after the promulgation of the 1959 Brunei constitution, with the amalgamation of 'the hands' and the royal regalias, at both sides of the crest. Other features include the royal umbrella, the wings, the centre mast and the crescent. The symbolic meaning of these features is described in some detail (in Malay and English). Although many government agencies today have formed their own departmental emblems, the state crest remains. Illustrations show the various changes in design.

256  **Selesilah (book of descent) of the rajahs of Brunei.**
Hugh Low. *Journal of the Straits Branch of the Royal Asiatic Society*, no. 5 (June 1880; Kraus reprint, 1965), p. 1-35.

This English translation of a Malay text traces the history of Brunei's rulers. These writings provide very detailed insights (in the form of anecdotes and events) into the lives and reigns of several rajahs who ruled the Sultanate in pre-European times. A chronological list (p. 24-31) of Muslim sovereigns of Brunei, assembled by Low from various sources at his disposal, is also included. Twenty-three sultans are described in terms of their position in the lineage, their accomplishments and place in history.

257  **Silsilah Raja-Raja Berunai.** (Genealogy of Brunei's sultans.)
Edited and annotated by P. L. Amin Sweeney. *Journal of the Malaysian Branch of the Royal Asiatic Society*, vol. 41, part 2, no. 214 (Dec. 1968), p. 1-82.

This description of two original 19th-century manuscripts, is written in Malay and annotated in English. The first, identified as MS No. 25023, is held at the School of Oriental and African Studies, London; the second, MS No. 123, is available at the Library of the Royal Asiatic Society, London. The original *silsilah* contains narratives on coronation ceremonies, accounts of processions, the procedures for building a mosque, trade regulations, information on the function of high officials, a history of Brunei and a list of the sultans.

258  **The Sultan of Brunei.**
Text by Joan Orendain; photographs by Joe Cantrell, Jaime Zobel de Ayala. Manila: Filipinas Foundation Inc. for Ayala International, 1983. 208p. 4 maps. bibliog.

A pictorial portrayal of the private and public life of His Majesty Sultan Hassanal Bolkiah.

259  **Titah, (speeches) 1959-1967.**
Omar Ali Saifuddin III, Sultan of Brunei. Bandar Seri Begawan: Brunei Dewan Bahasa dan Pustaka, 1971. 505p.

Contains the text, in Malay, of 105 speeches given by Sultan Omar Ali Saifuddin III during his reign, from 1959 to 1967. Throughout this period he formulated the constitution, promoted Islam and composed poetry (Sha'er) containing advice concerned with peace, government and contemporary problems. As such, the twenty-eighth Sultan was known as the 'Architect of Modern Brunei'. He abdicated voluntarily in favour of his son on 4 October 1967.

The Sultans

260   **Tomb of the 'King of Brunei' in Nanking.**
Tun Mohamed Suffian. *Journal of the Malaysian Branch of the Royal Asiatic Society*, vol. 56, no. 2 (1983), p. 1-6.
The author relates his impressions of a visit made in 1983 to the burial site of a Brunei Sultan in Nanking, China. The Sultan 'Manaregarna' (or Maharaja Karna) visited China in 1408, fell ill and died there. The Chinese built a mausoleum outside the city gates of Nanking which, after 600 years, is still standing and is being preserved by the Cultural Relics Preservation Committee of the Yuhua District in Nanking.

261   **The tributes paid in former days to the Sultan of Brunei by the then dependent Province of Sarawak.**
Edward Parnell. *Sarawak Museum Journal*, vol. 1, no. 1 (Feb. 1911), p. 125-30.
A short, but rare, account of the tax collection system and practices of extortion carried out by provincial feudal chiefs to support the Sultan who ruled the greater part of Borneo. The information is derived from an old document dated 1148 and pertains only to the Province of Sarawak.

262   **The world's richest man: Brunei's free-spending Sultan of oil.**
Louis Kraar. *Fortune*, vol. 116, no. 8 (12 Oct. 1987), p. 132-33.
In a series which covers the world's billionnaires, the Sultan of Brunei is featured as the richest man with his fortune in oil and gas and $20 billion in foreign investments. Kraar highlights the major events since independence, the Sultan's family and his palace.

**Memperingati penukaran nama Bandar Brunei menjadi Bandar Seri Begawan.** (Commemorating the name change from Bandar Brunei to Bandar Seri Begawan.)
*See* item no. 14.

**Sultan Mumin's will and related documents.**
*See* item no. 159.

**Pg. Anak Hashim's role in Brunei affairs prior to his accession to the throne in 1885.**
*See* item no. 216.

**The Royal *nobat* of Brunei.**
*See* item no. 575.

# Population and Minorities

## General

263 **Brunei: report on the census of population taken on 10th August, 1960.**
Laurence Walter Jones. Kuching, Sarawak: Government Printing Office, 1961. 182p. 2 maps.

Censuses of population were held in 1921, 1931 and 1947; the first two as part of the censuses of the Straits Settlements of which Brunei then formed one unit; and the last in conjunction with that of Sarawak with which Brunei, in 1947, had close administrative ties. This 1960 census of Brunei is again in conjunction with Sarawak. The total population enumerated on 10 August 1960 was 83,877, as compared to 40,657 for the previous census of 1947. The current census report consists of 10 chapters, containing information on the administration of the census, the population by districts, community services, age structure, sex and marital status, literacy and level of education, religion, place of birth, occupation, industry and housing. Statistics are presented in the form of 36 tables.

264 **The Chinese in Borneo 1942-1946.**
Thomas H. Harrisson. *International Affairs*, vol. 26, no. 3 (July 1950), p. 354-62.

In Sarawak and Brunei, the Chinese are a significant minority, primarily active as merchants, middle-men and, in some cases, in pepper planting, mining and specialized agriculture. This article, however, focuses on a very different activity: the involvement of Chinese people in the war efforts during the Japanese occupation of the 1940s. When the Japanese took control of northern Borneo, the Chinese, in general, favoured passive resistance. There was a tendency for some Chinese to move away from their centres of commerce on the coast and become farmers in the less accessible places. This resulted in a considerable curtailment of

**Population and Minorities.** General

trading activities; the effect of the war on the Japanese economy emphasized this as the occupation continued. The paper also singles out several Chinese individuals who made remarkable contributions to organized resistance against the Japanese, especially during the allied landing in Labuan and Brunei and during the terrible Sandakan 'death march'.

265   **The Chinese in Sarawak (and Brunei).**
Lee Yong Leng.   *Sarawak Museum Journal*, new series, vol. 11, nos. 23-24 (1964), p. 516-32. 2 maps. bibliog.
Using census data from 1947, 1951 and 1960 the author analyses the Chinese population, their history, migration patterns and distribution in Sarawak and Brunei. Some attention is given to Chinese linguistic groups, their occupational structure and changes in settlement and land-use patterns brought about by Chinese settlers in the past.

266   **Hereditary rank and ethnic history: an analysis of Brunei historiography.**
Donald E. Brown.   *Journal of Anthropological Research*, vol. 29 (1973), p. 113-22. bibliog.
This paper argues that ethnicity in Brunei is fostered by a system of hereditary rank (status by descent), the reverse of assimilation in a society with open hierarchies (the coming together of ethnically diverse people). Two themes are presented in this paper. The first theme is that ethnic diversity varies with the hereditary closure of ranking systems. The people of a given locality, the Brunei River for example, came to dominate people of other localities in Borneo and the Philippines. In this case the rulers and the ruled engaged in extensive cultural borrowing and, consequently, are not biologically distinct. The second theme, in contrast, describes an open society characterized by cultural variation between strata. Bruneians traditionally perceive their society as a collection of *bangsa* (people, race, stock, etc.), each with distinct origins. Hence, societies with hereditary ranking systems may describe their past with a rhetoric of ethnic diversity, but the rhetoric may bear little or no relation to historical facts. Brunei, therefore, possesses a historiography which is unreliable with respect to traditional accounts of its ethnic origin.

267   **The Kedayans.**
P. M. Shariffuddin.   *Brunei Museum Journal*, vol. 1, no. 1 (1969), p. 15-23.
The Kedayans of Brunei are Muslims and comprise about one-fourth of the whole population. They extend northwards along the coast and the river deltas of Sarawak as well as across the Sabah border. The Kedayans are characterized by a tendency to keep to themselves. This article describes their culture, language, folklore, housing, appearance and gives details regarding their methods of hunting, fishing and rice cultivation. According to the author, this article is one of very few about the Kedayans. He lists three of these works in his notes.

268 **Laporan banchi pendudok Brunei 1971.** (Report on the census of
population 1971.)
State of Brunei. Bandar Seri Begawan: Bahagian Ekonomi dan
Perangkaan Jabatan Setia Usaha Kerajaan, [1972]. 260p.
Contains an introductory text which describes the organization and administration
of the census. This is followed by a statistical analysis for the population by
districts, ethnic groups, age and sex ratios, levels of education, religion, place of
birth, labour force, occupation and industry. Part II presents 44 tables showing
population data by year, sex, levels of education, age categories, marital status,
etc. A sample of the household questionnaire used in this census is included in the
appendix.

269 **Origins and attitudes of Brunei, Tutong-Belait-Bukit-Dusun, North
Borneo 'Dusun' and Sarawak 'Bisayan', Meting and other
peoples.**
Thomas H. Harrisson. *Sarawak Museum Journal*, new series,
vol. 8, no. 11 (1958), p. 293-321.
The naming of communities by river is a common occurrence in Borneo because
many of them tend to be located in valleys with which they become intimately
associated. When they move to another site they change their name, though it
may take governments many years (or never) to register their change. The author
argues, however, that this does not take into account those who live on the coast
or in the interior highlands. One conclusion drawn in this article, therefore, is that
different local environments within Brunei and Sarawak present a major obstacle
to the understanding of the origin and changing distribution of ethnic groups in
the area.

270 **The population of Borneo: a study of the peoples of Sarawak, Sabah
and Brunei.**
Laurence Walter Jones. London: Athlone Press, 1966. 213p.
map. bibliog.
Several censuses have been conducted throughout northern Borneo, yet little has
been published on the demography of the region. This book, the first to be
written on this subject, is by a man who was administratively responsible for the
1951 and 1960 enumeration process. The book is divided into two parts: the first
deals with the situation in the pre-war years, whilst the second covers the period
of rapid growth since World War II. While much of the data comes from the 1951
and 1960 censuses some population characteristics, such as density, fertility,
mortality and migration, are included for the period 1910 to 1930. The last
chapter is devoted to population projections into the 1980s. All statistics
presented in this study are shown separately for each state. The appendix shows
the ethnic variation of the 1960 population and methodology for computing
projections for the economically active population.

271 **Population of British Borneo.**
Y. L. Lee. *Population Studies*, vol. 15 (1962), p. 226-43. 7 maps.
bibliog.

A geographical interpretation of population characteristics for Brunei, Sarawak
and North Borneo. One outstanding feature of the population distribution in
these areas is the coastal concentration of immigrant groups (Chinese, Malay), set
against the concentration of the indigenous people in the interior. Such
differences accentuate the differences in ethnic, social and economic status
between the two populations. Migration to British Borneo is significant, not only
because it has contributed to a numerical imbalance but also because of the
powerful economic position assumed by the newcomers. It will take a long time
before this plural society will become assimilated into a homogeneous regional
population.

272 **Population policy compendium.**
United Nations, Department of International Economic and Social
Affairs, Population Division. New York: United Nations, 1985.
1 vol. bibliog.

This publication attempts to present, country by country, both updated
information on population policy and basic population data for the member states
of the United Nations and its specialized agencies. The demographic indicators
from 1975 to the year 2000 are population size, mortality, morbidity, fertility,
internal migration and spatial distribution. The information pertaining to Brunei
covers four pages. The loose-leaf binder format allows for easy updating.

273 **Sarawak and Brunei: a report on the 1947 population census.**
J. L. Noakes. London: Crown Agents of the Colonies, 1950.
282p. 2 maps. bibliog.

The introduction to this work states that the aim of the 1947 census was not only
to provide factual data, but also to supply the governments of both territories with
a demographic profile which could be used to predict population trends and to
initiate social planning. The text provides an account of census operations, a
comparison with earlier enumerations (the 1931 census for Brunei) and an
interpretation of the data (for both states separately), emphasizing population
growth, ethnic composition, occupation, fertility, literacy and housing. The
statistical section includes 72 tables showing social, demographic and economic
data grouped according to administrative divisions, ethnic groups, urban-rural
location, age, education and other categories. Appendix 10 presents a socio-
cultural classification of the population, written by Thomas Harrisson (p. 271-79).
Another analysis of this census data, emphasizing the indigenous population, has
been published by Noakes under the same title in the *Sarawak Museum Journal*
(new series, vol. 5, no. 3 (1951), p. 624-44).

274 **The Sea Dayaks before white rajah rule.**
Benedict Sandin, with a preface by Tom Harrisson and an
introduction by Robert M. Pringle.   East Lansing: Michigan State
University Press, 1968. 134p. 7 maps. bibliog.
For more than twenty years, the author, a Sea Dayak himself, has collected the
folklore and traditions of his own people. In this work he traces their history from
approximately the fifteenth generation, using oral history to examine Iban
migration from the Kapuas valley, in Indonesia, to the Sarawak–Brunei
territories. Accordingly, these migration movements occurred along major rivers
from the interior of Borneo to the northern coast. As the Ibans made contact with
other people who were generally weaker, less numerous and aboriginal, they were
gradually displaced or absorbed. The last part of the book deals with the patterns
of raiding and retaliatory warfare along the coast.

275 **Social classification and history.**
Donald E. Brown.   *Comparative Studies in Society and History:*
*an International Quarterly*, vol. 15, no. 4 (1973), p. 437-47. bibliog.
A theoretical interpretation of the relationship between ethnicity and social
stratification in Brunei society. As an anthropologist, the author naturally focused
on traditional organization and government. Historically, the most important
stratificational boundary was between the nobles and the commoners. How these
two groups were internally classified by rank and office in the bureaucracy, is the
subject of this paper. The data on Brunei is compared to change and continuity in
the Nigerian emirate of Zazzau.

276 **Some demographic characteristics of the Iban population of Brunei.**
Robert F. Austin.   *Brunei Museum Journal*, part I, vol. 3, no. 4
(1976), p. 64-69. bibliog; part II, vol. 4, no. 1 (1977), p. 1-6.
bibliog.
Part I (1947-60) of this analysis deals with the rapid growth of the Iban population
in Brunei. The author attributes the increase of almost 200 per cent between 1930
and 1960 to heavy in-migration and a higher natural growth rate than other tribal
groups. In Part II (1960-71), the 1971 census figures for Brunei are analysed. The
growth of the Iban population during the 1960 to 1970 period was less dramatic
than before due to new restrictions in migration policy and a greater emphasis on
temporary resident workers.

277 **Through many subcultures: a view of the subcultural units in a
typical Brunei Malay life cycle.**
Linda A. Kimball.   *Borneo Research Bulletin*, vol. 12, no. 1
(April 1980), p. 19-24.
An examination of life-cycle stages or subcultures as experienced by individuals in
the course of their lifetimes. Members of a typical Brunei Malay riverine village in
the Temburong District were studied as they passed through childhood, formal
schooling, marriage, professional career and old age. These subcultures are also
viewed from a larger temporal and areal perspective – beyond the world of the
traditional Brunei village.

278    A world of women: anthropological studies of women in the societies
        of the world.
        Edited by Erika Bourguignon.    New York: Praeger, 1980. 364p.
        bibliog.
Several case-studies present the lives of women in various socio-cultural settings
throughout the world. The descriptions are based on original field-work carried
out by researchers who have maintained long-term associations with their people.
According to Linda A. Kimball in chapter three, *Women in Brunei* (p. 43-56),
most Brunei Malay women today follow a life-style that has remained essentially
unchanged despite a strong drive toward modernization in that country. Marriage,
child care and housekeeping activities are compared in both rural and urban
settings. Additional responsibilities of local women may be gardening, producing
handicrafts, or running a small business. Although some women hold technical or
administrative jobs in the modern sector, most remain oriented toward their
domestic role. In their family, however, women make important economic and
social contributions.

**Wijaya (=victory) Merdeheka (=independence) Brunei.**
**(Commemorative issue on Brunei's independence).**
*See* item no. 18.

**The population geography of the Chinese communities in Malaysia,
Singapore and Brunei.**
*See* item no. 43.

**Brunei, the structure and history of a Bornean Malay sultanate.**
*See* item no. 150.

**Allah, Shell and the Sultan.**
*See* item no. 348.

**The pagan tribes of Borneo: a description of their physical, moral and
intellectual condition, with some discussion of their ethnic relations.**
*See* item no. 553.

**The pagans of North Borneo.**
*See* item no. 554.

**Urang Darat, an ethnographic study of the Kadayans of Labu Valley.**
*See* item no. 560.

**Annual Report.**
*See* item no. 589.

**Report on the census of population 1971.**
*See* item no. 595.

**A bibliography of the demography of Malaysia and Brunei.**
*See* item no. 640.

# Settlements

279 **The city of many waters.**
Lee Yong Leng. *Hemisphere*, vol. 8, no. 6 (May 1964), p. 8-11.
An examination of the physical site of Brunei Town and the land-use pattern as it existed in the 1960s. As an administrative capital and seat of the Sultan it has attracted people from many cultural backgrounds, but Malays have always formed the majority. While Brunei Town (now known as Bandar Seri Begawan) declined with the arrival of the European traders, the rehabilitation of the oil industry since 1947 has brought the city back into prominence.

280 **Historical aspects of settlement in British Borneo.**
Y. L. Lee. *Pacific Viewpoint*, vol. 2 (1961), p. 187-212. 3 maps. bibliog.
A comparative analysis of the settlement history and economic development for Sarawak, Brunei and North Borneo. The author provides a useful introductory survey of early Indian, Chinese and Malay contacts with northern Borneo. European explorations were made purely for commercial purposes and did not leave any lasting effects on settlement in the region. With the coming of Brooke's rule and the Chartered Company, aboriginese and Chinese immigrants began to settle the coast, working in mines, farms and trading posts. Eventually the regional economy came to depend on the production of raw materials, the extension of a transportation network and inter-territorial trade. These economic factors have been of prime importance in effecting the settlement patterns in all three territories.

281 **Kampong Ayer: the conservation of a living community.**
Jodie K. Hruby Beggs. Master's thesis, Heriot-Watt University, Edinburgh, 1985. 191p. 19 maps. bibliog.
A study of Kampong Ayer as the living derivative of Brunei's cultural and architectural heritage. The author provides development history, together with proposals which suggest a present-day role for the settlement as part of the modern capital, Bandar Seri Begawan. Realistic ideas for its future existence are also suggested. Many coloured photographs are included.

282 **Living on stilts in Brunei.**
Henry J. White. *Oceans*, vol. 19, no. 2 (March-April 1986), p. 22-27.
A study of the people and their unusual community, Kampong Ayer, built entirely on stilts in the shallow waters of the Brunei River. White describes the context in which this water village has survived the influences of the shoreside city for more than 400 years. The author, an oceanographic engineer, was quite intrigued by the widespread use of motorized water taxis. Their construction is based on a long tradition of boat builders who developed their own method of design and fabrication, using native mahogany. While many modern improvements have been introduced in the water village in recent years, the people still have a deep respect for the river fostered by a long maritime background.

283 **The long house and Dayak settlements in British Borneo.**
Y. L. Lee. *Oriental Geographer*, vol. 6 (1962), p. 39-60. map.
bibliog.

A comparative settlement geography of the Muruts, Dusun, Iban (Sea Dayaks) and Land Dayaks focusing on the indigenous community organization: the long house. The structural features of the long house and its role in social organization are discussed. Topography and religion are both factors responsible for the siting and forms of many long-house settlements. The general distribution of long-house settlements is typically associated with the practice of shifting cultivation. While some groups have given up this form of habitat, many still cling to the long-house domicile with remarkable resilience, even in the face of modernization.

284 **North Borneo (Sabah): a study in settlement geography.**
Lee Yong Leng. Singapore: Eastern Universities Press, 1965.
156p. 30 maps. bibliog.

A well-organized, descriptive study of settlement patterns of an undeveloped equatorial region, based almost entirely on field-work. The first three chapters provide an introduction to the physical, historical and economic geography of North Borneo. The remaining five chapters present a more detailed analysis of population, land use, rural and urban settlements in relation to physical, historical and economic factors. Brunei plays an important role in the analysis of historical aspects of settlements and population distribution. Twenty-six photographs are included.

285 **The port towns of British Borneo.**
Y. L. Lee. *Australian Geographer*, vol. 8 (1962), p. 161-72.
2 maps.

Lee analyses the urbanization process in Sarawak, Sabah and Brunei using statistics gathered from the 1951 and 1947 censuses. Some emphasis is given to the ethnic composition of the urban population and to the distribution and size of towns. While the region as a whole is only twenty-five per cent urbanized, the largest urban concentration (eighty-three per cent) for Brunei is mainly due to the oil industry. At the same time, Brunei seems to have the lowest proportion of Chinese in its population. Characteristically, all towns in British Borneo are distributed throughout the coastal zone which is at once a reflection of the undeveloped and inaccessible interior. (This article is also reprinted in: *Changing South-East Asian cities: readings on urbanization*. Edited by Y. M. Yeung, C. P. Lo. Singapore: Oxford University Press, 1976, p. 82-90).

286 **Spatial prognosis of the rural population.**
Zaharah Haji Mahmud. In: *Brunei in transition: aspects of its human geography in the sixties*. Khoo Soo Hock [et al]. Kuala Lumpur: Department of Geography, University of Malaya, 1976.
p. 1-51. 9 maps. (ITS Occasional Papers, no. 2).

Brunei's rural population is widely distributed in four major river valleys and their tributaries; the Brunei, Tutong, Belait and Temburong valleys. The author presents some generalizations as to the distribution, origin and change of human settlement in each valley even though generations of isolation have resulted in marked variations in settlement and land-use patterns. Ethnic, racial and communal considerations are also indispensable in understanding the rural population in Brunei.

287 **The traditional economic activities in Kampung Air, Brunei.**
Syed Hasjim bin Abdullah Alhabshi. Thesis, National University of Singapore, 1983. 180 leaves. 9 maps.
Based largely on original field research in Kampong Air, this thesis has three objectives: to trace 400 years of settlement history, to identify functional and morphological changes, and to describe the origin and characteristics of indigenous cottage industries (fishing, metal works and *nipah* crafts) and explore the reasons why some have vanished whilst others persist to this day.

288 **Urban settlements.**
Lam Thim Fook. In: *Brunei in transition: aspects of its human geography in the sixties.* Khoo Soo Hock [et al]. Kuala Lumpur: Department of Geography, University of Malaya, 1976. p. 52-75. 5 maps. (ITS Occasional Papers, no. 2).
The main urban centres in Brunei are the capital, Bandar Seri Begawan, Tutong Town and the oil towns of Seria and Kuala Belait. In 1970 these areas accounted for 63.6 per cent of the country's total population. In this chapter the author discusses these communities with regard to their land use, public facilities, population growth and demographic characteristics. The emphasis is on the capital city and adjacent Kampong Ayer which are expected to remain the growth centres of the country.

289 **A vanishing heritage: the old traditional Malay houses.**
Kamaruddin Md. Ali. MA thesis, University of York, 1983. 102 leaves. 5 maps. bibliog.
States that the Nurul Iman Palace, the Foreign Ministry, the Supreme Court, the Brunei Museum and many other public buildings situated in the capital of Brunei bear many distinct features of traditional Malay architecture. In this thesis the author examines the origin, design concepts and conservation of this vanishing style of architecture. The necessity for preserving vernacular structures is argued on the basis that they are a link with the past and reflect a time-tested technology. In a current effort to preserve this valuable heritage, two problems must be addressed: providing an inventory on the subject and, ultimately, establishing a conservation policy.

290 **Variations and changes in the names and locations of the wards of Brunei's Kampong Ayer over the last century.**
Abdul Latif Haji Ibrahim. *Brunei Museum Journal*, vol. 2, no. 3 (1971), p. 56-73. 3 maps. bibliog.
Historically the water village (Kampong Ayer) consisted of several wards, each with its own name and different headman (ketua). The people's recognition of

each ward was also associated with the individual social and cultural character of that ward. This study examines the changes in names, boundaries and socio-economic fabric of some 30 residential units within Kampong Ayer. By comparing historical descriptions with the present conditions, the author discovered that wards are no longer differentiated by occupational activity, social status or title. Many of the trades, occupations and titles in use during the last century have declined or died out completely. The present population of the water village has become more homogeneous as a result of increased mobility and a higher standard of living.

**The development of resources in British Borneo and its impact on settlement.**
*See* item no. 359.

# Politics and Government

291 **Background to a revolt: Brunei and the surrounding territory.**
Thomas H. Harrisson.   Bandar Seri Begawan: Light Press, 1963.
38p. map.

The aim of this booklet is to briefly explain the history and the complexities of human geography which brought about the rise and fall of the Brunei Sultanate. Obviously its proud tradition has greatly influenced a variety of people both in and outside Brunei. The Kedayans, Bisayas, Ibans, Muruts and Punans are described in terms of their material culture and their relation to the environment. Since this pamphlet was designed for use by the military personnel of the British forces in Borneo, everyday phrases in Malay and some 'dos and don'ts' are also included.

292 **The Borneo response to Malaysia, 1961-1963.**
James P. Ongkili.   Singapore: Donald Moore, 1967. 148p.
2 maps. bibliog.

A concise history of the political developments in British territories during the early 1960s. Since the events and territories are greatly intertwined, the three political units Sabah, Sarawak and Brunei are not treated as separate entities in this book. Ongkili presents 'an impartial study of reactions and feelings in the territories of Northern Borneo to the idea of federation with Malaya and Singapore.'

293 **Brunei 1839-1983: the problems of political survival.**
D. S. Ranjit Singh.   Singapore, Oxford, New York: Oxford
University Press, 1984. 260p. 2 maps. bibliog.

A well-written and documented political history of Brunei, covering the past 150 years. This book focuses on the James Brooke period; its survival and diplomacy in the 19th century; the Japanese period; the Independence era; and international

## Politics and Government

politics in the 20th century. The author traces the evolution of Brunei's relationship with Britain and shows how, despite the suffocating embrace of British protection, her rulers struggled to maintain the vestiges of autonomy and to control her destiny. Written by a Malaysian, the book sets out to examine developments from the Asian, as opposed to the Western, point of view and the results are a generally sympathetic survey of Brunei's modern diplomatic history. While the first few chapters weave together the accounts of other writers (e.g. Keppel, Low, Irwing, Tregonning, Tarling and Wright), later chapters rely more on newspaper material and recently published scholarly studies. The nine appendixes contain various relevant treaties. For a review of this work, see Ernest Chew in *Journal of Southeast Asian Studies* (vol. 16 (1985), p. 166-67).

294 **Brunei and the Malaysia negotiations.**
D. S. Ranjit Singh. *Jernal Hubungan Antarabangsa*, vol. 3, (1975/76), p. 19-34. bibliog.

In 1961, when Malaysia showed open enthusiasm for a Malay–Brunei merger, one of the foregone conclusions was that Brunei, which had close ethnic and dynastic ties with Malaysia would automatically become a member of the new federation. However, much controversy and secrecy surrounded the negotiations between the two governments which resulted in Brunei not joining the federation. This paper, therefore, is an attempt to provide a deeper insight into the areas of compromise and conflict that highlighted the inter-governmental negotiations. The major issues discussed during the negotiations centred around the status of the Sultan of Brunei, the federal seat allocation for Brunei, the special position of Brunei's residents and taxation and revenues. The author also attempts to analyse the factors that led to the Sultan's controversial decision. The article is written in English, with an abstract in Malay.

295 **Brunei Darussalam in 1986: in search of the political kingdom.**
K. U. Menon. *Southeast Asian Affairs*, (1987), p. 85-101.

As a result of declining world oil prices, negative growth rates in 1986 finally confirmed the urgent need to restructure the economy. This is precisely the theme of the Fifth National Development Plan (1986-90) which recommends that Brunei's industrial policy be aimed at reducing imports and boosting export-oriented commodities. On 7 September 1986 Sultan Omar Ali Saifuddin III died. Two legacies of his period of government remain: the negotiation of Britain's commitment to the security of Brunei; and the replacement of the Residency system with the 1959 Constitution. Under the new Sultan the line-up of ministers has changed little and, according to the Cabinet reshuffle which occurred three years after independence, the kingdom is very much a modernizing autocracy. The year 1986 was also important for the Royal Brunei Armed Forces (RBAF), which assumed its first Bruneian commander and celebrated its 25th anniversary. The goals for a more effective defence posture are to upgrade the fighting force and increase troop strength to 5,000 men by 1995. In foreign affairs Brunei's first priority after independence was to uphold the international legitimacy of the new state. Clearly its membership in ASEAN was a major instrument of that policy, and it is now fully integrated into ASEAN activities. Other conscious efforts were directed toward expanding links with Brunei's neighbouring states, such as Singapore and Indonesia. Brunei also continued to improve its relations with Nepal, the homeland of the Gurkhas. Perhaps the most intriguing relationship in

1986 was forged with the United States, beginning with a visit by the US Secretary of State, George Schultz, and culminating in the transfer of several million dollars to the Contras. In all, the short period of nationhood has certainly promoted a measure of internal cohesion, legitimacy and stability in Brunei.

296  **Brunei in 1984: business as usual after the gala.**
Kent Mulliner. *Asian Survey*, vol. 25, no. 2 (Feb. 1985), p. 214-19. bibliog.

It is the purpose of this article to identify some of the problems, opportunities and responsibilities the government of Brunei must recognize with the coming of independence. The make-up of the government, at a ministerial level, is briefly outlined. The predominance of the royal family in key positions demonstrates the Sultan's commitment to retaining tight control. The author expresses concern as to whether all members of the royal family have such a commitment and, aside from losing touch with the people of Brunei, another hazard in this form of government is corruption. There is also no recognizable opposition party within Brunei, since the Brunei People's Party has been exiled. Another critical issue since independence has been the status of the Gurkha battalion, which must remain under British control. In the economic sphere petroleum earnings are reassuring but they also restrict the diversification of other sectors. It is estimated that about two-thirds of the citizens employed work for the government and the remainder is employed by Brunei Shell Petroleum. In foreign affairs this mini-state looks to international bodies to amplify its voice. ASEAN, for example, provides an ideal medium for improving relations with Brunei's larger neighbours, like Indonesia and Malaysia, who cast an envious eye on Brunei's wealth and resources.

297  **Brunei in 1985: domestic factors, political and economic externalities.**
D. S. Ranjit Singh. *Asian Survey*, vol. 26, no. 2 (Feb. 1986), p. 168-73.

A concise overview of the international and domestic policies of Brunei since independence. According to this paper, the state is currently concerned with four major problems: political survival, cultural identity, oil wealth and control of political power. For example, the government, in order to legitimize its position in the eyes of the populace, puts forward the idea that Brunei is a traditional Malay state as well as an Islamic state. The leadership wants an economically satisfied but docile population served by an élite and absolutely loyal bureaucracy. There does appear to be some relaxation by the government – it adopted bilingualism for all schools and allowed the formation of a new political party, the Brunei National Democratic Party (BNDP). Membership in ASEAN is seen as a symbiotic relationship – Brunei needs it to safeguard its cardinal interests and ASEAN cannot allow Brunei to remain apart since it is at the centre of that region. Brunei's security, therefore, is ASEAN's security.

## Politics and Government

298 **Brunei in comparative perspective.**
Donald Edward Brown. *Sarawak Museum Journal*, vol. 26, (1978), p. 135-60. bibliog.
This analysis deals with the structure of Brunei society and polity in the 19th century. A polity is seen by the author as a type of institution endowed with identity, membership, common affairs, autonomy and organization. There is a very simple formula which expresses the relationship between the institutions of Brunei and their neighbouring societies in the last century. Whereas, in general, Bornean societies were larger than their polities, Brunei's polity was larger than its society. The author uses ethnology and history to explore this peculiar feature of North Borneo.

299 **Brunei in international cross-currents 1946-1963.**
D. S. Ranjit Singh. *Jernal Hubungan Antarabangsa*, vol. 2, (1974/75), p. 95-109.
The rise of nationalism, decolonization and the emergence of independent states in Southeast Asia also dragged Brunei into international politics after World War II. These political changes brought about a desire for Brunei to have its own destiny and identity. In this article, the author considers three alternatives for Brunei: (a) to achieve independence (b) to merge with other entities in a federation of some sort; and (c) to continue a *status quo*, i.e. remain a British protectorate. These issues are discussed from the perspective of two political groups: the monarchists, led by the Sultan and representing a kind of guided, paternalistic type of nationalism; and the mass-based nationalistic group, led by Azahari and his partai Ra'ayat. During the 1950s and 1960s, Brunei became a classic example of the interplay between internal and external politics. In the end Brunei remained what it was, a protectorate. What course the country was to take if the British decided to withdraw was by no means clear at the time.

300 **Brunei – independence for whom?**
Michael Beckett Leigh. Canberra, Australia: Legislative Research Service, Department of the Parliamentary Library, 1984. 13p. map. (ITS Current Issues Brief, no. 1).
Decribes Brunei as an anomaly in many respects: the Sultan maintains an autocratic system of rule; the economy is prosperous; the Gurkha regiment provides protection; and foreign relations with ASEAN are viable. The author asks the question: full self-government for whom?

301 **Brunei: istoriya, ekonomika, politika.** (Brunei: history, economics, politics.)
Edited by A. N. Ionova. Moscow: Far Eastern Institute, 1984. 124p.
A detailed examination (in Russian, with an English summary) of Brunei's political development after World War II with special emphasis on the foundation of political parties, the Constitution of 1959, and Brunei's stand toward the Federation of Malaysia.

302   **Decolonization and international status: the experience of Brunei.**
M. Leifer.   *International Affairs*, vol. 54, no. 2 (April 1978),
p. 240-52.

An examination of the negotiations between the British government and the
Sultanate, leading to the Anglo–Brunei Agreement of November 1971. Furthermore, the author looks at the impact of this agreement on Brunei in the 1970s.
The first part of the paper surveys the roles of the British Resident, the High
Commissioner and the People's Party (Partai Ra'ayat). The second portion, which
attempts to clarify the international status of Brunei in the light of the request for
independence, reveals that the issues are complex. Britain sought to change its
relationship with the Sultanate by withdrawing the Gurkha battalion and by
introducing democratic institutions. Brunei, on the other hand, concerned with its
vulnerability because of its powerful neighbours, Malaysia and Indonesia,
believed that the Gurkhas served as a deterrent against external military
intervention. The Sultan preferred to retain a bilateral association despite the
wealth at his disposal. The Malaysian government felt that the British connection
sustained an anachronistic political system and, consequently, denied Brunei's
self-determination. Other countries in the region believed that political change in
Brunei could serve as a catalyst for a separate North Borneo, with similar goals to
those of the 1962 revolt. Brunei saw its predicament of international status not in
terms of a lack of legal sovereignty but rather a lack of sufficient capability to
ward off neighbouring states.

303   **The disturbances in the Tutong and Belait districts of Brunei (1899-
1901).**
A. V. M. Horton.   *Journal of Southeast Asian Studies*, vol. 18,
no. 1 (March 1987), p. 93-107. 2 maps. bibliog.

This paper comprises an inquiry into the unrest in the Belait and Tutong districts
of Brunei at the turn of the 20th century. After outlining the nature and causes of
the disturbances, the author attempts to explain why the recrudescence of
violence led to a departure in British policy toward the Sultanate. Once the
factors which had given rise to the original disaffection were removed, peace was
restored under a reformed administration in 1906.

304   **How the dominoes fell: Southeast Asia in perspective.**
John H. Esterline, Mae H. Esterline.   Lanham, Maryland;
London: Hamilton Press, 1986. 429p. 11 maps. bibliog.

Chapter seven, entitled 'Brunei', provides a concise political history of Brunei
from the earliest times, becoming a more detailed account of events and
developments from the close of World War II through to mid-1985. It emphasizes
characteristics of indigenous and colonial political culture and examines the
influence of nationalism on defence and the economy.

305 **Information submitted to the United Nations by her Majesty's**
**Government in the United Kingdom under article 73(e) of the**
**Charter of the United Nations for the year 1970.**
State of Brunei. London: Her Majesty's Government, [1970].
33p.
Three topics are covered in this report: economic, social and educational
conditions and activities in Brunei for a particular year.

306 **The internal politics of Brunei in the 1950's and 1960's.**
D. S. Ranjit Singh. In: *Proceedings of the 8th Conference of the*
*International Association of Historians of Asia, August 25-29, 1980.*
Kuala Lumpur: International Association of Historians of Asia,
1980. 27 leaves. bibliog.
A study of the impact of external forces and foreign relations on Brunei's internal
politics.

307 **Malaysia and Singapore; the building of new states.**
Stanley S. Bedlington. Ithaca, New York; London: Cornell
University Press, 1978. 285p. map. bibliog. (Politics and Inter-
national Relations of Southeast Asia).
Part IV is devoted to the Sultanate of Brunei (p. 257-68). The author discusses
Brunei's history and future status. He predicts that political change could make
Brunei part of Malaysia within one or two decades.

308 **Modern Brunei: some important issues.**
Timothy Ong Teck Mong. *Southeast Asian Affairs*, (1983),
p. 71-84. map.
In assessing Brunei's efforts to make its way into the 'modern era', the author
examines the issues of democracy and common good, the economic prospects for
the 1980s, and international diplomacy within ASEAN. The absence of
institutionalized popular participation in Brunei government has led to the
questioning of the viability of the existing political structure. A polity is frequently
judged by the extent to which it serves the common good. In Brunei, although the
Sultan and the royal family rule, the welfare features of the country range from
free education and medicine to the absence of personal income tax. In the
economic sphere, the challenge for the next decade is to expand employment
opportunities through the diversification of the economy. Another cause for
concern is Brunei's small size and, therefore, vulnerability. Thus, one of the
country's external priorities, upon which its diplomacy must centre, is security
and, indeed, its survival as a state.

309 **Political development in Brunei with reference to the reign of Sultan**
**Omarali Saifuddin III (1950-1967).**
Matassim bin Haji Jibah. MA thesis, University of Hull,
England, 1983. 90 leaves. map. bibliog.
This thesis reviews developments in three areas of domestic politics in the 1950s
and 1960s: the origin and implementation of the first written constitution; the role

of political parties in Brunei; and how that role was perceived by Sultan Omar Ali Saifuddin III. Within this context the author examines: why the political parties, the Partai Ra'ayat Brunei (PRB – Brunei's People Party) and the Barisan Kemerdekaan Ra'ayat (People's Independence Party), failed to meet the terms of the constitution; why the PRB launched an armed uprising in December of 1962; and the causes for Brunei's refusal to join the Federation of Malaysia in 1963. The information used in this thesis was obtained from local newspapers; the PRB's monthly newsletter, *Suara Ra'ayat* (The People's Voice) of January to July 1957; and the State Archives of the Brunei Museum.

310  **Political history of Brunei.**
B. A. Hamzah.  *Asian Defence Journal*, no. 3 (May-June 1980), p. 70-74 (Part I); no. 4 (July-Aug. 1980), p. 18-22 (Part II). map. bibliog.

This two-part essay explores the history of Brunei's contact with China, and the more turbulent relations with the West and Great Britain, in particular. The fact that Brunei sustained itself for four hundred years, despite some ups and downs, must be attributed to its internal strength. Likewise, the fact that the Sultanate disintegrated in the fifty years after contact with Great Britain must be attributed to external factors. For example, the annexing of Limbang could be construed as a British conspiracy supported by Charles Brooke's action. Furthermore, anything that was obstructing the English seaborne trade was considered piratical and deserved to be suppressed. In short, the author argues that while several internal factors, such as factions, politics and avaricious sultans, have played a prominent role in the early history of Brunei, the most important cause of the crumbling of the Brunei empire was Great Britain.

311  **Politics in the ASEAN states.**
Edited by Diane K. Mauzy.  Kuala Lumpur: Maricans, 1984. 343p. bibliog. (Maricans Academic Series).

A collection of eight essays featuring governments' efforts to achieve political stability and economic development. Each chapter, devoted to a specific country, includes an historical section providing socio-political and economic background information, an analysis of major policies, and a discussion centred around the complex questions: who rules, by what means, and on behalf of whom? 'Brunei, ASEANS's newest member' (p. 294-305), by Diane K. Mauzy, features a brief description of the royal family and the government, the people, the economy, defence and internal security, and contemporary problems and prospects.

312  **The price of loyalty.**
James Wong Kim Min.  Singapore: Summer Times Publishing, 1983. 230p. map.

The personal recollections of a former member of the Malaysian parliament and leader of the opposition, detained for several years without trial, accused of trying to cede the territory of Limbang to Brunei.

## Politics and Government

313 **Report on Brunei in 1904. Introduced and annotated by A. V. M. Horton.**
Malcom Stewart Hannibal McArthur. Athens: Ohio University, Center for International Studies, Center for Southeast Asian Studies, 1987. 283p. map. (Monographs in International Studies).

In 1904 the British Protectorate of Brunei had reached the nadir of its fortunes. It was reduced to an isolated enclave, bankrupt and threatened with complete takeover by Sir Charles Brooke of Sarawak. During that same year M. S. H. McArthur, a British official in the Malayan Civil Service, was sent to Brunei with instructions to assess the situation there and to make recommendations concerning the country's future administration. Published here, for the first time, together with an introduction and commentary by A. V. M. Horton, are two reports which resulted from McArthur's six-months stay in Brunei: 1. *Notes on a visit to the Rivers Belait and Tutong, dated 14 June 1904;* and 2. *Report on Brunei in 1904, dated 5 December, 1904.* These manuscripts were written by a comparatively unprejudiced, but not uncritical observer, and offer an exhaustive insight into the history and geography, as well as the constitution, economic and political conditions prevailing in Brunei on the eve of the British Residency there (1906-59). The text deserves the attention of a wider audience, not only in Brunei itself, but also including researchers and historians abroad.

314 **Das Staatsangehörigkeitsrecht von Brunei, Indonesien, Malaysia, Singapur, und den Philippinen.** (Nationality law of Brunei, Indonesia, Malaysia, Singapore and the Philippines.)
Hellmuth Hecker. Frankfurt, GFR: Metzner Verlag, 1978. 297p. (Sammlung Geltender Staatsangehörigkeitsgesetze, Bd. 36).

This work (in German and English) covers in detail the laws and legislation regarding citizenship, nationality and naturalization requirements for these five Southeast Asian nations. A summary of the constitution of each country is included. Brunei's Nationality Enactment of 1961 is fully described in English.

315 **Sultan Hassanal comes of age as a ruler.**
Nigel Holloway [et al]. *Far Eastern Economic Review*, vol. 135, no. 9 (26 Feb. 1987), p. 20-25.

A Brunei-based correspondent looks at Sultan Hassanal as a man in charge, who watches domestic affairs carefully and is sensitive to his subjects' problems. Following his father's death, it is the Sultan's turn to ensure the continuity of the dynasty. The new form of government now more closely resembles that of a modern state with the prime minister presiding over a cabinet. The Sultanate now has much closer control over its foreign reserves. It has presented its credentials as a developing country in the form of a five-year Development Plan, with a twenty-year programme to follow. There is also a university which is, as yet, at a fledgeling stage. All this has been achieved by a gradual assertion of the Sultan's power. At the same time, according to Western observers, it is an obsession of the Sultan not to let Brunei develop too quickly, as the resulting social and economic turbulence would destroy his power. Brunei has also been scared by the collapse of several financial institutions, all managed by foreigners. The shortage of labour also limits the rate of 'Brunei-zation' of the private sector. Leaders of the major political parties in the country urge the Sultan to bring about the alleviation of poverty and the nationalization of Shell Petroleum. Lastly, the author discusses the royal feud between Sultan Hassanal and his father which nearly caused a crisis in leadership.

**Brunei, the structure and history of a Bornean Malay sultanate.**
*See* item no. 150.

**British policy in the South China Seas area, with special reference to Sarawak, Brunei and North Borneo, 1860-1888.**
*See* item no. 188.

**The British Residency in Brunei, 1906-1959.**
*See* item no. 189.

**Nineteenth century Borneo: a study in diplomatic rivalry.**
*See* item no. 208.

**Brunei in transition.**
*See* item no. 231.

**Nervously into the world.**
*See* item no. 243.

**Agreement between Her Majesty the Queen of the United Kingdom of Great Britain and Northern Ireland and His Highness the Sultan of Brunei amending the Agreement of 29 September 1959.**
*See* item no. 317.

**Brunei: the ASEAN connection.**
*See* item no. 338.

**Treaties and engagements affecting the Malay States and Borneo.**
*See* item no. 344.

**The Borneo three.**
*See* item no. 350.

**Brunei Darussalam in 1985: a year of nation-building.**
*See* item no. 352.

**Brunei: the constraints on a small state.**
*See* item no. 356.

**Brunei asserts its independence.**
*See* item no. 386.

# The Constitution
# and Legal System

316 **Het adatrecht van Borneo.** (Customary law of Borneo.)
   J. Mallinckrodt. Leiden, The Netherlands: M. Dubbeldeman,
   1928. 2 vols. map. bibliog.

Although written some years ago, this is still the standard work, in Dutch, on this
subject. It represents an inquiry into the jurisdictions and legal rights of
indigenous groups in Borneo. The early history of customary law; the
classification of tribes; land and water rights; family inheritance; political
influence and Dayak legal terminology are some of the subjects covered. External
forces, such as Islam and Christianity, are also noted.

317 **Agreement between Her Majesty the Queen of the United Kingdom
   of Great Britain and Northern Ireland and His Highness the Sultan
   of Brunei amending the Agreement of 29 September 1959.**
   London: Her Majesty's Stationery Office, 1972. 17p.
   (Parliamentary Papers. Miscellaneous, no. 12).

This agreement came into force on 23 November 1971, and was presented to the
British Parliament by the Secretary of State for Foreign and Commonwealth
Affairs by command of Her Majesty. It spells out the responsibilities and
provisions concerning both parties, Her Majesty, the Queen of the United
Kingdom of Great Britain and Northern Ireland and His Highness Sultan
Hassanal Bolkiah Mu'izzaddin Waddaulah, Sovereign and Chief of the State and
Territory of Brunei Darussalam, in relation to the future development of the
country. It was decided that, under the status of 'protectorate', Her Majesty
should continue to be responsible for the external affairs of the state and that,
subject to consultations, provisions for the defence and security of the state
should be a task shared between Her Majesty and His Highness. Furthermore,
the state should enjoy full internal self-government, and additional amendments
to the 1959 Agreement should be made as necessary. These amendments spell out
in further detail the responsibilities for internal and external affairs. The
agreement is made and expressed in both the English and Malay languages.

318 **Brunei and the Commonwealth.**
*Commonwealth Law Bulletin*, (April 1981), p. 771-76.

Traces the political developments throughout history which have brought about a change in Brunei's position, from one of dominance to various forms of foreign allegiance. Close association with Britain dates back to 1847 and, in 1888, Brunei came under British protection. In the early 20th century a system of government was introduced whereby legislation was enacted by a Legislative Council presided over by the Sultan. Further constitutional development was interrupted by a period of Japanese occupation during World War II. Indirect elections to the Legislative Council under the new constitution were held in 1962 for the first time. The United Nations has also taken an interest in the affairs of Brunei with regard to its declaration of independence. This paper provides a good outline of the present constitutional arrangement, with the Sultan as supreme executive authority assisted by the *Mentri Besar* (Chief Minister) and five councils: the Religious Council, the Privy Council, the Council of Ministers, the Legislative Council and the Council of Succession.

319 **Brunei: cabinet reorganization.**
Kent Mulliner. *Southeast Asia Business*, no. 11 (fall 1986), p. 14-15.

A short article which describes the reorganization of the Brunei cabinet after the death of Sultan Omar Ali Saifuddin III, who reigned from 1950 to 1967, and voluntarily abdicated in favour of his son, the current Sultan. In the new cabinet the Sultan, who continues to serve as Prime Minister, now replaces his late father as Minister of Defence. His brothers will also continue to hold key cabinet posts. The new cabinet includes four new ministries and a number of non-royal deputy ministers. All positions and names are listed.

320 **Brunei constitutional documents.**
State of Brunei. Kuala Lumpur: Government Press, 1960. 276p. (Treaties. Miscellaneous Public Documents).

Contains all constitutional documents which came into force on 29 September 1959 and before 1 July 1960. The most important agreement made by Her Majesty the Queen, His Highness Sir Omar Ali Saifuddin Saadul Khairi Waddin and the High Commissioner established the constitution of the state of Brunei in 1959. This is the official document spelling out the establishment, function and procedures of the Privy Council, the Executive Council and the Legislative Council. It provides guidance on: the powers required to legislate and to authorize expenditures; the establishment of a public service structure; the Attorney-General; and the state seal.

321 **The laws of Brunei.**
Compiled by Robert Yorke Hedges. London: [n.p.], 1952. rev. ed. 2 vols.

The preface states that 'this edition of the laws of Brunei has been prepared in accordance with the revised edition of the laws enactment, 1951. It contains the enactments of the state which had been enacted on or before the 22nd day of March 1952, except such as are omitted under the authority of that Enactment.' The two-volume set is divided into nineteen subject areas, containing ninety-two chapters. Volume one covers: revision of the laws; application and interpretation of the laws; administration of justice; public order; and criminal law. Volume two covers: currency and finance; mining; forestry; medicine and health; the police and prisons; the postal service and telegraphs; education; local government; regulation and control; commerce and industry; family law; statistics; public officers; and the military and defence.

322 **The laws of the State of Brunei, 1906-1930.**
State of Brunei. Singapore: Government Printing Office, 1931. 410p.

This edition represents the enactments of the State of Brunei which came into force on 31 December 1930. Forty-two enactments are printed in this volume, as amended, and range in subject from population registration to stamping procedures, powers of law, classification of land, protection of employers and labourers, the postal service, extradition of individuals, and laws related to mining, sanitation and excise tax. In 1952 a two-volume revised edition was prepared in accordance with the revised edition of the Laws Enactment of 1951. Volume 1 contains chapters 1-31 of the enactments and volume 2 covers chapters 32-91.

323 **Malaya and Singapore, the Borneo Territories: the development of their laws and constitutions.**
Edited by Lionel Astor Sheridan, with specialist contributors. London: Stevens & Son, 1961. 510p. 2 maps. (British Commonwealth. The Development of its Laws and Constitutions, vol. 9).

In the words of the author, this legal textbook is a pioneering effort; its nature has been influenced by the general lack of publications in the legal profession. Those who have contributed to this volume, therefore, attempted not only to sketch the development of Malaya's law and constitution but also indicated how the information could be applied. Despite the title of this book, Brunei is quite extensively covered, particularly in Chapter 5, entitled 'The Borneo Territories', written by R. H. Hickling (p. 115-50). It covers the constitutional structure, the civil service, nationality and citizenship, the legal system and local government as they existed in 1960. Local government in Brunei is, generally, regulated by the Municipal Boards Enactment, which contains, in thirty-nine brief sections, a basic law regulating municipal boards, rates and by-laws. A list of Brunei's enactments is also provided (p. 498-99).

324 **Memorandum upon Brunei constitutional history and practice.**
R. H. Hickling. s.l.: 1955. 96p. bibliog.

An excellent interpretation of constitutional development in Brunei since 1906, including its later reform (1946), the role of the British High Commissioner, and the naturalization of aliens and citizenship law. This typewritten manuscript is marked confidential but appears in many bibliographies and libraries.

325 **The nature of Malay customary law.**
Joseph Minattur.   *Malaya Law Review*, vol. 6, no. 2 (Dec. 1964),
p. 327-52. bibliog.

Malay customary law, called *adat*, generally means right conduct, and in common usage stands for all things connected with proper social behaviour. Thus, it may connote rules of etiquette, and ceremonies for special occasions, as well as those customs which have legal consequences. It is in this last sense that the word *adat* is generally used in this paper. After defining the fundamental rules of *adat melayu* (Malay custom) the concept is applied to the constitutional structure, land tenure and marriage. Brunei Malay society adheres to the same form of customary law, *adat perpateh*.

326 **Some historical aspects of local and sovereign rights in 19th century Brunei.**
Colin N. Crisswell.   *Journal of Oriental Studies*, vol. 10, no. 1
(1972), p. 51-61. bibliog.

An important feature of the earlier sultanates was the existence of a system of local rights similar to those of the European feudal system. All inhabitants of Brunei owed allegiance to an overlord to whom they were obliged to render a wide range of dues and services. The power of the Sultan rested upon his ability to pay, or otherwise persuade loyal subjects to punish those who disobeyed his commands. The decline of his authority was paralleled in the 18th and 19th centuries by the impoverishment of the Sultanate and the consequent cession of territories inhabited by those who resisted the claims of their overlords. The establishment of the state of Sarawak by James Brooke and the North Borneo Company by the British government created rivals that competed vigorously in the acquisition of the declining domain of the Sultanate. Several cases are presented where these two entities, in pursuit of their goals, applied whichever interpretation of customary law best suited their interests. By its very nature customary law afforded considerable scope for interpretation even more so when the Sultan's right to arbitrate was challenged. In 1888 Britain strengthened her position in northern Borneo by establishing several protectorates. The author describes how, by the end of the century, the ultimate sovereign powers in the area were in reality wielded by British officials, the Foreign and Commonwealth Office (FCO) and Governors of the Straits Settlements.

327 **The status of women in the family law in Malaysia and Brunei.**
Ahmad bin Mohamed Ibrahim.   *Malaya Law Review*, vol. 7,
no. 1 (July 1965), p. 54-94; vol. 7, no. 2 (Dec. 1965), p. 299-313;
vol. 8, no. 1 (July 1966), p. 46-85; vol. 8, no. 2 (Dec. 1966),
p. 233-69.

A substantial article, published in four consecutive issues of this journal, focusing on family law of non-Muslim women and their status, as recorded in the local statutes of Malaysia and Brunei. Five subject areas are analysed: marriage, parental authority, legal status of unmarried women, inheritance rights and social factors affecting the status of women in the family.

328  **The subsidiary legislation of Brunei. 1956-.**
State of Brunei.  Kuching, Sarawak: Government Printing Office,
1956-1958; Kuala Belait, Brunei: Brunei Press: 1959-.
This publication, which supplements the *Government Gazette*, contains a wider
range of notifications and enactments than the *Gazette* itself. They include labour
enactments, dangerous drug enactments, air navigation enactments, court
enactments and income tax enactments, to name just a few. Many of these have
been continuously improved and changed, hence the revised editions.

329  **The Supreme Court enactments.**
State of Brunei, Supreme Court, 1963.  [s.l.]: S. M. Buse,
Government Printer of Brunei, 1970. 354p.
Contains some 64 enactments which are modelled after the Singapore Supreme
Court of 1934. These orders and rules may be cited as 'The Brunei High Court
(civil procedure) rules, 1970', and have the approval of the Sultan.

330  **Water laws in Moslem countries.**
Dante A. Caponera.  Rome: Food and Agriculture Organization
(FAO), Water Resources and Development Service, Land and
Water Development Division, 1973. 223p. bibliog. (FAO Irrigation
and Drainage Paper, no. 20/1).
Irrigation in the Moslem world has traditionally received legal protection and,
over many generations, has developed into the present system of water rights.
These laws and customs are documented in this volume together with twelve
country case-studies. The general discussion covers the origin of Moslem law,
water use and ownership, concepts of water legislation, customary water laws and
codified law. The Brunei case-study is given on pages 62-73. The water legislation
of Brunei is rather complex since it derived from the constitution of the state
(1959), the land code of 1907 and the water supply enactment of 1962. Other
topics covered in some detail are water rights, protection of waterworks, water
administration and pollution control.

**Brunei** *adat.*
*See* item no. 538.

**Annual Report.**
*See* item no. 589.

# Foreign Relations
# and Defence

331 **Borderline in Brunei.**
Michael Page. *Far Eastern Economic Review*, vol. 43, no. 4
(23 Jan. 1964), p. 158, 163-64.
Traces the events of the 1962 revolt and the attempted formation of the
Federation of the Borneo Territories. The revolt was crushed and the concept of
the Federation rejected, leaving certain scars on Brunei's relations with its
neighbours. The exiled leftist Partai Ra'ayat was still a perceived threat; there
were sporadic raids over the border from Indonesia; Chinese propaganda was
spread through newspapers published in Sarawak; and there could have been
trouble from thousands of Indonesians living in Sabah if they had joined up with
the Communists in Sarawak. None of these situations were discounted as
potential threats to the national security of Brunei at the time.

332 **Brunei and Britain.**
Leonard Rayner. *Roundtable*, no. 290 (April 1984), p. 153-58.
A critical interpretation of Britain's attitude toward and role in Brunei's changeover from the status of protectorate to that of sovereign state. The author,
Honorary Regional Correspondent for the Confederation of British Industry,
stationed in Hong Kong, feels that the handling of Brunei is somewhat analogous
to Britain's withdrawal from Malaya (1957) and Singapore (1963). In all three
countries no attempt was made either to protect or to seriously consult British
commercial interests. Critics claim that in the case of Brunei the British supported
a régime that ruled by emergency decree, that the British-owned share in the
oilfields is declining and that the Crown Agents who managed the Sultan's foreign
investment are losing their business to American banking firms. In short, unlike
other nations, Britain has failed to coordinate its overseas commercial activities
with its diplomatic initiatives. At the same time, with Britain's departure, the
State of Brunei, with all its advantages, seems to have been left ill-prepared for
the endemic confrontations that are part of everyday life in Southeast Asia.

103

**Foreign Relations and Defence**

333   **Brunei: ASEAN's reluctant independent.**
T. M. Burley.  *Insight: Asia's Business Monthly*, (Dec. 1981),
p. 38-40.

The author argues that, despite its enormous oil-based wealth, Brunei has favoured reliance on British protection for fear of being absorbed by its larger neighbours. However, this view has changed since independence.

334   **Brunei in ASEAN; the viable choice?**
Pushpathavi Thambipillai.  *Southeast Asian Affairs*, (1982),
p. 105-12.

The author considers the options available to Brunei in terms of its regional relations with the member states of ASEAN. Several factors make the small Sultanate so significant: its large oil reserves, its potential for trade with neighbouring countries and its crucial location on one of the busiest sea routes in the South China Sea. From the ASEAN point of view, the political considerations of Brunei's membership seem more important than the economic ones. Inclusion of Brunei would enable ASEAN to encompass the entire region and, therefore, provide better coordination in both political and security matters.

335   **Brunei joins ASEAN: its expectations.**
B. A. Hamzah.  *Asian Pacific Community: a Quarterly Review*,
no. 24 (spring 1984), p. 1-13. bibliog.

Addresses the problems associated with intra-ASEAN politics which are likely to emerge from the entry of Brunei into the organization. Topics covered include: the extent to which the membership of Brunei will shift the balance of power within ASEAN; the benefits from joining ASEAN, such as political security and access to international forums; and an evaluation of whether Brunei has the capacity to fully undertake ASEAN's obligations. The author concludes that Brunei's membership will enhance ASEAN's prestige, bargaining position and regional stability.

336   **Brunei – newest and richest in Asia.**
Bruce Burton.  *International Perspectives: the Canadian Journal on World Affairs*, (Jan.– Feb. 1984), p. 27-29.

Prime Minister Trudeau's visit to Brunei, in January 1983, was designed to enhance Canada's export performance and political profile within Southeast Asia. With this background in mind the author outlines the economic and political climate in Brunei and how this relates to Western nations, ASEAN and the United Nations. Like others who have written about Brunei, Burton asks the question: how long can the oil dependency and absolute monarchy, based on the Persian Gulf model, last within the setting of contemporary Southeast Asia? According to the author if the problems related to the nature of the present political system can be resolved, however, the long-term prospects for Brunei look favourable.

337  **Brunei: prospects for a 'protectorate'.**
Lim Joo-Jock.  *Southeast Asian Affairs*, (1976), p. 147-64. map.
Reviews three critical issues faced by Brunei in the 1970s. The author first of all focuses on the efforts to diversify the economy in the light of a continued dependency on, and dominance of, the oil industry. Another source of contention was the Sultan's policy of 'Malaynization', which, together with the Limbang claim, brought about a continued state of tension between Brunei and Malaysia. Finally, the country's external defence and internal security, which were both shared with Britain, were critical factors in planning for the future. The author concludes with a possible scenario for the time when Brunei will have to face Britain's ultimate withdrawal.

338  **Brunei: the ASEAN connection.**
Donald Weatherbee.  *Asian Survey*, vol. 23, no. 6 (1983), p. 723-35. bibliog.
Explores the internal and external political and economic situation of Brunei on the eve of independence. Brunei was set on a course of full sovereignty under the twin pressures of Malaysian hostility and British policy. Malaysia attempted to destabilize the régime by providing clandestine assistance to the exiled Partai Ra'ayat Brunei. The Malaysian pressure on Brunei and the sentiments in the United Nations were congruent with the British government's desire to terminate its semi-colonial role in the region. Brunei's unwillingness to sever ties with Britain stemmed partly from its precarious relations with Malaysia and Indonesia. Even though Brunei's defence posture is one of the most advanced in the region, the author argues, its best guarantee for security may be the kind of international order which currently exists in the region. However, he points out that joining ASEAN will undoubtedly have consequences for both Brunei's internal politics and ASEAN itself.

339  **The confrontation in Borneo.**
E. D. Smith.  *Army Quarterly and Defence Journal*, part I, vol. 105, no. 4 (1975), p. 479-83; part II, vol. 106, no. 1 (1976), p. 30-36.
A survey, from a military perspective, of the Brunei–Indonesian border conflict in 1962. At that time, Malay and Gurkha soldiers on the one hand and Indonesian border terrorists on the other, made incursions into Malaysian territory. The military tactics of the Borneo campaign are seen as a model of inter-service cooperation, with all three branches of the military services successfully working together. The author presents a chronological analysis of the events and outcome of Indonesia's confrontation with Brunei and Malaysia which lasted almost four years, ending in August 1965. Part I, entitled 'The revolt in Brunei leads to "confrontation"', focuses on the formation of the North Kalimantan National Army (Tentara Nasional Kalimantan Utara – TNKU) which was to establish a union of the Borneo States of Sarawak, Sabah and Brunei. The TNKU in Brunei was under the political leadership of Azahari. Part II, entitled 'The incursions of the undeclared war', provides tactical details of the 'undeclared war' adopted by British and Malaysian troops.

340    **Gurkhas to withdraw from Brunei in 1983.**
*Asia Research Bulletin*, vol. 8, part 6 (31 July 1978), p. 468-69.
Describes the pre-independence nerves of the government with regard to such
issues as defence and future relationships with its neighbours, Indonesia and
Malaysia.

341    **The Kennedy Initiatives in Indonesia, 1962-63.**
Frederick Philip Bunnell.    PhD thesis, Cornell University, Ithaca,
New York, 1969. 335p. bibliog; University Microfilms, Ann Arbor,
Michigan, 1970.
In the wake of the settlement of the West Irian dispute Indonesia continued its
militant anti-imperialist confrontation policy which emphasized national unity and
a commitment to the creation of the New Emerging Forces against its northern
neighbours. The Kennedy Administration tried to persuade Indonesia to avoid a
policy of confrontation for a Western-financed economic stabilization programme.
Sukarno, however, exhibited only intermittent interest in abandoning confrontation for stabilization. Chapter III (p. 224-72), entitled 'The genesis of confrontation' (December 8, 1962-March 2, 1963), presents a good historical account of the
Brunei revolt and its immediate consequences for Washington, DC, Jakarta and
Manila.

342    **The Pandaruan issue (1884-1920).**
A. V. M. Horton.    *Sarawak Gazette*, vol. 110 (July 1984),
p. 26-30. bibliog.
The Pandaruan River forms part of the international frontier between Limbang
(Sarawak) and Temburong (Brunei). In the 19th century families living in the
district paid taxes to Sarawak despite the fact that Brunei claimed sovereignty
over the area. The conflict between Charles Brooke and the British authorities
was finally settled in 1920 when control of the left bank of the river was vested in
the Sarawak government and the right bank in the Brunei government. According
to the author, the establishment of the river itself as the international boundary
would have presented a more favourable outcome for Sarawak.

343    **Southeast Asia's second front: the power struggle in the Malay
Archipelago.**
Arnold C. Brackman.    London: Pall Mall Press, 1966. 341p.
bibliog.
This book traverses considerable ground in the multi-complex struggle for
regional leadership and identity, racial tension between the Chinese and Malays,
and the rivalry between authoritarian and representative systems of government
in the Malay-speaking archipelago. It is the writer's intention to present the
schemes and stratagems of the protagonists, whenever possible, in an expository
manner. The reason for this approach is that the power struggle can neither be
appreciated nor understood without a knowledge of the various 'pieces', their
limitations, and their position within the conflict. Thus, some of the issues
addressed in this study, resulting from a process of decolonization are: (1) the
Brunei revolt and its relationship to the power struggle between Indonesia,
Malaysia and the Philippines; (2) the creation of a makeshift Malaysia, a daring

political and social experiment which sought to melt Malays, Chinese, Dayaks and Kadazans into unity between China and Indonesia; (3) the Philippines' claim to North Borneo and search for an Asian identity; and (4) Indonesia's 'crush Malaysia' campaign, first punctuated by an armed attack against Borneo and later against the Malay Peninsula. Within a yet larger context the book also addresses the emergence of the Jakarta–Peking axis, Soviet policy, the role of the United Nations (UN), and even the Australian and American responses to the course of events.

344 **Treaties and engagements affecting the Malay States and Borneo.**
William George Maxwell, William Sumner Gibbon. London: J. Truscott & Son, 1924. 276p.

This important document contains some 136 treaties and agreements which influenced the political future of the Malay Peninsula and the States under British protection in Borneo between 1800 and 1920. With respect to Brunei the following agreements are included: Agreement with Muda Hashim, 1841, and the Confirmation by the Sultan of Brunei, 1842; Cession of Labuan, 1846; Treaty with Great Britain, 1847; Confirmation of grant of Sarawak, 1853; Cession of the Baram (Sultan Abdul Mumin), 1882; Cession of the Baram (Sultan Hashim), 1885; Agreement for British Protection, 1888; Agreement of the appointment of Resident, 1905 and 1906; and Agreement with Sarawak regarding the Pandaruan River (westbank of Limbang), 1912 and 1920.

345 **US–ASEAN dialogues resume in Washington.**
Linda Droker. *Business America*, vol. 8, no. 7 (1 April 1985), p. 2-4.

High-level officials from the United States and ASEAN met in Washington, DC, on 2-3 April 1985, to discuss a broad range of economic subjects with implications for American business. Topics include: trade expansion, investment, development cooperation and technical assistance. A profile of each of the six ASEAN members shows that they are economically among the most dynamic countries in the world. A country profile of Brunei (by Jeff Hardee and Savanna Jackson) follows this article (p. 5). It summarizes the objectives of the current National Development Plan and the transfer of technology in both agriculture and the oil industry.

346 **US frigate *Constitution* in Borneo, 1845.**
William Craig Chaplin. *American Neptune: a Quarterly Journal of Maritime History*, vol. 4, no. 3 (July 1944), p. 217-23.

This account consists of two letters written by a lieutenant of the US Navy describing the hydrological conditions of the Sambas River and the Bay of Brunei in 1845. A trip to the 'Sultan of Borneo Proper' is also reported.

347 **The United States Consul and the Yankee Raja.**
H. G. Keith. Kota Batu, Brunei: Brunei Museum. [1980]. 256p.
map. bibliog. (Brunei Museum Journal Monograph Series, no. 4).
An account of Charles Lee Moses and Colonel Joseph William Torrey and their attempt to form an American colony in northern Borneo. This work describes the personalities involved and the political events which took place between 1864 and 1881.

**Coastal zone protection in Southeast Asia.**
*See* item no. 23.

**Visit of the 'King of Brunei' to the Emperor Yung Lo of China: contemporary and ancient accounts.**
*See* item no. 172.

**Revolt in Borneo.**
*See* item no. 219.

**Commemorative booklet on the admission of Brunei Darussalam into ASEAN (Association of Southeast Asian Nations).**
*See* item no. 236.

**Internationalization of the Brunei question and its implications.**
*See* item no. 239.

**Background to a revolt: Brunei and the surrounding territory.**
*See* item no. 291.

**Brunei Darussalam in 1986: in search of the political kingdom.**
*See* item no. 295.

**Brunei in 1985: domestic factors, political and economic externalities.**
*See* item no. 297.

**Brunei in international cross-currents 1946-1963.**
*See* item no. 299.

**Decolonization and international status: the experience of Brunei.**
*See* item no. 302.

**The internal politics of Brunei in the 1950's and 1960's.**
*See* item no. 306.

**Modern Brunei: some important issues.**
*See* item no. 308.

**Politics in the ASEAN states.**
*See* item no. 311.

**Brunei Darussalam in 1985: a year of nation-building.**
*See* item no. 352.

**Oil and independence in Brunei: a perspective.**
*See* item no. 363.

**Oil-state Brunei steps out from British protection to join the world.**
*See* item no. 364.

**Oil and security in Brunei.**
*See* item no. 409.

# Economics and
# Development

348  **Allah, Shell and the Sultan.**
Friedemann Bartu, with photographs by Sandra Maire Prem.
*Swiss Review of World Affairs*, vol. 33, no. 11 (Feb. 1984),
p. 11-15.

Brunei's modern economic and political structure rests almost entirely on three supports: Allah, Shell Oil and the Sultan. This has not always been the case. The author explains why Brunei was threatened with extinction on several occasions during the past 400 years. This essay also deals with the anticipated changes in the country brought about by independence. While the populace seems quite content with the *status quo* the future position of the ethnic minorities is quite unclear. The Sultan has already informed the 40,000 Chinese subjects that only citizens of Brunei will have claim to the country's passport. In the long term, however, pressures are bound to increase in Brunei from Islamic fundamentalists dissatisfied with the country's modern life-style or from politically engaged citizens demanding a greater voice in public affairs. With independence the Sultan will have full responsibility for dealing with these and other domestic issues.

349  **ASEAN economies.**
Viraphong Vachratith.  *Bangkok Bank Monthly Review*, vol. 25
(April 1984), p. 148-54.

ASEAN, as a whole, has of late been in the limelight, receiving global acclaim as one of the world's fastest growing regions. Despite an overall satisfactory picture, however, the economic performance of individual member nations differs widely. This article discusses the economic background and performance of each nation, including the newest member, Brunei.

350 **The Borneo three.**
Derrick Sington, Jeannine Stephens. *New Commonwealth Trade and Commerce*, vol. 39 (Feb. 1961), p. 85-92. map.

A comparative description of the social, economic and political conditions in Sarawak, Brunei and North Borneo at the time a federation was contemplated for the British Borneo territories. While local circumstances differ considerably between the three territories, they have many problems in common. These include difficulties in achieving economic self-sufficiency, improving physical communication and narrowing the gap between rural and urban areas. Several reasons are presented as to why Brunei needed to begin to develop its economy and, at the same time, was reluctant to join a federation.

351 **Brunei.**
Michelle Misquitta. In: *Asia and Pacific Review*. Saffron Walden, England: World of Information, 1987. 8th ed., p. 62-64. map.

A current account of the economy, government and business climate in Brunei. The author concentrates on issues related to oil production, national politics, manpower problems and plans to diversify the economy. The previous annual editions contain similar material, including a map, key facts about the country and a business guide which provides information on working hours, telecommunications, hotels and banking services.

352 **Brunei Darussalam in 1985: a year of nation-building.**
Sharon Siddique. *Southeast Asian Affairs*, (1986), p. 43-51. map.

Siddique argues that the year 1985 did not equal 1984 in terms of historical significance, rather it was dedicated to nurturing the one-year old nation. The political scene was dominated by the promotion of the concept of 'Malay Islamic Monarchy', which emphasizes the fact that Islam is the official religion, Malay the official language and that native Malays enjoy a pre-eminent position in society. Issues which remain unclear include: the position of indigenous groups, the role of political parties and the problem of foreign workers. In foreign affairs, Brunei established full diplomatic relations with several nations, strengthened its military cooperation with Australia, became more fully integrated in ASEAN activities and hosted the '*Merdeka Games*' for the first time. Economically, despite a decline in oil production and sales, the year was capped in December with the publication of the Fifth National Development Plan (1986-90).

353 **Brunei: development problems of a resource-rich state.**
Christopher Colclough. *Euro-Asia Business Review*, vol. 4, no. 4 (Oct. 1985), p. 29-32.

Brunei has sustained very rapid growth over the past decade, based exclusively on revenues from the export of oil and gas. The government must now face the question of how to maintain the productive capacity of the economy over the long term. Ironically, the present oil-based development strategy is the main obstacle toward promoting a variable industry outside the oil sector. The author anlayses the main choices faced by the government, concluding that the present high-technology, labour-saving strategy of Singapore may be a useful lesson for Brunei.

# Economics and Development

354 **Thé Brunei economy.**
Sritua Arief. East Balmain, New South Wales: Rosecons, 1986.
233p. map. bibliog.
Provides a comprehensive analysis of Brunei's economy based on a variety of
information derived from agencies in both the public and private sectors. Part I
contains a review of the economic structure of Brunei and development planning.
An overview of the major productive sectors (agriculture, petroleum, gas and
manufacturing) is presented in part II. Public finance, external trade, and money
and banking are the subjects of part III. The concluding part covers income
distribution, population, employment and physical infrastructure. The author, an
economist, prepared this report in 1985-86 in conjunction with his involvement in
the National Development Plan.

355 **Brunei seeks to diversify its economy.**
Bernard Long. *Singapore Trade and Industry*, (Dec. 1974),
p. 39-42.
Provides an evaluation of the 1975-79 National Development Plan which is aimed
at creating 10,000 new jobs by 1978 and diversifying the predominantly oil-based
economy. Under the 1962-66 plan Brunei built a new airport, a deep-water
harbour, a water supply scheme for the capital and a road network to isolated
areas. This infrastructure was to serve industrial and agricultural developments
envisioned in the 1975-79 plan. Although much of the investment in this plan was
expected to come from overseas, the government was also seeking to encourage
the growth of the state's own small private sector.

356 **Brunei: the constraints on a small state.**
A. J. Crosbie. *Southeast Asian Affairs*, (1978), p. 67-79.
The survival of Brunei is discussed in terms of its resources, government
performance, and the challenges faced in the rapidly changing international
environment. Crosbie argues that Brunei's small size and population places
limitations on its political affairs, social change and development potential. A
heterogeneous population, traditional restraints, lack of skilled labour and high
wages in the service sector all detract from attempts to induce industrialization
and stimulate agriculture in order to diversify the economy. Brunei is fortunate,
however, in terms of its capital reserves and energy resources which are used to
provide revenues for infrastructure improvements outlined in the National
Development Plan. The author concludes that Brunei's economic and political
stability will largely depend on external rather than internal independent
variables.

357 **Charcoal production in Brunei.**
J. S. Lim, P. M. Shariffuddin. *Brunei Museum Journal*, vol. 3,
no. 3 (1975), p. 201-19. map.
The earliest reference to charcoal in the literature on Brunei is found in the 1946
Brunei *Annual Report*. Even today few people are aware that charcoal is
produced solely on the island of Berbunut in Brunei Bay where the first kiln was
built in 1930. In this account the author presents the history of the charcoal
industry in Brunei and describes the method of production used today. The data

112

were collected through interviews with charcoal producers on Berbunut in 1975. The information presented gives rise to three important questions: (a) why is Berbunut the only place in Brunei where charcoal is produced, (b) why is charcoal which has been manufactured from mangrove logs still in demand, and (c) what is the future outlook for this industry? The author provides some speculative answers. Sixteen plates illustrating various phases of charcoal production accompany this article.

358  **Country Profile: Malaysia, Brunei.**
London: Economist Intelligence Unit, 1986/87. 43p.
This annual country report provides some basic economic information and analyses current trends in primary production, employment, manufacturing, construction and foreign trade. Statistics on revenues, interest rates and money supplies are also included. Brunei is covered on pages 32-42.

359  **The development of resources in British Borneo and its impact on settlement.**
Y. L. Lee.  *Sarawak Museum Journal*, new series, vol. 10, nos. 19-20 (1962), p. 563-89. bibliog.
British Borneo (North Borneo, Brunei and Sarawak) is largely undeveloped. Economic exploitation has so far only taken place in the coastal region. Developments such as smallholding commercial agriculture in Sarawak and Sabah, off-shore oil production in Brunei and timber exports are, however, receiving much greater support from governments than has been the case in the past. The chief obstacle to these development efforts seems to be the shortage of labour, access to the interior and fluctuation in world demand. For a more detailed discussion of Brunei's coastal region see *The coastal environmental profile of Brunei Darussalam: resource assessment and management issues*, edited by Chua Thia-Eng, Chou Loke Ming and Marie Sol M. Sadorra (Bandar Seri Bgawan: Fisheries Department, Ministry of Development; Manilla: International Center for Living Aquatic Resources Management, 1987. 196 p. 44 maps. bibliog.). This publication provides much needed data for an integrated strategy to protect, develop and control the coast and its resources. The first three chapters assess the physical environment and its resources, such as mangroves, beaches, reefs and minerals. Other topics covered include: traditional uses of the marine environment; land use patterns; aquaculture; recreation; and major pollution problems, both on- and off-shore.

360  **Focus on Brunei.**
Don Taylor.  *New Commonwealth Trade and Commerce*, vol. 48, no. 3 (1969), p. 9-21. map.
A general review of the economy with an emphasis on primary production and infrastructure developments. In the 1960s Brunei emerged as a developing economy with potential for growth through the diversification and expansion of the private sector. The author records how agriculture, fisheries, forestry, trade and tourism have progressed by the end of that decade. In addition to the construction of a new international airport and deep-water port as a means of furthering the development of industry, the government also embarked on a

programme to expand on telecommunications, education and social services. Also included is a short biography of the present Sultan, some economic statistics and a chronology of events.

361   **Independence of wealth.**
      Patsy Lim.   *Singapore Business*, vol. 8, no. 1 (Jan. 1984), p. 6-7.

An analysis of various sectors of the economy in the early 1980s, including agriculture, and the construction, manufacturing and service industries.

362   **Industrial development: Asia and the Far East. Vol. II –**
      **Afghanistan, Australia, Brunei, Burma, Cambodia, Ceylon,**
      **Republic of China, Hong Kong, India, Indonesia, Iran, Japan,**
      **Republic of Korea.**
      United Nations. Economic Commission for Asia and the Far East.
      Selected documents presented to the Asian Conference on
      Industrialization. Manila, December 6-20, 1965.   New York:
      United Nations, 1966. 454p.

Prior to the adoption of national planning in 1962, industrial development in Brunei was of an *ad hoc* nature. Since then, various National Development Plans have provided for the planning of industrial activities and infrastructure developments. Industrial policy is not yet clearly delineated, but some basic legislation exists with respect to investment regulations for both domestic and overseas investors. No data are currently available on the mobilization of capital for industrial growth. Several joint ventures with Japanese companies and domestic entrepreneurs are, however, mentioned. The institutional framework for industrial promotion is provided by the National Development Plan. At present only Brunei Shell Petroleum is engaged in manpower training but since the publication of this report the government has established several training institutions to mobilize the country's labour resources. The chapter on Brunei covers pages 55-61.

363   **Oil and independence in Brunei: a perspective.**
      B. A. Hamzah.   *Southeast Asian Affairs*, (1981), p. 93-99.

The aim of this article is to show the linkage between oil and the question of independence, especially in terms of oil being a factor in retarding Brunei's progress toward independence. Continued access to Brunei's oil has been an important consideration in Britain's colonial policy. At the same time the Sultan was genuinely worried about his vulnerable position in both defence and leadership. Finally, with regard to ASEAN, Brunei's possible membership was seen as an asset to the further development of ASCOPE (ASEAN Council on Petroleum) and a guarantee of the region's energy needs.

364   **Oil-state Brunei steps out from British protection to join the world.**
      V. G. Kulkarni, Susumu Awanohara.   *Far Eastern Economic*
      *Review*, vol. 123, no. 4 (26 Jan. 1984), p. 28-34. map.

This cover story surveys every aspect of domestic and foreign affairs at the time when Brunei became the world's 169th sovereign state. Now that its ruler, Sultan

Sir Muda Hassanal Bolkiah, has taken the Sultanate's destiny into his own hands, many problems are now faced, including: external security, internal stability, relations with its neighbours and the management of natural resources. Clearly, Brunei's foreign policy, despite the British defence link, will be shaped mainly by its relations with ASEAN. Economic cooperation with Singapore which provides a skilled workforce is also stressed. On the domestic front there is concern over maintaining internal harmony and diversifying into a non-oil economy. The Malays and other indigenous groups who form the majority of the population are generally well cared for, but the Chinese have become a non-citizen minority who do not receive welfare and are only marginally represented in the country's administration. Throughout the population there is a significant gap between the urban rich and the rural poor, compounded by the ostentatious life-style of the royal family. Culturally, Brunei faces the difficult task of adapting its traditional ways to the necessities of a contemporary world.

365 **Pengakajian [sic] ekonomi bagi perusahaan2 perniagaan, 1979. Economic survey of business undertakings, 1979.**
Economic Planning Unit, Brunei.   Bandar Seri Begawan: Bahagian kira2 negara yunit peranchang ekonomi pejabat setia usaha kerajaan Brunei, 1980. 115p.

This report, carried out by the Economic Planning Unit in 1978, presents the results of a survey of corporate and quasi-corporate enterprises in Brunei. The data presented are for the years 1974-78. Apart from economic accounts, tables on capital formation, employment, organization and number of establishments by economic activity are presented. In addition, information on ownership of paid-up capital by locals and foreigners is included. Since 1978 the data generated from the business census have been published in the *Brunei Statistical Yearbook* (q.v.).

366 **Ranchangan kemajuan Negara, 1975-1979. (National Development Plan, 1975-79).**
State of Brunei.   Bandar Seri Begawan: Star Trading & Printing, [1976], 63p.

The third five-year National Development Plan (in Malay and English), outlines public and private sector involvement in improving the economic, social and cultural life of the people of Brunei between 1975 and 1979 at a cost of 500 million Brunei dollars. The first chapter summarizes the achievements of the 1962-66 plan; chapter two addresses socio-economic problems and long-term development perspectives; chapter three looks at growth targets and investment programmes; chapter four estimates government expenditure; and chapter five outlines private investment. The last part of the plan touches on administrative policy and development planning.

**Economics and Development**

367 **Ranchangan kemajuan Negara, 1980-1984. (National Development Plan, 1980-84).**
Bandar Seri Begawan: Yinit Peranchang Ekonomi, Pejabat Setiausaha Kerajaan Brunei (Economic Planning Unit, State Secretariat), [1980]. 79p.

The Fourth National Development Plan (in Malay and English) is, in some respects, similar to previous plans in that it focuses on public sector projects and only provides a general framework for the development of the private sector. Four basic objectives are stated: increase the flow of goods and services and hence improve per capita income; modernize the economy; develop complementarities between the public and private sectors; and integrate the public elements with adequate coordination. A review of the 1975-79 plan is also provided.

368 **Ranchangan kemajuan Negara yang kelima, 1986-1990 – Fifth National Development Plan, 1986-1990.**
Bandar Seri Begawan: Yinit Peranchang Ekonomi, Kementerian Kewangan (Economic Planning Unit, Ministry of Finance), [1985]. 109p.

The Fifth National Development Plan has been formulated not only to cater for the development of the next five years but also for long-term growth up to the year 2005. As this is the first plan since the country assumed its full independence, greater emphasis is placed on nation building. In reviewing the economy, the report states that the worsening of the current oil market clearly signals for immediate action in the diversification programmes, particularly in the field of industry. Comparative statistics on population, government expenditure, oil production, trade and manufacturing are used to project future trends in various sectors of the economy. The text of the report concludes with a series of proposed strategies and action programmes for the next five years. Appendix 8 itemizes 355 projects in agriculture, education, construction, housing, health, public building and other areas to be carried out during the next five-year period.

369 **A review of brickmaking in Brunei.**
R. B. Tate. Kuala Belait, Brunei: Geological Survey, State of Brunei, 1968. 18 leaves. map. (ITS Technical Report no. 2).

The first successful commercial brick production in Brunei began in 1960. Since that time a steady increase in demand has resulted in an expansion of activities to nine factories, all located in coastal areas, where abundant deposits of clay were found. This report covers various aspects of brickmaking, the nature of the raw material, clay preparation, fuel sources, the kinds of kilns used, firing procedures and the quality of bricks. Unfortunately, most bricks produced in Brunei tend to be of a poor quality. Various reasons for this are given in this report and recommendations are made on methods to improve the quality and strength.

370 **The Sultan takes his place in the sun and the world.**
Robert Kroon. *ICC Business World: Magazine of the
International Chamber of Commerce*, vol. 3 (July-Sept. 1985),
p. 26-30.
An informative article which reviews Brunei's recent spending pattern related to
defence, infrastructure development, the royal family and government. The
author is critical of the Sultanate's one-man system of rule and how it copes with
an ever-growing budget surplus. Many photographs are included.

371 **Thinking of the future from day one.**
*Economist*, vol. 290 (7 Jan. 1984), p. 61-62.
Outlines several domestic problems in Brunei, including the shortage of skilled
labour, the imbalance between imported and exported goods, the economic
dependency on Brunei Shell and the lack of investment opportunities outside the
petroleum industry.

**The Brunei Darussalam State Chamber of Commerce review.**
*See* item no. 11.

**The geography of the State of Brunei with special reference to agriculture
and agricultural systems.**
*See* item no. 41.

**The development of Brunei during the British residential era 1906-1959: a
sultanate regenerated.**
*See* item no. 193.

**Brunei: what changes will independence bring?**
*See* item no. 235.

**Sarawak and Brunei: a report on the 1947 population census.**
*See* item no. 273.

**Brunei Darussalam in 1986: in search of the political kingdom.**
*See* item no. 295.

**Brunei in 1984: business as usual after the gala.**
*See* item no. 296.

**Modern Brunei: some important issues.**
*See* item no. 308.

**US–ASEAN dialogues resume in Washington.**
*See* item no. 345.

**Malaysia and Brunei handbook.**
*See* item no. 382.

**Oil and economic development issues in Brunei.**
*See* item no. 408.

**The political economy of oil in Brunei.**
*See* item no. 412.

**Annual Report.**
*See* item no. 589.

**Brunei: statistischer Gesamtüberblick und neuer Entwicklungsplan 1986-1990.** (Brunei: statistical overview and the new development plan 1986-1990.)
*See* item no. 593.

# Trade and
# Transportation


372  **ASEAN economies and investment opportunities.**
Viraphong Vachratith, Pairote Wongwuttiwat, Kanitha
Srisilpavongse.  *Bangkok Bank Monthly Review*, vol. 25
(Oct. 1984), p. 399-406.
The Association of Southeast Asian Nations (ASEAN) was established to
accelerate development through close cooperation and mutual assistance among
its six members in the Southeast Asian region. The Association represents a
market of 277 million people. In 1983 the regional gross domestic product (GDP)
reached US$205.3 million. Per capita income ranges from a high of US$22,000 in
Brunei to a low of US$560 in Indonesia. After a general introductory survey of
the ASEAN Finance Corporation (AFC), the report gives a nation-by-nation
evaluation of the ASEAN economies for the benefit of potential investors.


373  **Brunei and camphor.**
Robert Nicholl.  *Brunei Museum Journal*, vol. 4, no. 3 (1979),
p. 52-74. bibliog.
Numerous historical accounts of Chinese, Indian and Arabic origin are cited in
this analysis to confirm the importance of the camphor trade in the history of
Brunei. For centuries Brunei was known for being the source of the world's finest
quality of camphor, a translucent crystalline obtained from the *kapur* trees and
used in medicine and the manufacturing of celluloid. Historically, the camphor
connections established early relations and trade with provinces of southern
China, Malacca, India and Sumatra.


374  **Brunei in ASEAN: implications for us.**
Patsy Lim.  *Singapore Business*, vol. 8, no. 1 (Jan. 1984), p. 3-6.
Focuses on the Singapore–Brunei trade pattern. Import-export data for the period
1978-83 for both countries is analysed. The article concludes that Brunei could
evolve into a satellite centre playing a complementary role to Singapore's
development as a major financial centre.

375 **Brunei joins ASEAN: a European perspective.**
   Brian Bridges. *Asia Pacific Community: a Quarterly Review*,
   no. 24 (spring 1984), p. 14-24. bibliog.

Brunei became the sixth member of the Association of Southeast Asian Nations
(ASEAN) in 1984. Bridges argues that although membership is not likely to make
any significant difference to the intra-ASEAN trade, there is considerable interest
in Brunei's capital for private sector ASEAN industrial joint ventures. Europeans
are also interested in Brunei's assets as banks in Europe, Japan and America
compete for the country's international reserves. European investment opportunities in manufacturing and other sectors are, however, likely to be affected by the
country's labour shortage. Brunei's high per capita income will also exclude it
from European aid. On a regional basis, however, the European Community
(EC) is considered an important trading partner for ASEAN, but EC imports
from ASEAN are marginal. The European countries have an interest in
ASEAN's strategic position across vulnerable sea-lanes which could affect the
movements of European goods to Asia. The author suggests that the Europeans
need to strengthen their relationship with ASEAN. As the ASEAN nations adjust
to their new member, the Europeans ought to reconsider how to enhance their
opportunities with this dynamic group of countries.

376 **The coastal boats of North Borneo and Labuan Bay.**
   C. A. Gibson-Hill. *Sabah Society Journal*, vol. 3, no. 4 (March
   1968), p. 190-204.

Based on a survey carried out in 1949, the author attempts to provide a
descriptive classification of native-built boats found in the coastal waters of Sabah,
Labuan and Brunei. The system of identifying the small crafts is based on the
form and method of hull construction. Accordingly, ten types of boats have been
identified. The Brunei boats fall into three major categories: the fishing boats
mostly employed on rivers, the deeper dug-outs known as *bagong* and the general
cargo carriers, the *tongkang*.

377 **Coastal problems encountered at Muara Port area in Brunei.**
   H. S. Goh, A. S. Rajendra, S. K. Pui. In: *International
   conference on coastal and port engineering in developing countries,
   Colombo, Sri Lanka*, vol. 1 (20-26 March 1983), p. 115-29.
   10 maps.

Muara Port, the only general cargo port in Brunei, is surrounded by shallow seas
which are prone to continued siltation. To avoid large-scale dredging and to
reduce navigational distance to the port, a channel was constructed in 1969 by
cutting through the Pelompong Spit. This paper describes some parameters of the
coastal environment and the problems experienced after the construction of the
new access channel. Methods applied to resolve some of the erosion and
sedimentation problems are also discussed.

378 **Commerce and international trade.**
Voon Phin Keong. In: *Brunei in transition: aspects of its human geography in the sixties.* Khoo Soo Hock [et al]. Kuala Lumpur: Department of Geography, University of Malaya, 1976. p. 222-60. 6 maps. (ITS Occasional Papers, no. 2).

Presents an analysis of import-export statistics for the period 1920 to 1965. The changing composition of imported goods and exported materials indicates the evolution of Brunei's economy from a virtually undeveloped country to one where development is steadily advancing. Despite this, the weekly *tamu* (market fair) where large numbers of indigenous farmers and merchants sell jungle products, handicrafts and other home-made articles remains a vital component of internal commerce and trade.

379 **Construction of [the] new international airport, Brunei.**
W. A. D. Sterling, C. B. Paget, J. M. Eddison, M. C. Earwaker. *Proceedings of the Institution of Civil Engineers*, vol. 62, part 1 (Nov. 1977), p. 605-22. map.

Deals with the particular problems of earthmoving and pavement construction involved in the building of the new international airport in Brunei. The airport was designed and constructed between 1966 and 1972 on a site some 8 kilometres outside the city of Bandar Seri Begawan. Surveys and construction procedures are described in detail and a brief mention is made of the terminal building complex and the radio-navigational equipment.

380 **Design and construction of Muara Deep Water Port, Brunei (Paper 8649).**
A. H. Beckett, S. Marshall. *Proceedings of the Institution of Civil Engineers*, vol. 74, part 1 (Aug. 1983), p. 349-64.

The development of the State of Brunei necessitated the construction of a deep-water port capable of handling general cargo vessels operating throughout Asia. It had long been realized that the waters off Muara, some 25 kilometres from Bandar Seri Begawan, offer a sheltered site, but access to the off-shore deeper waters was hampered by a series of mobile sandbars. Tidal models were developed to study various means of access, and a gap through the Muara Spit was found to be self-scouring and needed little maintenance dredging. This paper describes the design and construction of the access channel and the principal features of the new port. Construction began in May 1968 and the first vessel arrived in February 1972. The cost of construction was approximately B$40.4 million. For a discussion on Paper 8649 see *Proceedings of the Institution of Civil Engineers*, vol. 76, part 1 (1984), p. 741-52. 3 maps.

381 **Export market study: export potential for Western Australian rural industries.**
Kevin R. Rutter, P. Smetana. Perth, Western Australia: Rural and Allied Industries Council, Department of the Premier and Cabinet, 1982. 46p. map.

An evaluation of the potential to increase trade in agricultural commodities between Western Australia, Malaysia and Brunei. The section on Brunei contains

121

**Trade and Transportation**

information on transportation links to Western Australia, and Brunei's requirement to import beef, rice and other agricultural products. Some statistics on Brunei's trade, livestock, crops and land use are also included.

382 **Malaysia and Brunei handbook.**
Department of Trade and Industry, New Zealand. Wellington: Government Printer, 1975. 87p. 4 maps.
An excellent review of the economy, trade and development in the early 1970s. A section entitled 'Selling to Brunei' describes the requirements for engaging in business activities in the country (p. 64-73).

383 **Perahu-perahu tambang yang berlainan jenis. Taxis with a difference.**
*Petroleum di Brunei*, (Jan. 1985), p. 12-18.
A bilingual article discussing the *tambang*, or water taxi, used to transport passengers across the Brunei River which separates the town's waterfront from Kampung Ayer, the nation's oldest settlement. Interviews with some of the boatmen reveal information on the hazards of this occupation, new traffic regulations introduced by the government, the services they provide and the costs associated with operating a *tambang*.

384 **Why companies should investigate opportunities in booming little Brunei.**
*Business Asia* (Hong Kong), vol. 6, no. 26 (27 June 1975), p. 201-03. map.
Based on the 1975-79 Development Plan, this article lists the government's spending plan for equipment and materials that could provide sales opportunities for suppliers overseas. For companies interested in selling to Brunei, a businessman's guide to Brunei provides some details on the population, labour and wages, money and taxes, and other useful facts.

**Longshore drift and its effect on the new Muara Port.**
*See* item no. 80.

**Focus on Brunei.**
*See* item no. 360.

**Pengakajian [sic] ekonomi bagi perusahaan2 perniagaan, 1979. Economic survey of business undertakings, 1979.**
*See* item no. 365.

**Brunei as an oil state.**
*See* item no. 397.

**Annual Report.**
*See* item no. 589.

**Statistics of external trade.**
*See* item no. 597.

122

# Finance and Banking

385 **Brunei: a guide for business and investors.**
Singapore: Coopers & Lybrand, 1985. 41p. 2 maps.
This guide, specifically prepared for clients of Coopers & Lybrand (an accountancy firm), is useful for anyone interested in knowing more about the business climate in Brunei. It includes information on the major industries, labour regulations, taxation, banking and finance. Business organizations and reporting requirements are also listed.

386 **Brunei asserts its independence.**
L. Goodstadt. *Euromoney*, (July 1984), p. 146-52.
Primarily addresses the economic and financial changes brought about by full independence. The creation of the Brunei Investment Agency (BIA) was a first logical step. The government also increased its equity in Brunei Shell Petroleum (BSP). The biggest budget item in recent years has been defence and several independence related construction projects are being completed. Public expenditure and private development have created something of a banking boom engaged primarily in recycling the 'oil dollars'.

387 **The Brunei mystery: how the world's richest man manages his money.**
Peter Koening. *Institutional Investor*, vol. 19, no. 12 (Dec. 1985), p. 138-48.
A well-written investigative report on Brunei's financial reserves and their management during the last decade. Initially, the country's assets were managed by the British Crown Agents. By 1975 the price of oil had quadrupled and Brunei's financial resources were attracting international interest. Over the next few years money managers the world over descended on Brunei to attempt to pursuade the royal family to diversify the management of the state's portfolio. In 1983 the Brunei Investment Agency (BIA) was established which has seven

**Finance and Banking**

investment firms under contract with varying mandates. On another front there is competitive tension between the old-guard British money managers and new American investors. The strength of Brunei's ruling family lies in its ability to play balance-of-power politics among international investment institutions.

388   **Brunei's Khoo d'état**
Nigel Holloway, James Bartholomew.   *Far Eastern Economic Review*, vol. 134, no. 49 (Dec. 1986), p. 54-57.
Correspondents from London and Singapore report on the government's takeover of the family-controlled National Bank of Brunei in November 1986. Charged with false accounting and conspiracy to defraud, the Malaysian businessman Khoo Teck Puat committed one of the most controversial banking scandals in recent Brunei history.

389   **Economic and social conditions in Brunei.**
Hong Kong and Shanghai Banking Corporation.   London: Hong Kong and Shanghai Banking Corporation, 1976-. (Country Reports).
Forms part of a country series summarizing the economic trends of the countries involved. Population, trade, finance and all sectors of the economy are interpreted for a particular year.

390   **Financial development in Malaya and Singapore.**
P. J. Drake.   Canberra: Australian National University Press, 1969. 253p. map.
This investigation of the financial system of West Malaysia and Singapore is concerned with two basic topics: the money supply and the allocation of credit. The study also concentrates on the developments from the 1950s to 1967 'when the common Malayan dollar gave way to the individual currencies of Malaya, Singapore and Brunei.'

391   **Financial institutions and markets in Southeast Asia: a study of Brunei, Indonesia, Malaysia, Philippines, Singapore and Thailand.**
Michael T. Skully.   New York: St. Martin's Press, 1984. 411p. bibliog.
Examines the financial sector of Southeast Asia in terms of the local money market, the stock exchange and foreign exchange markets. The information provided should prove invaluable for researchers in financial economics and international business. Pages 1-48 are devoted to Brunei.

392 **A guide to doing business in the ASEAN region:
Brunei-Indonesia-Malaysia-Philippines-Singapore-Thailand.**
Department of Commerce, International Trade Administration,
Office of Pacific Basin, United States.   Washington, DC: US
Government Publications Office, 1985. 65p. map.
This booklet outlines in very broad terms the countries' economic growth rates,
development plans and trade policies. Brunei became a member of ASEAN in
January of 1984 upon being granted full independence. Several important
addresses in the United States pertaining to the various countries are provided as
well as addresses in the countries themselves. Brunei is covered on pages 5-9.

393 **Major companies of the Far East 1986. Volume I: Southeast Asia.**
Edited by Jennifer L. Carr.   London: Graham & Trotman,
3rd ed. 1986. 319p.
A comprehensive guide to business establishments, listing their addresses,
principal activities and financial information, of all Southeast Asian countries. For
Brunei (p. 3-7), seventy-seven companies are listed. There are plans to annually
update this book.

394 **The Sultan and the financier.**
Eric Gelman, Ronald Henkoff, Melinda Liu, Simon Ingram.
*Newsweek*, vol. 106, (21 Oct. 1985), p. 60-62.
Traces the controversial relationship between the Sultan of Brunei, the Egyptian-
born businessman Mohamed al Fayed, and British real estate owners. In this
account, East and West meet in some strange ways: an Asian Sultan visits the
business leader of a nation that once dominated his land and now is a declining
power, possibly in need of his help. To navigate these waters the Sultan relies on
men like Mohamed al Fayed and Saudi financier Adnan Khashoggi to serve as
intermediaries.

**Fiscal system and economic development: the ASEAN case.**
*See* item no. 29.

**Country Profile: Malaysia, Brunei.**
*See* item no. 358.

**The Sultan takes his place in the sun and the world.**
*See* item no. 370.

**Brunei joins ASEAN: a European perspective.**
*See* item no. 375.

**Annual Report.**
*See* item no. 589.

# The Oil and Gas Industry

395  **Assessment of undiscovered conventionally recoverable petroleum resources of Malaysia and Brunei.**
Keith Robinson.   Reston, Virginia: US Department of the Interior, Geological Survey, 1984. 19 leaves. 3 maps.
A geological investigation prepared to assess the likely extent of, as yet, undiscovered conventionally recoverable petroleum resources of Malaysia and Brunei. This report was conducted as part of the World Energy Resources Program of the US Geological Survey. It primarily contains maps, statistics and probability graphs projecting resources.

396  **Brunei and the Seria oilfields.**
Hedda Morrison.   *New Commonwealth Trade and Commerce*, vol. 21, no. 7 (April 1951), p. 498-501.
This illustrative article presents a brief account of Brunei and its oil industry at the time of recovery from the destructions of World War II.

397  **Brunei as an oil state.**
J. W. Moffatt.   *Trade and Industry*, vol. 17, no. 10 (5 Dec. 1974), p. 516-18.
A survey of Brunei's economy and oil industry of the mid-1970s intended for the British business community. The article elaborates on the development of the state's infrastructure, including a deep-water port, an international airline and various municipal services. The oil industry constitutes an obvious target for British exporters, although the competition is strong, especially from foreign (mainly American) companies with extensive experience in oil and gas exploration.

398 **Brunei Shell Petroleum.**
Seria, Brunei: Brunei Shell Petroleum Co., Public Affairs
Department, 1986. 44p. 2 maps.

This annual report of Brunei Shell Petroleum discusses the oil industry
exploration, production and engineering. Historical background information on
the country is also provided.

399 **Brunei: the forgotten state of Southeast Asia.**
Srikant Dutt. *China Report*, vol. 17, no. 6 (1981), p. 33-41.
bibliog.

Written prior to independence, the author saw Shell Oil as a unique example of
how the narrow commercial interests of a company can override the national and
even international interests of several states, namely those of Great Britain and
Brunei, respectively. First, by bolstering an absolute monarchy, the Sultan
through his oil wealth is able to stifle opposition and buy off potential dissenters.
Related to this strategy has been Shell's desire to retain a cheap security presence
for itself by maintaining protectorate status for the country. This brings other
benefits to Shell. Not only are high corporate profits maintained, the company can
also sell oil to South Africa with impunity. This curious anomaly in Brunei was,
however, running out of time when independence changed the status of Shell Oil.

400 **China's offshore energy policy and its implication for the Japanese
market oriented ASEAN producers.**
Lam Lai Sing. *ASEAN Economic Bulletin*, vol. 1, no. 3 (March
1985), p. 209-22. bibliog.

Using foreign capital and advanced technology to develop its off-shore energy,
China began its exploration activities on an unprecedented scale in 1984. This
paper considers the implications of China's future energy production on the
ASEAN oil market. In the case of Brunei, the highest proportion of exports in
both crude oil and Liquid Natural Gas (LNG) go to Japan. Japan's oil imports
from Brunei and other ASEAN nations has been falling in recent years, however,
with an increasing supply coming from China. This has made China an effective
competitor, especially against Brunei and Indonesia, and it is likely to accelerate
when China's off-shore oil appears on the market in the late 1990s with its
'preferential prices'.

401 **Country profile: Brunei.**
*OPEC Bulletin*, (1984/85), p. 35-42. map.

A state-of-the-arts assessment of Brunei's oil and gas reserves, exploration efforts
and policy regarding production, consumption and trade. While the precise extent
of Brunei's reserves is a state secret, at the current rate of extraction, oil should
last well into the next century. Activities are described for several important
offshore production sites. Additional discoveries are unlikely but the government
is encouraging other companies (besides Brunei Shell Petroleum [BSP]) to
become involved in prospecting. Another vital source of Brunei's prosperity is
natural gas and there are currently efforts underway to expand LNG facilities and
processing plants. However, Brunei will not involve itself in the manufacturing of
oil products and petrochemicals. There has been no major shift in policy and

The Oil and Gas Industry

cooperation with BSP since independence and the nationalization of the oil industry is not contemplated by the government. The government is attempting to increase the 'Brunei-zation' of BSP, improve its share in joint ventures and reduce the rate of long-range production.

402　The discovery and development of the Seria fields.

G. C. Harper.　Kota Batu, Brunei: Muzium Brunei, 1975. 99p. (Muzium Brunei Penerbitan Khas, bil. 10 [Brunei Museum, Special Publication, no. 10]).

An interesting narrative of the hardships, environmental conditions and technological difficulties encountered in the development of Brunei's largest onshore oilfields.

403　In the wake of political independence: Seria brings Brunei up to self-sufficiency in oil.

[A correspondent].　Petromin, (Feb. 1984), p. 16-18.

Describes the technical aspects and economic benefits of the state's first refinery completed at Seria in November 1983. With a capacity of 10,000 barrels per day, the plant will meet Brunei's demand for jet fuel, kerosene and diesel well into the 1990s.

404　Independence renews drilling offshore.

Nick Longworth.　Petromin, (Oct. 1984), p. 22-29. map.

This cover story reveals several new activities in the oilfields of Brunei. First, the independent American company, Jasra Jackson, is making a second attempt to drill for oil, this time with the cooperation of Brunei Shell Petroleum (BSP) and to gain more accurate information on the local geology. This geology is, however, very complex and may have been the cause of a blow-out due to sudden overpressure experienced by BSP at the Iron Duke field. Finally, the author reports on a planned decrease in output by BSP. The company has the capacity to raise production to levels of up to 200,000 barrels per day, but is working toward a target of 150,000 barrels by 1988.

405　Kilang penapis minyak Brunei. The Brunei refinery.

Petroleum di Brunei, (Oct. 1984), p. 4-13.

A new $104 million refinery, officially opened in August 1984, dramatically increased refining capacity in Brunei. This bilingual article describes the contribution this facility is expected to make and how refined products are used domestically.

406　Laporan Tahunan. (Annual Review).

Bandar Seri Begawan: Public Affairs Department, Brunei Shell Group of Companies, [n.d.]. annual.

Represents the official report of the Brunei Shell Group of Companies, which includes Brunei Shell Petroleum Company, Brunei LNG, Brunei Coldgas and the Brunei Shell Marketing Company. This report discusses the activities of each company for a particular year, gives information on personnel changes, oil trading, exploration, engineering and development for the industry as a whole. The public affairs activities of the Brunei Shell Group of Companies, particularly those involving education, are also mentioned. A map, coloured illustrations and statistics are usually included.

### 407 The offshore petroleum resources of South-East Asia. Potential conflict situations and related economic considerations.

Corazon Morales Siddayao. Kuala Lumpur: Oxford University Press, under the auspices of the Institute of Southeast Asian Studies, Singapore, 1978. 205p. 6 maps. bibliog.

This work examines the potential for conflict or cooperation among the Southeast Asian nations arising from the search for petroleum resources. Chapters consider such topics as the value of petroleum to these nations and actual territorial disputes, and include reference to Brunei.

### 408 Oil and economic development issues in Brunei.

B. A. Hamzah. Singapore: Institute of Southeast Asian Studies, 1980. 34p. bibliog. (Research Notes and Discussions Paper, no. 14).

This paper focuses on the interaction between oil and national development in Brunei. The author's purpose is to examine to what extent the oil and gas resources contribute to the continued economic development. Through many years of political autonomy and consolidation Brunei Shell has managed to create for itself a mini state within a Sultanate. The Brunei model is not unique but in present-day international petroleum nomenclature, it is extraordinary. The anomalous state–company relationship that has arisen in the Sultanate is a source of political embarrassment which, Hamzah argues, Britain can no longer ignore. It is recommended that Brunei considers joining OPEC and ASEAN, in order to gain access to petroleum knowledge. This course of action is also likely to raise the state's credibility in its continuing relationship with Brunei Shell. To maximize benefits the author suggests that the government renegotiate the present financial provisions with Brunei Shell. The new contractual relationship could be in the form of concessions, leases, joint ventures, service contracts or profit sharing. See also *The political economy of oil in Brunei* (q. v.).

### 409 Oil and security in Brunei.

Ahmad Hamzah. *Contemporary Southeast Asia*, vol. 2, no. 2 (Sept. 1980), p. 182-91. bibliog.

Reviews the trade-off whereby the British provide basic security in exchange for continued access to Brunei's petroleum resources. The author suggests, however, that the oil–security linkage is asymmetrical. Through many years of political consolidation, Brunei Shell has made itself indispensable to the local economy and, thus, the company is frequently regarded as a state within a sultanate. On the other hand the author questions the kind of security arrangement the British government provides in exchange for oil and other privileges. First, the Gurkhas guarding the oil installations do not form a British defence contingency. Secondly, the regiment is maintained at an exorbitant cost, particularly when it does not have an offensive capability. In the final analysis, the British have got a good bargain in Brunei. To be fair, the British did not promise more than what they were willing to provide. It is most unfortunate, according to the author, that Brunei has taken a different view.

### 410 Petroleum in Borneo.
A. Redfield. *Economic Geology*, vol. 17, no. 5 (Aug. 1922), p. 313-49. 3 maps. bibliog.

For centuries the natives of Borneo have used mineral oil obtained from surface seepage for the purpose of domestic remedies and fuel. This evidence prompted the establishment of commercial oil and drilling activities by British and Dutch companies as early as 1885. This lengthy study is devoted to the first three decades of oil exploration and drilling activities in Borneo with particular emphasis on three areas: the Koetei, Tarakan and British Borneo oil districts. Each district is described in terms of its location, physiography, stratigraphy, structural geology and petroleum development. The oil-bearing territories of the British portion of Borneo included the Miri oilfields, the Belait area of northwestern Brunei, the island of Labuan and the Klias Peninsula near Brunei Bay where the first well was drilled in 1887. Intensive commercial production in Brunei's off-shore oilfields started in 1929.

### 411 The petroleum resources of Indonesia, Malaysia, Brunei, and Thailand.
Energy Information Administration Office of Oil and Gas. Washington, DC: US Department of Energy, 1984. 183p. 3 maps. bibliog. (Foreign Energy Supply Assessment Program Series).

Chapter three provides an overview of Brunei's oil and natural gas resources, their distribution, reserves, pattern of recovery and trade. A summary of all countries is given in chapter five.

### 412 The political economy of oil in Brunei.
Ahmad Hamzah. PhD thesis, Tufts University, Fletcher School of Law and Diplomacy, Medford, Massachusetts, [1980]. 300p. 2 maps. bibliog.

Presents an indepth study of the complex relationship between oil politics and economic interests in Brunei during the 1970s. Ironically, although oil has given the Sultanate the highest per capita income in Southeast Asia, it has also interfered with Brunei's progress toward independence. According to the author, continued access to Brunei's petroleum resources is the single most important factor for Britain's reluctance to cut ties with the Sultan. In turn, the Protectorate accepted a passive role in its dealings with Brunei Shell. Thus, the oil and gas industry's investments have created a dependency state with the characteristics of an enclave economy. The country's oil bounty is the primary reason for neglecting the agricultural sector which has turned the country into a net importer of most basic food needs. The impact of oil imperialism as a result of the government's inferior bargaining position, is one theme analysed in this thesis. Some corrective measures are also suggested, such as increasing the economic rent and royalties, or by restructuring income tax regulations. Brunei should also move to obtain a majority equity control and equal participation in the policy-making apparatus in the petroleum industry. Aside from the central theme outlined above, the dissertation presents an excellent coverage regarding the political history of Brunei, the oil mining laws and economic development policies. For an abbreviated version of this study, see items no. 408 and 409.

413 **A review of the oil economy of Brunei; with particular reference to the arrangement concerning government revenue from oil production operation.**
Walter J. Levy.    Zug, Switzerland: Walter J. Levy, 1962. 75p.
Deals with government oil revenues, petroleum legislation, leases and tax allowances. It also provides a good introduction to the legal basis for oil development in Brunei.

414 **Report on the utilization of natural gas for the production of nitrogenous fertilizers in the State of Brunei.**
London: L. H. Manderstam & Partners, 1957. 159p.
A comprehensive analysis of the potential for using natural gas to manufacture nitrogenous fertilizer in Brunei. The possibilities in Brunei are compared to the supply of natural gas in Iraq, Pakistan, Canada, the United States, Italy and France.

415 **Shell builds an island.**
Ralph Shaw.    *Journal of the British Association in Malaya*, (July 1957), p. 27-30.
Describes the preparation of an oil-drilling platform which was lowered into the sea at Hankin 'F', a potential drilling site 112 miles offshore in the China Sea.

416 **Shell in Brunei.**
Seria, Brunei: Brunei Shell Petroleum Co. Ltd, [1973]. 1 vol. map.
This booklet summarizes the development history of oil and gas production by the Brunei Shell Petroleum Company in Brunei.

417 **South-East Asian seas: oil under troubled waters: hydrocarbon jurisdictional issues, and international relations.**
Mark J. Valencia.    Singapore, New York: Oxford University Press, 1985. 155p. 18 maps. bibliog.
Issued under the auspices of the East-West Environment and Policy Institute, The East-West Center, Honolulu, Hawaii, the author describes the petroleum geology of Southeast Asia in relation to the jurisdictional claims and disputes with particular reference to oil potential, national interests and international relations. Of particular interest is the chapter entitled 'The off-shore Brunei: Brunei, Malaysia, China, Vietnam, Philippines' (p. 75-89). This chapter discusses Brunei's efforts in establishing its new maritime boundaries in the light of the recently declared 200-nmi EEZ (Exclusive Economic Zone).

**The Oil and Gas Industry**

418   **Shell loses its Brunei monopoly.**
      Ian Gill.   *Insight: Asia's Business Monthly*, (Oct. 1980), p. 45-50.
      A detailed assessment of Brunei's oil and gas industry and the state's relationship
      with the Royal Dutch Company or Shell Oil, as it became known, at the end of
      the 1970s. Even today, the two partners will say publically that their relationship
      is close and cordial. Privately, however, Shell has long been concerned over the
      government's increasing participation. The state has 50 per cent equity in Brunei
      Shell Petroleum and Brunei Shell Marketing and a one-third stake in Brunei LNG
      and Brunei Coldgas. Also discussed are the problems associated with being rich;
      in view of Brunei's current wealth, there is little incentive to diversify. This will
      become increasingly important as the oil and gas reserves decrease.

419   **Two trends [are] clear as Brunei steadies course for independence.**
      Ian Gill.   *Petromin*, (Oct. 1983), p. 15-20. map.
      A Brunei independence special and optimistic report about Brunei's oil
      production and political stability, and the changing relationships between the
      government and the British-owned Brunei Shell Petroleum Company (BSP). Two
      trends are becoming evident in Brunei's oil and gas industry; on the one hand
      production is slowing down in order to conserve the known reserves, whilst on the
      other hand, the government is encouraging foreign interests to look for more
      hydrocarbons. The US-based oil company, Jasra Jackson, has stepped in to break
      BSP's stronghold on offshore operations. Also mentioned is an experiment in
      tertiary recovery, the first of its kind in the Asia–Pacific region.

420   **What independence means.**
      Louise do Rosario.   *Petroleum News: Asia's Energy Journal*,
      vol. 14, no. 11 (Feb. 1984), p. 61-65. map.
      A survey of the present status and future outlook of Brunei's oil and gas industry.
      While the government continues to request a greater share from petroleum
      ventures, exploration and production remain in the hands of foreign companies
      as they have been for the past 70 years. An interview with Brunei Shell Petroleum
      (BSP) answers some questions regarding the potential reserves in oil and gas.
      With a recoverable supply for some 25 years and a foreign reserve of $14 billion,
      Brunei is, clearly, not in a rush to exploit its most valuable resource. A lingering
      problem for Brunei continues to be a shortage of qualified civil engineers and the
      fact that the majority of the workforce are still non-citizens of Brunei. These non-
      citizens give Shell Petroleum a strong leverage in any negotiations with the
      government.

**Petroleum di Brunei.**
*See* item no. 16.

**Allah, Shell and the Sultan.**
*See* item no. 348.

**Oil and independence in Brunei: a perspective.**
*See* item no. 363.

**Oil-state Brunei steps out from British protection to join the world.**
*See* item no. 364.

# Agriculture, Forestry and Fisheries

421  **Agricultural land use.**
Khoo Soo Hock.  In: *Brunei in transition: aspects of its human geography in the sixties*. Khoo Soo Hock [et al]. Kuala Lumpur: Department of Geography, University of Malaya, 1976. p. 74-149. 4 maps. (ITS Occasional Papers, no. 2)
Generally, the pattern of agriculture is discussed in terms of shifting and sedentary cultivation, subsistence and commercial activities, wet and dry rice, and rubber production, and according to the type of farmers: Malay, Chinese, or indigenous groups. More specifically, however, the agricultural systems of Brunei involve a multiplicity of crop associations, elements of commercialism and farming households. Furthermore, land utilization is based on the four districts of Temburong, Brunei, Tutong and Belait for it is apparent that statistical information and topographic features are determined on that basis.

422  **The agricultural systems of Temburong District, Brunei in 1972.**
R. B. Hewitt.  *Brunei Museum Journal*, vol. 5, no. 4 (1984), p. 203-14.
Describes the history and ecological relationships of subsistence agriculture in Temburong, one of four administrative divisions of Brunei. Three major ethnic groups are mentioned: the Iban shifting cultivators, and the Kedayan and Murut who adopted permanent wet rice cultivation methods.

423  **Annual Report 1984.**
Sinaut Agricultural Training Centre.  Tutong, Brunei: Sinaut Agricultural Training Centre, 1985. 76p. map.
This is the ninth report produced by the staff of the Sinaut Agricultural Training Centre, jointly sponsored by the Brunei government and Brunei Shell Petroleum Company, since its initiation as a full-time training centre in January 1976. Details of agronomic practices and husbandry techniques are not included, but yields and

133

production costs for a range of crop and livestock enterprises on the teaching farm are detailed. A thorough discussion of the training programme and curriculum in agriculture is included.

424 **Bercucuk tanam tanpa tanah. Farming without soil.**
*Petroleum di Brunei*, (April 1985), p. 24-29.
This well-illustrated essay examines (in Malay and English) the attempts to use hydroponic facilities at Sinaut Agricultural Training Centre for growing a variety of vegetables. A small project team evaluates both the technical and commercial feasibility of selected crops, and trains citizens to be commercially successful in hydroponics.

425 **Brunei: a first annotated list of plant diseases and associated organisms.**
W. T. H. Peregrine, Kassim bin Ahmad. Richmond, England: Commonwealth Mycological Institute, 1982. 87p. 2 maps. bibliog. (Phytopathological Paper, no. 27).
Provides an extensive history of plant diseases, together with an index of fungi and bacteria. The introduction describes soil deficiencies and the major diseases which affect fruit and vegetable crops. The work also includes a list of common names of host plants and their botanical equivalents.

426 **Brunei Bay penaeid prawn keys.**
David J. Currie. Bandar Seri Begawan: Department of Fisheries, 1980. 23p.
This report is one of a series of technical reports issued by the Department of Fisheries. Eleven species of penaeid prawns are reported to occur in Brunei Bay, three of which are here described in detail.

427 **Brunei Malay rubber beginnings.**
E. C. Janardanan. *Sarawak Museum Journal*, new series, vol. 10, nos. 19-20 (1962), p. 598-99.
A short account of the activities of two brothers with a very keen business sense who started the first rubber plantation in the capital of Brunei and, subsequently, became very successful. They brought the first ever rubber seeds and seedlings from Malaya to Brunei in 1908 and started with 300 trees around their house. Some of the estates extended very close to the present site of the Omar Ali Saifuddin Mosque in the centre of Bandar Seri Begawan.

428 **Demersal fish resources in Malaysian waters: 6 fish trawl survey off the coast of Sarawak and Brunei and the west coast of Sabah**
Mohammed Shaari bin Sam Abdul Latiff [et al]. Kuala Lumpur: Ministry of Agriculture and Rural Development, 1976. 64p.
Presents the results of a sampling analysis of prawn and demersal fish resources in the offshore waters of Brunei. The sea-floor throughout the surveyed region generally consisted of sandy mud with only isolated patches of clay, and was, thus, very suitable for trawling.

429 **Effects of lime, drainage, manganese dioxide and seedling conditions on rice in acid sulphur soil in Brunei.**

C. N. Williams. *Experimental Agriculture*, vol. 16, no. 3 (1980), p. 313-20. bibliog.

Acid sulphur soils which occur extensively in the deltaic and riverine environment of Brunei are generally considered unsuitable for agriculture. This paper reports on a study carried out at the Mulaut Experiment Station where five lime levels and two drainage conditions were investigated over three consecutive seasons. The results showed that yields of swamp rice on acid sulphur soil increased by liming but were unaffected by drainage and differences in hydrogen sulfide in the soil.

430 **Evaluation of smallholder farming enterprises 1965-1974.**

J. St. J. Groome. Sinaut, Brunei: Brunei Shell Petroleum Company, 1975. 112p. 2 maps. bibliog.

In an effort to diversify the economy of Brunei an investigation into small-scale farming was carried out under the sponsorship of the Brunei Shell Petroleum Company. This report presents the first results of four experimental farming units designed to produce pepper, rubber, oil palm, rice, vegetables and fresh-water fish. Management, marketing and day-to-day guidance were provided by the Brunei Department of Agriculture and Fisheries.

431 **Fertilizer response of Napier grass under different soil conditions in Brunei.**

C. N. Williams. *Experimental Agriculture*, vol. 16, no. 4 (1980), p. 415-24. bibliog.

Seasonal fertilizer responses to Napier grass were measured on various types of soil in Brunei. Napier grass is an exceptional producer of forage using fertilizer and appropriate cutting or grazing régimes. Since responses were obtained from various levels of fertilizer applications, it therefore became important to determine the optimal economic level under different conditions.

432 **Fisheries development in Brunei.**

Elmar Birkenmeier. *Brunei Museum Journal*, vol. 1, no. 1 (1969), p. 192-96.

Presents an evaluation of Brunei's fisheries resources in the late 1960s as seen from both an economical and a biological perspective. Surveys in Brunei's offshore waters have produced catches in commercial quantities. There are also large resources of prawns in coastal areas which are not yet fully utilized. A fish farm which was under construction at that time aimed to investigate the potential of freshwater resources. The author looks at the opportunities and possible problems in the production of these fisheries. The subject of the gradual replacement of traditional fishing methods with more modern techniques is also investigated. In improving the utilization of marine resources the government must play an active role which will not only help fishermen and pond owners but also assist in the diversification of the economy.

## Agriculture, Forestry and Fisheries

433 **Fishing crafts.**
J. S. Lim. *Brunei Museum Journal*, vol. 5, no. 3 (1983),
p. 155-67.

Eight traditional fishing vessels used in Brunei waters are decribed in this article. The crafts range from the very primitive dug-outs used on the rapids of rivers, to sailing vessels for use in offshore waters and recently introduced trawlers. Each description is accompanied by an illustration.

434 **Forest trees of Sarawak and Brunei and their products.**
F. G. Browne. Kuching, Sarawak: Government Printing Office,
1955. 369p. map. bibliog.

The forests of Sarawak and Brunei contain some 3,000 different kinds of trees and, therefore, rank among the richest areas of vegetation in the world. This book, however, is restricted to botanical descriptions of trees which are of some importance to the timber industry. Forty-seven families of trees are covered and their description on a species level includes details on: characteristics of the tree, silviculture and type of wood. The introduction includes remarks on the environment and stratification of the tropical rainforest. The author states that this is not a 'scientific work' but rather a preliminary guide for use by foresters and timber workers.

435 **Growth and yield of cabbage cultivars in a lowland tropical**
**environment.**
C. N. Williams. *Tropical Agriculture*, vol. 56, no. 2 (1979),
p. 99-104.

The cultivation of cabbage in the equatorial tropics has, traditionally, been confined to land at high elevations. In recent years, however, certain cultivars have been successfully developed for cultivation in lowlands. This agricultural experiment describes the results of several cultivars of cabbage grown at lowland sites in Brunei. Data was obtained on their capacity for head formation, plant diameter and survival rates.

436 **Hedge row pepper production in Brunei.**
J. St. J. Groome. *Singapore Journal of Primary Industries*, vol. 5,
no. 1 (1977), p. 49-61. bibliog.

Pepper has been grown in Brunei for over 100 years but cultivation is now restricted to an area of 20 hectares and production is poor. The state farm management unit at Sinaut began an experiment to improve pepper production by developing the cultivation of hedge row pepper as opposed to the traditional mound pepper cultivation method. However, because of higher capital costs, difficulties in controlling disease and greater labour output, the Department of Agriculture has recommended not to develop hedge row pepper cultivation during the 1975-79 National Development Plan period.

437   **History of shifting cultivation of Brunei 1906-1939.**
Charles O. Flemmich.   *Malayan Agricultural Journal*, vol. 28,
no. 5 (1940), p. 234-39.

The practice of shifting cultivation (known locally as *tebasan*) has caused extensive damage to soil and forest cover in the highlands of Brunei. The government in the 1920s and 1930s attempted to reduce *tebasan* practices and increase wet rice cultivation. This article looks at the systematic efforts to control shifting agriculture and evaluates the introduction of wet rice in coastal areas. Reduced payments to the Sultan and government incentives gradually changed the agricultural system in Brunei, but domestic rice production is still inadequate to meet local consumption. This article was reprinted from the *Malayan Forester*, vol. 9, no. 1 (Jan. 1940).

438   **The inter-relationship of technology, economy and social organi-zation in a fishing village of Brunei.**
Jock Seng Lim.   Master's thesis, London School of Economics and Political Science, London, 1981. 259p. 3 maps.

Provides a study of a small fishing village called Batu Marang. The author examines the organization of fishing and various factors which contributed to the introduction of modern technology in 1952 and which, subsequently, brought about social and economic changes.

439   **Investigations into fisheries resources in Brunei.**
Richard W. Beales, David Currie, Robert H. Lindley.   Kota Batu, Brunei: Brunei Museum, 1982. 204p. 18 maps. bibliog. (Brunei Museum Journal, Monograph Series, no. 5).

Consists of six separate papers which present the results of biological field-work carried out by members of the Brunei Department of Fisheries and technical consultants from England. The purpose of this investigation was to provide baseline data on trawlable demersal fish resources for the formulation of fisheries management policy. The report does not, however, include recommendations concerning the government's development options for offshore trawl fisheries.

440   **Notes on some 'coral fishes' in Brunei waters.**
Elmar Birkenmeier.   *Brunei Museum Journal*, vol. 2, no. 1 (1970), p. 294-317. bibliog.

Almost the entire eighty-mile coastline of Brunei consists of sandy beaches; moreover, the best place to observe coral fish is Pelong Rock, which lies two miles offshore. Despite these ecological limitations quite a large number of different coral fish can be found in Brunei waters. Based on visits to Pelong Rock and a small collection of fish in tanks kept at the Department of Fisheries some twenty-two common varieties of coral fish are described. Each species identifica-tion is accompanied by an illustration.

441   **A preliminary report on the species of planktonic marine diatoms found in Brunei waters.**
Teng Seng Keh.  *Brunei Museum Journal*, vol. 2, no. 1 (1970), p. 279-93. bibliog.

Marine diatoms are microscopic unicellular organisms which provide the basic food source for many species of fish. A full understanding of diatoms and plankton is, therefore, of some importance to the development of the fishing industry in Brunei. This paper provides full descriptions and illustrations for forty-seven species, embracing fifteen families found in Brunei waters.

442   **A preliminary survey of storage practices in Brunei.**
Bakri bin Haji Momin, Kamis bin Haji Tamin, Md. Zain bin Abdul Ghafar.  *Brunei Museum Journal*, vol. 3, no. 3 (1975), p. 226-33.

The authors report on an investigation related to insect-damaged produce in farm stores, commercial premises and state-owned stores. The structural features and storage practices are detailed for each facility. It was concluded that farmers and shopkeepers were more concerned with losses caused by rodents rather than those caused by insects. Also, state stores were found to be far more efficient in moving their stock with the result that their produce revealed virtually no insect infestation.

443   **A red tide in Brunei's coastal waters.**
Richard W. Beales.  *Brunei Museum Journal*, vol. 3, no. 4 (1976), p. 167-82. 3 maps. bibliog.

On 11 March 1976, the first red tide (a sudden population explosion of toxic dino-flagellates resulting in a reddish discoloration of the sea) was observed in the nearshore waters of Brunei. This report describes the incident, the measures taken by the departments of Fisheries and Health to inform the public and the procedures and results of a scientific survey of this phenomenon. On 17 March, health authorities placed a complete ban on the sale of all seafood since an increased number of illnesses were reported in Brunei and Sabah. Eighteen days later the ban was lifted. Although the red tide was a natural and temporary event, it demonstrated the fact that the traditional fishery is still of some economic importance and that only if it fails to meet the local demand do people take notice of it.

444   **Report on the 1964 census of agriculture.**
[Bandar Seri Begawan].  Government Printer, 1966. 330p. fold-out map.

When the 1962-66 National Development Plan was prepared, it was realized that detailed statistical data for a sound agricultural policy was needed. To meet this need, the government, in cooperation with the Food and Agriculture Organization (FAO), carried out the first agricultural census of Brunei. This project provided useful information on the number, size, and type of farm households, land cultivated, crops grown, livestock raised, labour employed, fertilizer, insecticides, and farm implements used, as well as data on transportation and marketing methods. The estimated 6,000 farm households were enumerated according to the four administrative districts: Brunei, Belait, Tutong and Temburong. The data has also been used by the UN Food and Agricultural Organization for the purpose of international comparison.

445 **Research report on the food economy of Malaysia and Brunei.**
Malcolm John Purvis.   Ithaca, New York: Department of
Agricultural Economics, Cornell University, 1965. 417 leaves.
map.

A statistical evaluation of agricultural data obtained from published census reports and field surveys conducted prior to 1964. The report is divided into four sections: (1) production and consumption of foodstuffs; (2) production and consumption of tobacco and cotton; (3) the relationship between income and consumption; and (4) projections of domestic production for the 1970s. Details of the method of analysis used are presented at the beginning of each section. Care has been taken throughout the report to point out the weaknesses and strengths of available information, and the reliability of estimates in production, demand and supply.

446 **Rice varieties in the Temburong District of the State of Brunei.**
R. B. Hewitt, Muhammad bin Yassin.   *Brunei Museum Journal*,
vol. 2, no. 3 (1971), p. 138-41.

This article discusses the possibilities of changing local rice varieties to new hybrids at the International Rice Research Institute in order to increase yields and desirable characteristics of local varieties.

447 **A short account of sago production in Kuala Balai – Belait.**
J. S. Lim.   *Brunei Museum Journal*, vol. 3, no. 2 (1974),
p. 144-55.

The sago palm, which grows extensively in the swampy coastal plains of Sabah, Brunei Bay and Sarawak, has remained the staple for the Punan, Bisayas, and Melanan people for centuries. In this article, Lim briefly discusses two aspects of making sago flour – the scraping of the sago tree trunk and the trampling of sago scrapings in water. The resulting sediments are left to settle in the water which is then drained, the deposits are dried and sieved, and these are then sold as flour. The twelve illustrations which accompany this article provide a useful visual explanation of the entire production process. See also Thomas H. Harrisson's 'The place of sago (and other palms) in Brunei and Borneo life' (*Brunei Museum Journal*, vol. 3, no. 3 (1975), p. 41-42). In this article, Harrisson attempts to establish the antiquity of sago utilization and its importance to indigenous agriculture.

448 **A soil survey of part of Brunei, British Borneo.**
G. Blackburn, R. M. Baker.   Melbourne: Commonwealth
Scientific and Industrial Research Organization, 1958. 84p. 3 maps.
(Soils and Land Use Series, no. 25).

Provides descriptions of the characteristics of soils, together with results from laboratory examinations of soil samples. These are discussed with reference to land use.

## Agriculture, Forestry and Fisheries

449 **Some aspects of the hydrology of the Brunei estuary.**
David J. Currie.  *Brunei Museum Journal*, vol. 4, no. 3 (1979),
p. 199-239. map.

The Brunei estuary supports an important artisanal fishery for prawns. As part of
a comprehensive study of the biology of the species involved in this fishery,
hydrological data were collected from stations in the two main channels of the
bay. The results of this study indicate that effluent from Bandar Seri Begawan
upstream is only slowly cleared from the estuary; the flushing time is calculated
from the salinity and tidal current data as being two to three days. Iron and
sulphate concentrations are also deposited into the estuary by the river. The
heavy metal concentrations provide a useful baseline for measuring the effects of
future industrial development involving such pollutants.

450 **Trends of change and development in the rural areas.**
Zaharah Haji Mahmud, Khoo Soo Hock.   In: *Brunei in transition:
aspects of its human geography in the sixties*. Khoo Soo Hock [et
al]. Kuala Lumpur: Department of Geography, University of
Malaya, 1976. p. 150-82. (ITS Occasional Papers, no. 2)

In this chapter, the author argues that the most important single element which
has affected the development of rural settlements and land use in Brunei was, and
still is, the construction of roads and communication facilities. Minor roads are
designed to connect rural settlements with each other and major links provide
access to the coast. Over a period of time the road construction programme
resulted in a number of physical and social changes, such as the introduction of
social services and public amenities. Some socio-economic changes can be traced
back as far as the establishment of the Brunei petroleum industry in the 1930s.

451 **Tutong area survey.**
J. St. J. Groome.  *Brunei Museum Journal*, vol. 3, no. 4 (1976),
p. 18-63. 18 maps.

In 1973 the Department of Agriculture in Brunei carried out an agricultural and
socio-economic survey of 659 rural households in the Tutong River District. This
paper reports the results of this survey which includes information on social
conditions, land tenure, agricultural practices, livestock, income and marketing of
agricultural products. The project was designed to help the Department initiate
new farm development programmes. Thirty-nine tables are included.

452 **Udang galah diternak. Udang galah (prawns) comes home.**
*Petroleum di Brunei*, (April 1985), p. 9-13.

The Department of Fisheries has started a pilot project to encourage farmers to
raise fish and prawns in their backyard ponds. This article reviews (in Malay and
English) various stages in the culturation of prawns from the construction of
ponds, to controlling water quality, raising larvae and harvesting. Since this type
of aquaculture is already widely practiced in other Southeast Asian countries,
Brunei's production, in the immediate future, is considered suitable only for
domestic consumption.

453  **Wandel in der Agrarstruktur.** (Agrarian change in Brunei.)
     Johannes C. Franz.   *Tropenlandwirt, Zeitschrift für die*
     *Landwirtschaft in den Tropen und Subtropen*, vol. 82, (April 1981),
     p. 53-59. map.
Statistics indicate that the importance of agriculture has declined in Brunei's
economy. Farmers have switched to jobs in government and construction which
offer more attractive salaries. This has resulted in a decrease in food production
and an increase in imports. The paper reports (in German) on the efforts of the
country to become more self-sufficient in agricultural production. Two of the
efforts underway include large rice schemes, which are being developed, and a
livestock joint venture that has been established. The National Development Plan
also advocates a reduction in food imports over the next five years.

**The geography of the State of Brunei with special reference to agriculture**
**and agricultural systems.**
*See* item no. 41.

**Water laws in Moslem countries.**
*See* item no. 330.

**The improving pattern of rice production in Brunei.**
*See* item no. 469.

**Annual Report.**
*See* item no. 589.

**Report on the buffalo census and survey in Brunei 1980/81.**
*See* item no. 594.

# Social Services, Health and Welfare

454 **Allergenic importance of house dust and storage mites in asthmatics in Brunei, S. E. Asia.**
A. A. Woodcock, A. M. Cunnington. *Clinical Allergy*, vol. 10, no. 5 (1980), p. 609-16. bibliog.

Mites have long been associated with allergic disorders of the respiratory tract. An examination of dust found in sleeping areas in homes showed that storage mites, especially Glycyphagid species, were predominant in various Brunei villages. The warm, humid conditions found in that country are favourable for the growth and development of storage mites. On skin testing sixty asthmatics with one per cent extracts of six mite species, *Dermatophagoides pteronyssinus* was found to provoke the greatest number of positive skin reactions. The author concludes that the role of storage mites in the causation of asthma in the tropics may have been underestimated.

455 **Borneo medicine: the healing art of indigenous Brunei Malay medicine.**
Linda Amy Kimball. Ann Arbor, Michigan: Published for the Anthropology Department of Loyola University of Chicago by University Microfilms International, 1979. 403p. 3 maps. bibliog. (Monograph Publishing: Sponsor Series).

This fascinating study of indigenous healing practices in Brunei is written in a literary style, enhanced with poetry and prayers. It was compiled by an anthropologist who lived in Brunei for three years and who was trained by a local *dukun* (medicine man). The traditional medicine men provide, for the most part, diagnoses and treatments in a systematic procedure, working from principle to application. As the principles they use differ from those used in 20th-century medicine, however, outsiders view their procedures as curiosities or magic panacea. At the same time, indigenous practitioners are all too aware that their treatment is limited and, in the end, the control of health does not lie in their hands. The author points out that much of modern pharmacy derives its substances from plants first used by indigenous medicine men. The twenty-one page index provides terminology with the Malay equivalent in parentheses.

456   **Brunei housing needs, 1986-2000.**
      Mohd. Jaman Mohamed.   *South East Asian Economic Review*,
      vol. 6, no. 3 (Dec. 1985), p. 149-63. bibliog.

Presents two methods of estimating future housing needs for Brunei. One of these, a formula used by the United Nations, is applied to 1960, 1971 and 1977 population statistics. Other relevant information, such as new housing and replacements, are, however, lacking, making it necessary to apply certain assumptions. According to several estimates the housing needs for Brunei over the fifteen-year period between 1986 and 2000 varies from 45,347 to 57,824 units. These figures, the author hopes, will provide a basis for a national policy and investment strategies in housing.

457   **The Brunei smallpox epidemic of 1904.**
      A. V. M. Horton.   *Sarawak Museum Journal*, new series, vol. 33,
      no. 54 (1984), p. 89-99. bibliog.

Horton examines the Brunei smallpox epidemic of 1904, the last natural disaster to have befallen the Sultanate. This disease decimated the population of the capital city as well as family members of Sultan Hashim within a fortnight. The circumstances which led to the outbreak of the epidemic, the efforts to cure it and the question of who was to pay for the relief mission are discussed in some detail.

458   **The concept of malaria in Brunei Malay indigenous medicine.**
      Linda A. Kimball.   *Borneo Research Bulletin*, vol. 7, no. 1 (April
      1975), p. 5-11.

The role of *dukun* practices is examined in the diagnosis and treatment of malaria. Quite clearly, indigenous practices still hold an important place in the total health care delivery system. Most frequently, however, villagers want both the efficacy of new medicine and the comfort of the traditional.

459   **Determination of SMA 12/60 reference values as the basis for diagnostic evaluation of biochemical profiling of the rural community in Brunei.**
      B. H. A. Rahman.   *Brunei Museum Journal*, vol. 4, no. 4 (1980),
      p. 238-50. bibliog.

Discusses the use of the technician multichannel auto-analyser (SMA 12/60) for biochemically investigating 608 medical patients and 903 pregnant women. The results detected patients with diabetes, hypercholestorolaemia, protein deficiency, renal disease and other symptoms.

460 **The development of health services in Brunei 1906-1970: a historical perspective.**
Ruth Lim. Bachelor of Science thesis, University College of Swansea, Swansea, England, 1974. 128p. 7 maps.
Traces the development of medical services in Brunei from 1906 to 1970 and constitutes the first attempt to bring various sources of information together into one body of literature. This thesis is based entirely on library and archival information from various government offices.

461 **An estimate of Brunei housing needs, 1980-2000.**
Mohd. Jaman bin Mohamed. *Brunei Museum Journal*, vol. 5, no. 3 (1983), p. 187-99. bibliog.
Reviews earlier housing projections made for the 1975-79 National Development Plan and provides a new, more realistic method of estimating housing needs which has been developed by the United Nations. Accordingly, the housing needs for the 20-year period vary between 45,000 and 57,000 units. These figures provide a basis for policy and investment in housing. In the conclusion, however, the author warns the reader that the estimates are inhibited by data problems and, consequently, certain assumptions had to be made which probably affected the estimates. This paper is an extract from Chapter three of the author's thesis, entitled *Housing problems in developing countries with special reference to Brunei* (M. Phil. University College, London University, 1981).

462 **Malaria eradication programme in Brunei State 1963-1970.**
Johar Noordin. Academic diploma in tropical public health. University of London, Department of Tropical Hygiene and Public Health, 1971. 70p. bibliog.
Assesses the health and medical facilities in the country. Anti-malaria activities and a malaria eradication project are described.

463 **Malaria in Sarawak and Brunei.**
Julian de Zulueta. *Bulletin of the World Health Organization*, vol. 15, nos. 3-5 (1956), p. 651-71. map.
A general survey of malaria in Brunei and Sarawak is provided in this article. In the course of the research more detailed observations on filariasis were made, and these are outlined in the author's follow-up report, entitled 'Observations on filariasis in Sarawak and Brunei' (*Bulletin of the World Health Organization*, vol. 16, no. 3 (1957), p. 699-705. map.) Contrary to what was expected because of the climate, the prevalence of malaria proved, on the average, to be low. The coastal areas were found to be practically free from the disease, although epidemics have occurred in recent years. Differences were also observed among various racial groups, but these were considered to be due to different habitats and customs rather than to race itself. Plans for a nation-wide malaria-control programme are briefly outlined.

464 **Postal services in Brunei's water town.**
J. A. Davidson. *Brunei Museum Journal*, vol. 3, no. 4 (1976),
p. 87-95. map.
Describes the postal service in Brunei with special emphasis on delivery problems
in Kampong Ayer, the water village. The postmen, for example, travel by
outboard motor boat and must have a good personal knowledge of the people in
their district. There are no street names or house numbers and households are
identified by a so-called MEP numbering system, devised during the Malaria
Eradication Programme. Mail deliveries by boat are also made up the Temburong
and Belait rivers to longhouses deep into the interior of the country.

465 **A preliminary study in medical anthropology in Brunei.**
Stewart Wolf, Thomas D. Wolf. *Pavlovian Journal of Biological
Science*, vol. 13, no. 1 (1978), p. 42-54. bibliog.
Nine rural communities in the tropical forests of Brunei were studied to ascertain
the possible effects of rapid social change on the health conditions of Iban, Dusun
and Punan families. The introduction since 1962 of modern communication,
medicine and schools, together with the encouragement to embrace Islam, have
posed difficult challenges for native people whose traditional pattern of life has
been established over many centuries. The results of the study indicate that
malaria, typhus and other infectious diseases have been virtually wiped out, and
that infant mortality has been reduced to the levels found in some of the more
medically advanced nations. Against this background there is, as yet, little
evidence of the major diseases of Western society, such as coronary artery disease
and hypertension, although most forms of cancer are commonly encountered. A
prediction is, therefore, offered that, as the newly educated youth of rural Brunei
grow up and as the anxiety relieving powers of old traditions are eroded, the
cardio-vascular diseases of Western society may make their appearance. Brunei
presents a splendid opportunity to test the putative relationship of chronic
vascular disease to social structure in the face of rapid modernization.

**Annual Report.**
*See* item no. 589.

# Employment

466 **The economics of labour shortage: three case studies from northern Borneo.**
Christopher Colclough, Martin Godfrey. *IDS Bulletin* (Institute of Development Studies), vol. 17, no. 4 (Oct. 1986), p. 48-56.

Briefly examines the causes of labour shortage in the oil-producing states of Brunei, Sabah and Sarawak. In Brunei, it is caused almost entirely by high public expenditure, financed by oil revenues. In the other two states, high levels of smallholders' productivity are also important causes. Governments face a range of policy options in response to labour shortages, the most common of which is the importation of foreign workers. Although this strategy appears to be in the interests of supplier states, it is only compatible with the employment objectives of importing states under special circumstances. This article is divided into three sections: the first defines the concept of labour shortage, the second describes the conditions in each country, and the third reviews some policy solutions.

467 **Economy and employment in Brunei.**
Warwick Neville. *Geographical Review*, vol. 75, no. 4 (Oct. 1985), p. 451-61.

Census data for 1971 and 1981, compiled by the author, show that the decline of employment in agriculture and food processing has not been matched by an expansion in non-service activities, such as manufacturing. Even the diversification that might have come from oil-based manufacturing did not materialize. The subsidy and welfare system in Brunei are the only means of distributing wealth in the absence of personal taxation. This study demonstrates that national achievements in economic development do not always agree with the need for employment or the welfare of all groups in the population, particularly non-citizens. The wealth of Brunei is narrowly based on the capital-intensive hydrocarbon industry, but employment in the industry, including backward and forward linkage, is modest. Government policy has given priority to economic growth rather than the generation of employment, a situation that has been reinforced by the high per capita cost of job creation in the oil industry and the lack of promotion of the agriculture and manufacturing sector for the local labour force. The principal benefits derived from the oil industry are through the multiplier effects generating tertiary occupations and subsidizing social services.

468 **Employment and labour.**
Voon Phin Keong.   In: *Brunei in transition: aspects of its human geography in the sixties*. Khoo Soo Hock [et al]. Kuala Lumpur: Department of Geography, University of Malaya, 1976. p. 184-221. (ITS Occasional Papers, no. 2).
Analyses the changing pattern of employment between 1921 and 1960. Clearly, over the years, employment has shifted from primary activities to secondary and, in particular, tertiary occupations. The most significant increase occurred in public administration, community services and commerce. Brunei's labour force has also experienced considerable changes in its racial composition, due to the recruitment of foreign workers.

469 **The improving pattern of rice production in Brunei.**
J. St. J. Groome, S. Soo Boon Ann.   *Brunei Museum Journal*, vol. 4, no. 1 (1977), p. 226-43.
This paper comprises a summary of the labour aspects of smallholder rice production at the farm management unit in Sinaut, Brunei. Through the introduction of power tillers, new harvesting methods and other forms of mechanization, considerable savings in working hours required at all stages of rice cultivation were achieved. The final labour input profile is compared with the traditional labour pattern of the previous decade. The experimental reduction in labour, according to the study, has been achieved with no unit area reduction in yield.

**Brunei: development problems of a resource-rich state.**
*See* item no. 353.

**Industrial development: Asia and the Far East.**
*See* item no. 362.

**What independence means.**
*See* item no. 420.

**Annual Report.**
*See* item no. 589.

# Education

470 **A critical exam of Brunei's higher education needs.**
Abdul Razak bin Haji Muhammad.    MEd thesis, University of
Birmingham, England, 1979. 204 leaves. map. bibliog.
Addresses the government's plans to set up an institution of higher education and,
in particular, focuses on the feasibility of a centre of higher education in Brunei.
It identifies the role and function such an institution can play in the light of
Brunei's educational problems and size of population.

471 **Curriculum innovation in Brunei since 1970 with special reference
to the introduction of Scottish integrated science.**
Abu Hanifah bin Mohd. Salleh.    MEd thesis, University of Hull,
England, 1980. 209 leaves. 2 maps. bibliog.
Examines the impact of a Scottish Integrated Science programme which was
introduced into secondary schools in 1969. The data are based on field-work
carried out by the author in 1979 when he visited several secondary schools in
Brunei. Other chapters in the thesis describe the history of formal education, the
secondary school curriculum before 1970 and the method of introducing the
Scottish Integrated Science programme into the school system of Brunei.

472 **The development of education in Brunei during self government
period, with special reference to primary education.**
Abu Bakar Haji Apong.    MA thesis, University of Lancaster,
England, 1980. 107p. bibliog.
Educational policy and the need for education are examined in the light of
Brunei's independence. The author focuses on the 1970-80 period.

### 473 Education in Brunei Darussalam: an outline.
Bandar Seri Begawan: Ministry of Education and Health, 1985.
11p.

A government document containing vital facts and figures for the educational system in Brunei. The present school system, the national objectives in education and the administrative structure of the Ministry of Education and Health are briefly outlined.

### 474 Education system of Negara Brunei Darussalam.
Bandar Seri Begawan: Jabatan Pelajaran Kementerian Pelajaran dan Kesihatan, Negara Brunei Darussalam, 1985. 43p.

Attempts to firmly establish the dominance of the Malay language whilst, at the same time, recognizing the importance of the English language. This study is based on the report of the Brunei Education Commission of 1972 which made the recommendation that the system of education in this country should not be diversified into different language streams. It deals with the concept and structure of the educational system in detail. The aims, according to the Brunei Education Commission, are to implement a single system of education in order to instill a sense of unity among the people of Brunei. A five- and a ten-year plan are included.

### 475 Educational policy in Brunei: with special reference to the national language.
Mustapha P. Metasan.   Bachelor's thesis, Faculty of Education, University of Birmingham, England, 1979. 115p. bibliog.

Examines the history of education and the present system as well as the role of a national language in education. Some of the problems which have resulted from the influence of Brunei's colonial heritage are also covered.

### 476 English in Brunei: second language or foreign language?
Guy Hill.   *World Language English*, vol. 1, no. 4 (Aug. 1982), p. 240-42.

In Brunei, many state secondary-school students are educated almost entirely in English while others have a complete Malay-medium education with a limited opportunity to study English. This system has created problems. Firstly, there are forces at work in Brunei which tend to undermine the position of the English language, such as the rise in national feeling and the increasing power of Islam. Secondly, certain strains may develop in the relation between students with regard to the use of English. Not only do students with an English-medium education have a better chance of further study abroad, but also the older generation still associates English with colonialism. Speaking English too well could be seen as betraying one's own culture and yet it is essential for economic development since English is the language of international communication. In view of these concerns, the author believes that the future role of English in Brunei is uncertain, it looks as though it may well become a foreign language for all students in a country where Malay is the national language.

# Education

477   An examination of disparity in educational provision with special
reference to Brunei.
Zainidi bin Haji Sidup.   MA thesis, University of Hull, England,
1979. 146 leaves. bibliog.

The objective of this research project is to isolate those factors primarily
responsible for the disparities in educational opportunities in the Brunei school
system. The analysis, however, is limited to the formal education system of the
Malay segment of society and excludes religious schools administered by the
Religious Affairs Department. As a result of this, many sources from Malaysia
were consulted for this study. The disparities investigated are seen in the context
of socio-economic, religious, linguistic and rural-urban characteristics.

478   An examination of the dysfunctional role and problems of education
in national unity and development with special reference to Brunei.
Nelson C. T. Chong.   MEd thesis, University of Hull, England,
1979. 133 leaves. 2 maps. bibliog.

Education is frequently regarded as an important agent in the process of national
unity, modernization and development. It is from this position that Chong's study
seeks to examine some of the issues in education in a multi-cultural society such
as Brunei. The emergence of a heterogeneous population has led to the
development of different school systems prior to World War II. Today's
impediments toward a national system of education are the disparities between
rural and urban schools, and unequal opportunities in post-secondary and college
education. The concept of a 'national language' is examined as a potential vehicle
in the unification of a nation-wide system of education.

479   History of Brunei for lower secondary schools.
Bandar Seri Begawan: Dewan Bahasa dan Pustaka, 1978. 79p.

An introductory text to the history of Brunei designed for elementary and junior
high-school students. It supplements other history text books currently used to
prepare students for their Lower Certificate of Education examinations. It covers
ancient Brunei (Kota Batu); the arrival of Westerners; the introduction of Islam;
the reign of prominent sultans; the Brookes; the Japanese occupation; and some
influential national personalities. Exercises are provided at the end of each
chapter. The original edition, in Malay, was published in 1976.

480   Laporan Surohanjaya Pelajaran Brunei. Report of the Education
Commission, Brunei.
Bandar Seri Begawan: Jabatan Setia Usaha Kerajaan, 1972. 54p.

In 1959 a commission was appointed to evaluate the progress of education in the
state. Subsequently, an education policy committee made recommendations to
the Council of Ministers. Several years later, in view of the rapid development of
education in Brunei, it became apparent that the education policy needed to be
revised. This bilingual report addresses the system of education from kindergarten
to the teachers' training college, in terms of curriculum, administration and
financial resources. The commission examined each topic and made policy
recommendations.

481   **Problems of education in rural societies with special reference to Brunei.**
Jamaludin bin Saman.   BEd thesis, University of Hull, England, 1982. 169 leaves. 3 maps. bibliog.

This thesis explores the widespread phenomena of rural disadvantages in the allocation of social resources, particularly education. As in other Southeast Asian countries, Brunei's urban bias has not led to equal opportunities in education for both city and rural populations. The government's objective, however, is to provide free primary and secondary education for all students. The remote Labi area in the district of Belait is used to illustrate the educational problems which exist in rural Brunei. A combination of demographic, environmental, social and political factors are explored in order to define the nature of education in rural areas. Some suggestions are made to improve the educational disparities in Brunei.

482   **Recent developments in international education: Indonesia, Malaysia and Brunei.**
Norman G. Goodman.   In: *Regional education profile: Asia: China, Hong Kong, Macau, Thailand, Indonesia, Malaysia, Brunei.* New York: Institute of International Education (IIE), 1986. 68p.

Written by the IIE representative in Jakarta, this discussion on Brunei (p. 61-63) concentrates on two topics: the education system in the country and overseas education for Bruneians. While the majority of Brunei students overseas still choose to study in Great Britain, that pattern may change since US educational information became available at the US Embassy from 1984. The *Regional education profile* is an Educational Resources Information Services Document: ED272047.

483   **Sedikit sebanyak mengenai komputer di sekolah. Bits and bytes come to school.**
*Petroleum di Brunei*, (Jan. 1984), p. 12-15.

Discusses how ten English-medium secondary schools in Brunei were introduced to the world of electronic information technology. Teachers were also given training in all aspects of computer education. According to this article, Brunei Shell's involvement in the project includes the purchasing of all hardware and the training of teachers.

**Annual Report.**
*See* item no. 589.

# Languages and Dialects

**484 The Bajau Darat language.**
Asmah Haji Omar. *Brunei Museum Journal*, vol. 4, no. 4 (1980),
p. 11-29.
Presents a linguistic treatment of the dialect used by the Bajau people. The
material focuses on idiosyncratic features of the language.

**485 The Bisayah language.**
Asmah Haji Omar. *Brunei Museum Journal*, vol. 4, no. 3 (1979),
p. 1-21.
The Bisayah language of Borneo is spoken in the area around Brunei Bay. It
should not be confused with the Bisaya of the Philippines, although the two may
have a genetic relationship. In the Philippines the term 'Bisayah' seems to refer to
various cultural linguistic groups, whereas in Brunei and Malaysia, Bisaya or
Bisayah refers to a single cultural linguistic group with dialectal variants. The
author discusses and gives examples of the grammar and morphology.

**486 'Bisayans' of Borneo and the 'Tagalogs' and 'Visayans' of the
Philippines.**
F. Araneta, M. A. Bernad. *Sarawak Museum Journal*, new
series, vol. 9, nos. 15/16 (1960), p. 542-64.
The people of the Visayan islands in the Philippines call themselves Bisaya; a
group of people also called Bisayans live along the Limbang River and around the
Bay of Brunei. It is speculated that the lowland Bisayans were at one time the
rulers of Brunei and Sarawak, and that it was this group that later inhabited the
Visayan islands and even Luzon. The anthropologist, Thomas Harrisson, goes
even further to suggest that the Belait, the Dusun and the Kedayans of Brunei
have some affiliation with the Bisayans. This conclusion drawn was based on
evidence from interviews with members of a Bisayan village in Limbang and other

ethnic groups in Seria, Tutong, Bandar Seri Begawan and Kuching. From this investigation a list of 100 words was prepared to find similarities in vocabulary and, more importantly, to discover what percentage of these words in each of the Borneo languages shows a recognizable relationship with Filipino words.

487 **Brunei and the modernization of the Malay language.**
In: *The modernization of languages in Asia. Papers presented at the Conference of the Malaysian Society of Orientalists held in Kuala Lumpur from the 29th of September until the 1st of October, 1967.* Edited by S. Takdir Alisjahbana. Kuala Lumpur: Malaysian Society of Asian Studies, University of Malaya, 1967. p. 140-45.

Addresses the question of when and how to modernize and standardize the Malay language. Once the Malay language is made capable of becoming an instrument of instruction in all fields, it is certain that the people will demand an amendment to the constitution to make it the sole official language. This issue, however, depends on the speed of development and modernization of the language itself. The Malay language today is far from efficient, lacks adequate vocabulary and is not standardized. In the process of modernization priority must be given to standardization of the idioms, rules, technical terms and new words. For the purpose of standardization, the author suggests that all countries concerned should join together for collective action and compile a 'master vocabulary'. Brunei, for example, could supplement the vocabulary in technical terms connected with the oil industry. This article concludes that no matter how small Brunei may be, it is able to contribute valuable assistance toward a common language.

488 **Brunei and the official language issue.**
Mahmud Bakri. In: *The modernization of languages in Asia. Papers presented at the Conference of the Malaysian Society of Orientalists held in Kuala Lumpur from the 29th of September until the 1st of October, 1967.* Edited by S. Takdir Alisjahbana. Kuala Lumpur: Malaysian Society of Asian Studies, University of Malaya, 1967. p. 134-39.

A debate over the need to have a national or 'official' language for the State of Brunei. A clause in the constitution of 1959 states that Malay shall be the official language of the state, but no target date for the implementation has been set. Historically, however, the Malay language has no roots in Brunei to feed a nationalistic ego. There is also no political or racial pressure to institute a national language as in Malaysia and Indonesia. In formulating a solution to the language issue Brunei puts practical considerations before emotional ones. This is one reason for the establishment of the Dewan Bahasa dan Pustaka (Language and Literature Bureau) which has among its objectives the development of the Malay language. Today, anyone wishing to gain the status of a Brunei national must speak Malay proficiently. On the administrative and academic side some difficulties can be expected in implementing Malay as the official language. Much of the law of the state is still in English and many professional jobs are filled by expatriate officers on contract who are primarily English speakers. The problem is further accelerated by the introduction of mass media which means wider contact with the technical and scientific world. If Malay is to become the official language and the coming generations come to depend largely on scientific knowledge then every effort must be made to 'equip the Malay language with modern devises to meet these modern challenges.' (p. 138)

489   **A critical survey of studies on Malay and Bahasa Indonesia.**
Andries Teeuw, with the assistance of H. W. Emanuels.   The Hague: Nijhoff, 1961. 176p. bibliog. (Koninklijk Instituut voor Taal-, Land-, en Volkenkunde. Bibliogr. Series no. 5).

A critical work of professional publications important to the study of language, literature and linguistics. The extensive bibliography (p. 91-157) is arranged alphabetically by author and covers works in English, Dutch, German, Malay and Indonesian. It includes a list of practical manuals and textbooks.

490   **Critical survey on studies of the languages of Borneo.**
Anton Abraham Cense, E. M. Uhlenbeck.   The Hague: Nijhoff, 1958. 82p. (Koninklijk Instituut voor Taal-, Land-, en Volkenkunde. Bibliogr. Series no. 2).

The introduction to this work provides a good overview of the linguistic situation on the island of Borneo. In view of the great scarcity of linguistic data on Brunei, missionary accounts and studies from ethnographic literature are included. The survey is organized both linguistically and geographically according to the languages and dialects spoken on the coast, in the interior and along the rivers. The content of the book is primarily derived from collections of the Leiden University Library and the Library of the Royal Institute in the Hague. While Dutch and German studies are included the majority of the 320 entries are in English.

491   **The early stage vocabulary and grammar acquisition of a Brunei Malay child.**
Shawna Craig, Linda A. Kimball.   *Borneo Research Bulletin*, vol. 18, no. 2 (Sept. 1986), p. 131-47. bibliog.

This paper explores the first stages of language learning for a Brunei male child. It focuses on three topics: (a) the child's interaction with his mother and siblings, (b) factors influencing his language acquisition and (c) some semantic and linguistic properties of Brunei Malay. The information was obtained from field observations conducted in Brunei between 1969 and 1971.

492   **The first words of a Brunei child.**
Linda Amy Kimball.   Brunei Museum Journal, vol. 2, no. 1 (1970), p. 67-86.

In this article, the author has produced a daily record of a child's first utterances and accompanying behaviour while living with a Bruneian family. The observations made during this project have since been published in three additional issues of the *Brunei Museum Journal* (BMJ). They are: 'More first words of a Brunei child' (*BMJ*, vol. 2, no. 3 (1971), p. 39-55); 'First phrases of a Brunei child' (*BMJ*, vol. 2, no. 4 (1972), p. 173-82); and 'More first phrases of a Brunei child' (*BMJ*, vol. 3, no. 2 (1974), p. 1-8).

493   **Kadayan evidence for word medial 'h' in Brunei Malay.**
Allen R. Maxwell.   *Borneo Research Bulletin*, vol. 6, no. 1
(1984), p. 3-12.

One of the most striking phonological characteristics of the Kadayan sub-dialect is
the presence of the voiceless glottal fricative 'h' in the position in which it has
been lost in other Malay dialects. In this article the author discusses the
occurrence of word medial 'h' based on his field-work with other sub-dialects of
Brunei Malay. The information presented is related to the author's PhD thesis:
*Urang Darat, an ethnographic study of the Kadayans of Labu Valley, Brunei*, Yale
University, Connecticut, (1980) (q.v.).

494   **The languages of Borneo.**
Sidney H. Ray.   *Sarawak Museum Journal*, vol. 1, no. 4 (Nov.
1913), p. 1-196. bibliog.

This lengthy paper examines in detail the geographical distribution and
grammatical structure of major Borneo languages. An extensive vocabulary of
Borneo dialects is included, together with a bibliography of 276 sources
containing some notes on languages. The subject is divided by the languages of
Lower and Upper Sarawak, the Netherlands Territories, North Borneo and
Malaya.

495   **The linguistic situation in northern Borneo.**
D. J. Prentice.   In: *Pacific linguistic studies in honour of Arthur
Capell*. Edited by S. A. Wurm, D. C. Laycock. Canberra:
Australian National University, 1970. p. 369-408. 7 maps. bibliog.
(Pacific Linguistic Series C, no. 13).

Discusses the major problem confronting research workers in Borneo, namely
that of ethnic and linguistic nomenclature. Prentice presents a tentative
classification of the indigenous languages in the area and summarizes the linguistic
research carried out so far in North Borneo. An extensive annotated bibliography
of linguistic sources is also provided.

496   **A list of Brunei–Malay words.**
H. S. Haynes.   *Journal of the Straits Branch of the Royal Asiatic
Society*, vol. 34 (1900), p. 39-48.

States that there are a number of obsolete Malay words still in common use in
Brunei. This list presents 295 Brunei lexical items. Unfortunately, the
transcriptions are often inaccurate.

497   **Malay–English dictionary (romanised).**
R. J. Wilkinson.   Mytilene, Greece: Salavopoulus & Kinderlis
Art Printers, 1933. 2 vols.

Represents the first official dictionary of the Malay language. In the preface the
author explains the painstaking work that goes into the creation of a dictionary. It
is a monumental work which was started in 1895 and which culminated in a
general-purpose dictionary of lexicographical literature.

## Languages and Dialects

498 **Notes on the early toponymy of Brunei.**
Robert Nicholl. *Brunei Museum Journal*, vol. 3, no. 3 (1975),
p. 123-30. bibliog.

The author relies on several historical writings and archival documents in an attempt to identify the early place-names of Brunei. There appears to be a linkage between the words Fo-shih, P'o-ni, Vijaya and Brunei. This being the case, the origins of Brunei can be traced back to at least the year 610 AD. Nicholl concludes that the last word on the manner in which these names evolved must be left to the linguists.

499 **On northern Borneo.**
C. de Crespigny. *Proceedings of the Royal Geographic Society*,
vol. 16 (1872), p. 171-83.

Reports on some interesting observations of customs and practices among the Muruts and the Bisayas in the Padass District on the northern border of Brunei. A vocabulary of 146 words in Malay, Brunei Low Dialect, Bisaya, Murut Padass, Murut Trusan and Dali Dusun is included.

500 **On the various spellings of the word 'Kadayan'.**
Allen R. Maxwell. *Brunei Museum Journal*, vol. 2, no. 1 (1970),
p. 87-103. bibliog.

Maxwell has recorded the use of the term 'Kadayan' as far back as 1735 and identifies ten different spellings given by the various authors in their references to this group of people who live around Brunei Bay. The reason for the concern over the different spelling is that there are so many other ethnic groups in Brunei with similar names, but which are, in fact, quite dissimilar both linguistically and culturally. Selections of variant spellings of Borneo ethnic groups are listed in the appendix. Reasons and explanations for accepting 'Kadayan' as the correct spelling are outlined in this paper.

501 **A possible example of ancient Brunei script.**
P. M. Shariffuddin, Robert Nicholl. *Brunei Museum Journal*,
vol. 3, no. 3 (1975), p. 115-22.

There has been much speculation as to what form the original Brunei script took and no example appears to have survived the conversion to Islam when it was replaced by Jawi. Recently, however, an inscription has come to light which may well prove to be written in the ancient Brunei script. In a local grave yard in Bandar Seri Begawan a small lotus-shaped stone was recently found bearing an inscription in Jawi on one side and an unidentified script on the opposite side. This article elaborates on the method of identification of the script which resembles ancient Balinese, a derivate of Sanskrit.

502   A short report on the linguistic situation in Sarawak, Sabah and
      Brunei.
      Robert Brock Le Page.   Kuala Lumpur: University of Malaya,
      Department of English, 1963. 15p.
An analysis of literacy rates of the major ethnic groups in the region. It is based
on the census reports and annual reports of the Department of Education for the
period 1947-65.

503   Some language aspects of Brunei Malay enculturation.
      Linda Amy Kimball.   *Borneo Research Bulletin*, vol. 10, no. 2
      (April 1978), p. 3-13.
Old and new methods of linguistic enculturation are described as they effect
Brunei Malay children today. Lullabies, tales and legends used by mothers are
seen as an important form of teaching and of developing identity. The increased
exposure to formal schooling, radio and television, however, is changing the
traditional patterns of linguistic enculturation. Children who once learned their
culture from traditional sources acquire different ideas from school books and the
media. The author argues that while these new influences lack traditional literacy
subtleties, the deepest emotions and feelings of the language are acquired in
childhood and will always carry the most responsive chord.

504   An unabridged Malay–English dictionary.
      R. O. Winstedt.   Kuala Lumpur, Singapore: Marican & Sons
      (Malaysia), 1965. 6th enlarged ed. 390p.
This standard Malay–English dictionary, first published in 1957, has passed
through numerous revisions and editions. This sixth edition contains more than
3,000 new captions, the result of the rapid development of modern Malay.

505   A vocabulary of Brunei Malay.
      H. B. Marshall.   *Journal of the Straits Branch of the Royal Asiatic
      Society*, vol. 83 (1921), p. 45-74.
An annotated list of 505 Brunei Malay words compiled over several years from
various sources and individuals. Many of the words, however, have their origin or
a parallel word in Sarawak Malay, Dayak or Malaysian Malay. Only 35 per cent
are true Brunei words, without any obvious connections with neighbouring
dialects.

**Education system of Negara Brunei Darussalam.**
*See* item no. 474.

**Educational policy in Brunei: with special reference to the national
language.**
*See* item no. 475.

**Dialek Melayu Brunei: catatan bibliografi.** (Brunei Malay dialect: a
bibliography.)
*See* item no. 646.

# Literature

## General

506 **Bahana rasa: antoloji cherpen.** (Anthology of short stories.)
Bandar Seri Begawan: Dewan Bahasa dan Pustaka, 1979. 202p.
A collection of short stories (in Malay) extracted from the journal *Bahana*.

507 **Bibliografi sastera kreatif Melayu. Jilid I: Brunei, Malaysia dan
Singapore 1920-80.** (A bibliography of Malay creative writings.
Vol. I: Brunei, Malaysia and Singapore 1920-80.)
Ding Choo Ming. Bangui, Philippines: Perpustakaan Universiti
Kebangsaan Malaysia, 1980. 497p. (Siri Bibliografi Umum, bil. 10.
[ITS General Bibliographies Series, no. 10]).
A comprehensive bibliography of short stories, dramas, novels and poems by
20th-century Malay writers. Entries are in Malay and an English introduction is
provided.

508 **Bunga rampai sastera melayu Brunei.** (A collection of Brunei
Malay literature.)
Abdullah Hussain, Muslim Burmat. Kuala Lumpur: Dewan
Bahasa dan Pustaka, Kementerian Pelajaran Malaysia, 1984. 386p.
A collection of short stories, poems and excerpts of novels by Brunei authors.
This publication may be regarded as a literary bench-mark in that the writers and
their work have exerted substantial influence on both national and regional
literature. This influence is, in part, the result of greater independence and wider
acceptance of Brunei writers in recent years.

509   **Hadiah sebuah impian.** (The prize of dreams.)
Muslim Burmat.   Bandar Seri Begawan: Dewan Bahasa dan
Pustaka, 1983. 153p.
This novel received second prize in the Writers' Competition organized by the
publisher. The competition was held in conjunction with the celebration of the
Muslim year 1400. The story concerns a religious propagator in a Bruneian
village.

510   **A history of classical Malay literature.**
Richard Olaf Winstedt.   Kuala Lumpur: Oxford University Press,
1969. 2nd ed. 323p. bibliog. (Oxford in Asia Historical Reprints)
Malay literature has been influenced by many cultures over the centuries: Sanskrit
came to Malaysia through Indians conversant with magic and the rituals of Hindu
religion; missionaries introduced writings in both Portuguese and Dutch; and even
folklore was borrowed from the vast storehouse of Indian legends and other
Oriental classics. This book covers the whole spectrum of Malay folklore,
histories and court literature. The reader will find a sampling of writings on
mythology, tales from Majapahit shadow plays. Muslim theology, and digests of law
and Malay poetry. An extensive bibliography provides suggestions for further
reading for the student of Malay language and literature.

511   **On the bank of the Baram.**
A. D. Galvin.   Singapore: Boy's Town, 1972. 201p.
The Baram River forms the border between Sarawak and Brunei and the
surrounding area is occupied by the Kayans, Kenyahs, Malays and the Punans.
The stories which are told in this book have been gathered from the Kenyah
people, their storytellers who recited them and members of the younger
generation who translated them. Every effort has been made to retain the original
form in which they were heard. Some, therefore, are written in prose while others
are in verse. The famous Balau Nyareng cycle of stories which is sung by men
who have not yet learned to read and write is included.

512   **Writing in Sabah, Sarawak and Brunei.**
T. Wignesan.   *Journal of Commonwealth Literature*, vol. 19,
no. 1 (1984), p. 149-52. bibliog.
The author addresses the problems faced by Borneo-born writers, writing in
English, as the states of northern Borneo became increasingly more 'Malaysian-
ized'. None of the indigenous languages have any written literary tradition, only
occasional oral forms are transcribed. In addition, the Borneo Literature Bureau,
which, until recently, was the only official publisher of local English writers, has
been absorbed into the Dewan Bahasa dan Pustaka, the official Malay Language
and Literature Bureau in Sarawak and Brunei.

513 **Land below the wind.**
Agnes Keith. Bath, England: Cedric Chivers, 1939. 318p.

An original description of the British empire-builders as seen through the friendly and amused eyes of an American. Having lived in northern Borneo for fourteen years, she writes about this region and its people with great affection.

**A critical survey of studies on Malay and Bahasa Indonesia.**
*See* item no. 489.

# Western fiction set in Brunei

514 **Abode of Peace.**
George J. Fernandez. Singapore: Scholastica Literary Service, 1975. 192p.

*Abode of Peace* is the survival story of a young Indian teacher and his family who lived for four years in a highly hypocritical and capitalistic society, and an international community in Brunei.

515 **Fuel for the flame: a novel set in the Orient.**
Alec Waugh. New York: Farrer, Straus & Cudahy, 1960. 468p.

There is something tropical in the way Alec Waugh writes. This tale is told in a slow-paced fashion where even violence is conditioned by the island atmosphere. He describes an imaginary island called Karak (Borneo) in the South China Sea where a kingdom (Brunei) is sustained by British consular assistance, but is, nevertheless, independent of Westminster. The ageing King welcomes his son, Prince Rhya, who returns to Karak with an English girl as his intended wife. The upcoming marriage is, thus, fuel for the flame that local Communists are determined shall destroy the monarchy and end British control of the Pearl Oil Company, which provides most of the kingdom's wealth. In short, the novel contains a multiplicity of characters, several happy endings, a number of intertwined short stories and some superficial essays on oil, government and modern colonialism.

516 **A prince of Borneo.**
R. H. Hickling. Singapore: Graham Brash, 1985. 206p.

An English schoolboy's adventure story about Brooke and the founding of Sarawak. Much of the material in this book also refers to the Brunei court of the day.

517 **You want to die, Johnny!**
Gavin Black (pseud. of Oswald Wynd).    London: Collins, 1966.
224p.

The fourth of Gavin Black's adventure novels about an importer-exporter whose
conventional methods of free enterprise involve him in organized crime and
international intrigue. The setting of the story takes place in an imaginary
Sultanate, Bintan (Brunei), the last surviving British Protectorate in Borneo. The
plot centres around the British Resident and his associates during a time of
political unrest and conflict (the 1962 revolt). The antagonists are the Chinese, a
member of the royal family and, secondarily, other groups which are woven into
the plot. This detective story is entangled with suspense and adventure. Two
other editions (1975 and 1979) are available from Harper & Row, New York.

**A checklist of English language fiction relating to Malaysia, Singapore
and Brunei.**
*See* item no. 643.

# Religion

518  **Adat istiadat diraja Brunei Darussalam.** (Customs and traditions of
the Brunei kingdom.)
P. M. Yusuf. *Brunei Museum Journal*, vol. 3, no. 3 (1975),
p. 43-108.

An outline of titles, appointments and rank of officials within the governmental
hierarchy of the old kingdom. The author also attempts to define the customs
during *lebaran* (the day ending a fasting period), the protocol related to an
audience with the Sultan and the material possessions passed on to a new Sultan
during inauguration. An editorial note indicates that this is a Rumi transliteration
by the author of the Jawi edition, published in 1958. An English translation is
anticipated.

519  **The advent of Islam to West and North Borneo.**
Thomas H. Harrisson. *Journal of the Malaysian Branch of the
Royal Asiatic Society*, vol. 45, part 1 (Jan. 1973), p. 10-20. bibliog.

The most accessible evidence for the introduction of Islam to northwestern
Borneo has nearly always been based on the Sultanate of Brunei. Most historians
believe that the Muslim Sultanate was founded at the end of the 15th century. On
the other hand, extensive sea trade by Arabic, Persian and Malay vessels had
already developed by 700 AD. One must also take into consideration the early
Sulu link to Brunei and the Sea Dayak connection with pre-1300 Sumatra which
appear in folklore. This paper, therefore, proposes to re-examine the Brunei and
Sea Dayak (Iban) material from this point of view; and also considers a native
text of the Idaham people on the northeast coast of Sabah. All three sources, the
Muslim Idaham text, the royal chronicles of Brunei and the Iban *tusut*
genealogical folklore, surprisingly indicate dates of about a century earlier than
that given by Western sources. While this evidence adds a new dimension to the
subject, the author urges that it should not be considered as final.

520 **Borneo: the land of river and palm.**
Eda Green, preface by the Bishop of Labuan and Sarawak,
forewords by Bishop Montgomery and Bishop Hose. [s.1.]:
Borneo Mission Association, 1911. rev. ed. 172p. 2 maps.
A detailed missionary account of the tribal people living in the Diocese of Labuan
and Sarawak, which, at that time, included parts of Brunei. Many photographs
and illustrations accompany the text. This work is also published by the Society
for the Propagation of the Gospel in Foreign Parts (London, 1912).

521 **Brunei.**
Peter Hsieh, Russell Self. In: *The Church of Asia*. Edited by
Donald E. Hoke. Chicago: Moody Bible Institute of Chicago,
[1975]. p. 96-100.
In this short essay the authors provide some interesting facts about the Christian
population in Brunei. Numerically, they make up less than four per cent of the
total population and the majority by far are Catholics. Christian communities
consist almost exclusively of local Chinese residents, and Philippine and Korean
migrant workers. The dominant and oldest Protestant group is Anglican, and is an
outgrowth of British settlement in the 19th century. Christian groups, today, are
described as small, lacking strong leadership, and are reluctant to be more
aggressive in a Muslim state. The Sultan is tolerant of other religions, but
government policy has been to allow a *status quo* for existing church groups and
no new missions are allowed to enter the country.

522 **Brunei's new mosque: one of the finest places of worship in the
Muslim world.**
*Malaya* (Nov. 1958), p. 27, 38.
Argues that the mosque is an expression of the Sultan's desire that the oil wealth
of the state should not only contribute to the material well-being of the people,
but also to the strengthening of the Muslim faith in Brunei. The cost, architecture
and the official opening ceremonies in 1958 of the Omar Ali Saifuddin Mosque in
Bandar Seri Begawan are also discussed.

523 **The discovery of an ancient Muslim tombstone in Brunei.**
Abdul Latif bin Haji Ibrahim, Dato P. M. Shariffuddin. *Brunei
Museum Journal*, vol. 4, no. 3 (1979), p. 31-37.
The arrival of Islam in Brunei is generally accepted by the West to be around the
16th century. This paper explains the recent discovery of an ancient Muslim
tombstone (found near the capital) dated 1048 AD. The authors conclude that
this tombstone would, undoubtedly, be the earliest evidence of Islamic activity as
well as an Islamic Sultanate to have existed somewhere in the region.

524 **Drunk before dawn.**
Shirley Lees. Kent, England: Overseas Missionary Fellowship,
1979. 215p. 5 maps.
Documents the experiences and accomplishments of missionaries stationed
throughout northern Borneo including the Limbang and Baram river watershed

near Brunei. With no roads into the interior, primitive living conditions, a lack of resources, internment by the Japanese, and problems of communication, the early missionaries faced many hostilities and agonizing defeats. The title of this book refers to the indulgence of potent rice beer, especially by the Lun Bawang people in the Limbang River area. It describes, however, how 'a breathtaking new dawn broke for them between 1928 and 1938 when God stepped in to build a church among them.' The theme of this book, therefore, focuses on the transformation of tribal groups into 'men and women of God' and the new problem created by the recently educated youth moving down to coastal towns for a more lucrative lifestyle. A subjective picture of missionaries working with tribes in a developing country is presented.

525 **Islam and development in the nations of ASEAN.**
Howard M. Federspiel. *Asian Survey*, vol. 25, no. 8
(Aug. 1985), p. 805-21. bibliog.

Examines the relationship between Islam and the national state in the ASEAN nations, concentrating on developments of the past decade. In particular, it stresses the relationship that exists between national leaders and leaders of Muslim communities and how these authorities view civic culture, and economic and political developments. The analysis is confined to Indonesia, Malaysia, Singapore, Thailand and the Philippines. Brunei lacks an adequate history as an independent nation to be fully included in this study. However, the four hypotheses presented by the author as a means to measure current thinking and attitudes in each country could be applied to Brunei as the value system and practices of the state leaders become better known.

526 **Islam and Malay kingship.**
A. C. Milner. *Journal of the Royal Asiatic Society of Great Britain and Ireland*, no. 1 (1981), p. 46-70. bibliog.

In this study the author looks in some detail at the influence of Islam on the political institutions of pre-colonial Malay culture. It is argued that after the 14th and 15th centuries Malay political life became strongly linked to developments elsewhere in the Muslim world (such as Indonesia and Brunei), which, eventually, threatened the ideological underpinnings of the Malay state. The evidence for this analysis comes from indigenous Malay writings and the accounts of European visitors to the region.

527 **Islam di Brunei: dari perspektif akiologi.** (Islam in Brunei: from an archaeological perspective.)
Matussin Omar. *Karya*, vol. 1, no. 1 (May 1979), p. 7-13. bibliog.

A synthesis of existing literature (in Malay) with a view toward providing a new interpretation of the introduction of Islam to Brunei. This Brunei writer disputes most Western evidence regarding the arrival of Islam in the 16th century. The most compelling indicators presented in this paper are Muslim stone sculptures found in Vietnam, dating back to 1035. It is postulated that Vietnamese Muslims could have been middlemen between Chinese and Brunei merchants. There is

also evidence that a prominent Chinese was buried in Brunei as a Muslim around
1264. The author concludes that Islam arrived in Brunei before the 13th century,
possibly as early as the 11th century, but certainly not during the 16th century.

528　**Islam in Brunei.**
Pehin Orang Kaya Amar Diraja Dato Seri Utama Dr. Awang
Haji Mohd. Jamil Al-Sufri. *Brunei Museum Journal*, vol. 4, no. 1
(1977), p. 35-42.
The belief that the Islamic religion was introduced to Brunei in the 16th century,
according to Western historians, is challenged by the author of this paper. Using
Spanish and Chinese sources he presents evidence indicating that Brunei rajahs
had embraced the Islamic faith much earlier. The author also argues that 'if we
look into the Genealogy of Brunei Sultans, during Pigafetta's visit (1512 AD)
Brunei was ruled by Sultan Abdul Kahar and he was the 6th Sultan, so surely
before Sultan Abdul Kahar there were five other Muslim Sultans' (p. 36).

529　**Islam in Brunei is a way of life, not a battle-cry.**
Suhaini Aznam. *Far Eastern Economic Review*, vol. 133, no. 35
(28 Aug. 1986), p. 36-38.
This article describes the effects the Sultan, government, tradition, education and
the Department of Religion have on cultivating a Brunei brand of Islam for sixty-
five per cent of the country's population. Thus, for the Brunei Malay, loyalty to
the King, country and Islam are one and the same thing. Unlike neighbouring
Muslim countries where many threads of Islam encourage debate, in Brunei Islam
binds rather than separates. Not even in this isolated country, however, do people
remain impervious to outside influences – changes in religious expression and new
*mazhab* (schools of interpretation) may be part of a trend.

530　**Islamic law in South-East Asia.**
Michael B. Hooker. Singapore, Oxford, New York: Oxford
University Press, 1984. 330p. bibliog. (East Asian Social Science
Monographs).
The intention of this book is to outline the main characteristics of Islamic law in
Southeast Asian countries. Subjects covered range from locally formulated
systems of prescription to the impact of colonialism and the post-war years of
Islamization, incorporating classical modes of reasoning into the judicial process.
Islamic law in Brunei is dealt with in chapter four (p. 173-88): 'Muslim law in
Brunei: the early legislation', and 'The religious council, state custom and Kathis
courts enactment'. This is a very thorough description of the development and
latest innovations of Brunei's legal history. The first modern law on Islam was the
Mohammedan Laws Enactment of 1912, a mixture of Muslim and local rules. This
act remained in force until 1955 when it was replaced by the existing legislation.
The author presents an extensive interpretation of all sections of the present
Enactment which provides for a *majlis* (religious authority), religious court,
marriage and divorce procedures, establishment of the Religious Fund, offences
and other religious matters.

531  **Khabar gembira = (The good news): a history of the Catholic Church in East Malaysia and Brunei 1880-1976.**
John Rooney.  Tunbridge Wells, England: Burns & Oates, 1981. 292p. bibliog.

Although Brunei is mentioned in the title of this work, relatively little attention is paid to it in the contents. It is, however, significant from the perspective of religious influence and conflict between Catholic missions in Sabah, Sarawak and Islamic Brunei.

532  **Pameran sejarah perkembangan Islam di Brunei. (Diffusion and development of Islam in Brunei).**
Bandar Seri Begawan: Dewan Bandaran, 1979. 46p. 2 maps.

A richly illustrated booklet (in Malay and English) depicting the impact of Islam on Brunei society. It traces Islamic influence through history, the arts, education and government. It also explains the organization and function of the Department of Religious Affairs, the Religious Council (*Muib*) and gives selected quotations from the Koran.

533  **A *Sebob Dirge* (sung on the occasion of the death of Tama Jangan Jau by Belawing Kupa).**
A. D. Galvin.  *Brunei Museum Journal*, vol. 2, no. 4 (1972), p. 1-158.

Argues that death is not an end, rather it opens the way for one's full self-consciousness and, when freed from the body, the soul becomes capable of expressing and actualizing all that it desired to do during the person's life. Reverend Galvin describes and interprets the elaborate death ceremonies and presents the complete text of the *Sebob Dirge* with a tentative translation. This paper is written in Malay and English.

534  **Singapore, Malaysia and Brunei: the Church in a racial melting pot.**
John R. Fleming.  In: *Christ and crisis in Southeast Asia*. Edited by Gerald H. Anderson.  New York: Friendship Press, 1968. p. 81-106. bibliog.

A useful summary of the origin and present status of Christianity in the Malay-speaking region of Southeast Asia, with special emphasis on the missionary activities of the Anglican, Presbyterian and Methodist churches. The contemporary challenges of the Church are explored within the context of such powerful forces as the emergence of nationalism, competition by Islam, and local cultural attitudes. In addition, the lack of Christian unity, and outdated mission services are seen as working against the true function of the Church in the region.

535   **The status of Muslim women in family law in Malaysia, Singapore and Brunei.**
Ahmad Ibrahim.   Singapore: Malayan Law Journal, 1965. 121p. bibliog.

An authoritative account of Muslim family law prepared at the request of the United Nations Secretariat for a seminar on the status of women in family law, held in Tokyo, May 1962. The status of women is discussed with reference to marriage, divorce, offences, guardianship of children and inheritance rights. The author hopes that the book will help in the understanding of Muslim law and foster among women an interest in social and public affairs, so that they can play a more active role in the life of their respective countries.

**The nature of Malay customary law.**
*See* item no. 325.

**Brunei *adat*.**
*See* item no. 538.

# Culture and Society

536 **The aims, approaches and problems in the study of folk literature or oral tradition with particular reference to Malay culture.**
Mohd. Taib Osman. *Brunei Museum Journal*, vol. 2, no. 4 (1972), p. 159-64. bibliog.
The post-war collections and scholarly efforts in the study of oral tradition have definitely shown a renewed interest in the Malay-speaking region, partly because of a strong feeling of nationalism. To further promote the rich field of oral tradition, the author suggests a well-planned combined effort of research of the nations in the region. Three kinds of activities are involved in the promotion of folk literature and traditional oral narratives: collecting, archiving and the interpretation of data. These approaches are discussed in some detail. Ultimately, the scholarly approach to oral tradition must be transformed into popular reading material and school texts so as to preserve both national identity and cultural continuity.

537 **Area handbook on British Borneo.**
General editor, Norton S. Ginsburg; edited by Irving Kaplan, Chester F. Roberts; authors, Bettyann Carner, Lois Grotewold, Zelda B. Hauser, C. Lester Stermer, John E. Trotter. Chicago: University of Chicago for Human Relations Area Files (HRAF), 1955. 443p. 19 maps. bibliog.
One of a series of area handbooks completed at the University of Chicago as part of a contract with the Human Relations Area Files during 1954-55. The purpose is to provide information of certain territories and people, their system of organization and patterns of activities. This volume on British Borneo (which includes Sarawak, Brunei and Sabah) provides an historical outline, together with information on resources, transportation, demography, education, health, economic activities and ethnicity.

538  **Brunei** *adat.*
Ibrahim bin Mohd. Jahfar.  *Brunei Museum Journal*, vol. 1, no. 1 (1969), p. 5-9.

*Adat* refers to the customary law and traditional beliefs which are still observed in the religion, life-cycle stages and daily activities of the people of Brunei. The author has selected three occasions where customary beliefs are observed: while constructing a sailing craft; during pregnancy and childbirth; and during the planting of rice. This paper, originally published in Malay (*Sarawak Museum Journal*, vol. 5 (1949), p. 100-03; and (1950), p. 256-61) by the same author, is considered an important landmark in Brunei scholarship, which was, heretofore, monopolized by non-Bruneians.

539  **Brunei cannon.**
P. M. Shariffuddin.  *Brunei Museum Journal*, vol. 1, no. 1 (1969), p. 72-93.

Describes the origin and history of the Brunei cannon, tracing it back to 1521 AD. The second and third parts of the article deal with the classification of cannons in the Brunei Museum and a discussion of Brunei terms relating to the cannon and its parts. Many plates and illustrations are included.

540  **Brunei cannon: their role in Southeast Asia (1400-1900 AD).**
Thomas H. Harrisson.  *Brunei Museum Journal*, vol. 1, no. 1 (1969), p. 94-118. map. bibliog.

Written in conjunction with Shariffuddin's article (see previous item) about the classification of the Brunei cannon. Whereas the latter went into detail about classification, Harrisson discusses the cannon, as well as the uses of guns and ammunition, in relation to the entire region from Burma to the Philippines, the European technical influence and the question regarding the spread of Brunei guns.

541  **Brunei Malay traditional ethno-veterinary practice.**
Linda Amy Kimball.  *Borneo Research Bulletin*, vol. 17, no. 2 (Sept. 1985), p. 123-50. bibliog.

Every culture has distinct concepts and attitudes regarding domesticated animals. An inherent conflict lies in the fact that although animals are cared for, their intended fate may be slaughter by human hands. This paper deals with that conflict as seen through the eyes of a Brunei farming community. Here animals form part of village life and such activities as the slaughter, castration or ringing of cattle, the training and fighting of cocks, and the veterinary care of animals are important events. In the medical treatment of animals, farmers have adopted practices derived from indigenous tribal groups (Muruts and Kadayans) and Western sources (agricultural extension service). According to local belief the lives of both man and beast are a passage through time and space, and sometimes medicine and care can help to smoothe the course of that life.

Culture and Society

542   The enculturation of aggression in a Brunei Malay village.
      Linda Amy Kimball.   PhD thesis, Ohio State University,
      Columbus, Ohio, 1975. 217p. (Available from University
      Microfilms, Ann Arbor, Michigan).
The purpose of this dissertation is to present a basic ethnography of Brunei Malay
culture with an emphasis on the process of enculturation, and especially the
enculturation of aggression. The data on enculturation begins with a description
of indigenous, social and psycho-sexual relationships of child development in a
farming village. Patterns of observable aggression in child behaviour were limited
to hitting, pinching and shooting. These patterns also permitted the utilization of
studies which have already been published for cross-cultural comparison of
aggression. Field-work was conducted in a Temburong village in eastern Brunei
from 1969-70.

543   The Iban of Sarawak under Brooke rule, 1841-1941.
      Robert Maxwell Pringle.   PhD thesis, Cornell University, Ithaca,
      New York, 1967. 679 leaves. 5 maps. bibliog. (Available from
      University Microfilms, Ann Arbor, Michigan).
This study explores the socio-political position of the Iban in Sarawak and
evaluates the effect of a century of Brooke government on Iban society. The early
chapters trace the gradual expansion of James Brooke's influence in the period
1840-60, relating this to his philosophy of personal rule. Chapters six and seven
discuss relations between the second Rajah and the remote upriver people,
unwilling to obey restraints imposed by the European overlord, and the
downriver Iban who served on primitive expeditions against upriver rebels for the
government. Thus, although there was a constant conflict between ruler and
ruled, a more basic harmony also existed. This theme is further developed in
chapter eight, which deals with Iban migration throughout Sarawak and Brunei,
and government methods to effect these movements. The final chapters discuss
the major social consequences of Brooke rule and the development of new
patterns of communal relations between the Iban, the Malay and the Chinese.
The text of the Brunei Treaty of 1847 is appended.

544   Inter-hierarchical commissions in a Bornean plural society.
      Donald Edward Brown.   *Southeast Asian Journal of Social
      Science*, vol. 1, no. 1 (1973), p. 97-116. bibliog.
The inter-hierarchical position which is examined here, pertains to the 'land
chiefs' (*menteri darat*) in Brunei. Twenty-eight of these rural-based traditional
appointees of the Sultanate were interviewed in 1967. This essay combines the
presentation of the data of what the author calls 'a pre-colonial inter-hierarchical
commission' with the development of the theory of structural types. In this case
the overall structure was that of the ethnically plural society in Brunei.

545 **Journal (from 29 April-25 May 1872) when on a trip from Sarawak
to Meri, on the northwest coast of Borneo in the Brunei territory.**
N. Denison. *Journal of the Straits Branch of the Royal Asiatic
Society*, vol. 10 (Dec. 1882), p. 173-88.
A day-by-day travel account which gives impressions of the native people and
their activities along the coast of the Baram River between Bintulu and Baram
(between Sarawak and Brunei).

546 **Malaya and Borneo in Malaysia?**
Thomas H. Harrisson. *Malayan Historical Journal*, vol. 1, no. 3
(Dec. 1954), p. 103-09.
The advent of the first publication of the *Malayan Historical Journal* in 1954
prompted the author to reflect on Borneo's relationship with peninsular Malaya
and how this has affected Borneo's history, linguistics and ethnography. In
Borneo today, for example, even the simple question of the nature of a Malay has
become obscure. North Borneo, Brunei and Sarawak have adopted different
attitudes and definitions for Muslim, Malay or Malaysian. This issue has a
powerful grip on the changing dynamics of human relations throughout Borneo.
The paper also refers to pre-European trade relations, colonial contact and
commercialization as factors which further obscured the position of Borneo *vis-à-
vis* Malaysia. In short, from the perspective of Borneo, some of Malaya's history
is interpreted differently than the new journal implies.

547 **The Malays. A cultural history.**
Richard Olaf Winstedt, revised and updated by Tham Seong
Chee. Singapore: Graham Brash, 1981. rev. ed. 221p. bibliog.
An excellent abridged ethnography of Malay culture which will serve well as a
general overview of the subject. The contents include chapters on the ancestral
origin of the Malay; their beliefs and religion; their social, economic, political and
legal systems; and their literature, arts and crafts. Tham Seong Chee's substantial
postscript deals with the changes in Malay society and culture since 1961, when
Winstedt's last edition had appeared.

548 **The Malays of southwest Sarawak before Malaysia.**
Thomas H. Harrisson. *Sarawak Museum Journal*, new series,
vol. 11, nos. 23-24 (1964), p. 341-511.
An anthropological interpretation of the land and the people in Sarawak's coastal
region, with some consideration of the Sarawak and Brunei Malay type, both past
and present. One section is devoted to the famed cultural hero, Datu Merpati,
who appears in Sarawak lore as the father-in-law of the first Malay Sultan of
Brunei; and, in a Brunei story, is the brother of the first Mohammedan Sultan.
Brunei also plays a role in the chapters devoted to 'White rajahs', and 'New
aristocracies'. Of general importance is a section entitled 'Growing Malay' which
attempts to trace the growth of the Malays as a people and tries to define the
Malay character and individuality.

## Culture and Society

549   **A mysterious find in Brunei.**
H. Hughes-Hallet. *Journal of the Malayan Branch of the Royal Asiatic Society*, vol. 16, no. 1 (1938), p. 100-01.

In 1933 timber workers on the banks of the Belait River discovered a living tree which embodied a cavity filled with human skulls, bones, beads, bracelets and pieces of earthenware. The find was thought to be of such significant ethnological interest as to warrant publication. The cut tree and its contents are illustrated in five photographs. Also mentioned are burials in dead trees, a once common practice among several tribes in Borneo.

550   **The natives of Sarawak and British North Borneo.**
Henry Ling Roth.   Kuala Lumpur: University of Malaya Press, 1968. (Reprint of the Truslove & Hanson 1896 ed.) 2 vols. 2 maps. bibliog.

An admirable compilation based on an incomplete manuscript by Hugh Brooke Low (1849-87), the son of Sir Hugh Low, Governor of Labuan. Despite its early publication date, this ethnography remains a valuable contribution to the history of Borneo. It contains a detailed description of the peoples of Sarawak (including Brunei) and British North Borneo at the end of the last century, shows the distribution of tribal groups and is well illustrated with drawings and a useful fold-out map. The twenty-eight chapters provide details on tribal populations, including their physique, religion, festivals, medical care, legends, agriculture, hunting and fishing, habitation, arts and crafts, head-hunting, human sacrifices, natural resources, music and language, and prehistory. Among the North Bornean tribes, the Bisaya, Murut, Dusun, Kedayan and Bajau, who are also found in parts of Brunei are covered. An appendix of English, Malay and Sea Dayak vocabulary is included.

551   **Notices of the city of Borneo and its inhabitants, made during the voyage of the American brig *Hammaleh* in the Indian Archipelago, in 1837.**
*Chinese Repository*, vol. 7, nos. 3 and 4 (1838), p. 121-36, 177-93.

A visitor's impressions of everyday life in Brunei in 1837 during a twenty-two-day stay in the capital city. The narrative covers meetings with the Sultan, etiquette in the palace, the people in Kampong Ayer and features of the natural landscape. The intent of this discussion was to bring Brunei culture into closer contact with the West and, in particular, with Christianity. A note at the end poses the question whether Brunei is a suitable place for a missionary station.

552   ***Padian*: its market and the women vendors.**
Abdul Latif Haji Ibrahim.   *Brunei Museum Journal*, vol. 2, no. 1 (1970), p. 39-51. 2 maps.

Women vendors in small boats (*padian*) have existed in Brunei for centuries but are, today, rapidly disappearing from the water village. This overview of the *padian* looks at the origin, function and present decline of this colourful group of peddlers on Brunei's waterfront. One of their most distinct features is the enormous straw hat used to obtain protection from the sun and rain. In their commercial role the *padian* provide an important link between local consumers, and the farmers and fishermen. They also control their own consumer market and specialize in certain products. With very few *padian* in business today, Brunei is on the verge of losing a unique cultural institution which can be traced back to pre-European times.

553  **The pagan tribes of Borneo: a description of their physical, moral and intellectual condition, with some discussion of their ethnic relations.**
Charles Hose, William McDougall.   London: Macmillan, 1912.
2 vols. 4 maps. bibliog.

A joint author publication which is the culmination of twenty-five years of field research on tribal culture carried out at the end of the 19th century. This two-volume study is now considered a classic treatise on the ethnology of northern Borneo. The first volume focuses on the geography and history of the area, its people, their material culture, social system, agriculture, decorative arts and warfare. The second volume covers animistic beliefs, burial practices, magic, legends, childhood, moral and intellectual peculiarities. Geographically, the emphasis is on the Baram and Rejang districts along the Sarawak–Brunei border. An appendix by Alfred C. Haddon features the physical characteristics of the tribes.

554  **The pagans of North Borneo.**
Owen Rutter.   Oxford, New York, Singapore: Oxford University Press, 1985. (Reprint of 1929 ed.). 288p. 2 maps. bibliog.

An authoritative and systematic description of the non-Muslim people of North Borneo. The objective of the book was to provide basic information for colonial policy-making in the 1930s. It represents a valuable source of information on traditional warfare, head-hunting, *adat* law and folklore. Seventy-five plates and eleven diagrams are also included.

555  **Principles of social structure: Southeast Asia.**
Donald Edward Brown.   Boulder, Colorado: Westview Press, 1976. 248p. bibliog.

This book grew out of an attempt to place the concept of corporateness in an ordered typology of social structure by drawing on various theories in social anthropology. Chapters 12 and 13 focus on Brunei and explore the relationship between structure and process, and between society and the individual. Much of the information included is based on the author's anthropological field-work carried out in Brunei during 1966 and 1967.

556  **Quer durch Borneo; Ergebnisse seiner Reisen in den Jahren 1894, 1896-97 und 1898-1900.** (Across Borneo; travel experiences during the years 1894, 1896-97 and 1898-1900.)
Anton Wilhelm Nieuwenhuis, in cooperation with M. Nieuwenhuis-von Osküll-Güldenbrandt.   Leiden, The Netherlands: E. J. Brill, 1907. 2 vols. map.

A descriptive travelogue which deals largely with ethnographic studies of the island of Borneo. It presents an anthropological perspective of Central Borneo, written in the 19th-century tradition of European explorers. This two-volume set includes a rich assortment of observations on customs, folklore and living conditions of tribes of the interior and traditional coast settlers.

557 **Seventeen years among the Sea Dayaks of Borneo; a record of intimate association with the natives of the Bornean jungles.**
Edwin Herbert Gomes, with an introduction by the Reverend John Perham. London: Seely, 1911. 343p. map.

In this book the author aims 'to give a complete account of the entire field of Sea Dayak life . . .'. It is not just a mere personal narrative of life among the natives of northern Borneo, but rather a full, systematic and comprehensive interpretation of Sea Dayak life, their work, thoughts, customs and ideals. The author knows these people intimately and writes from a storehouse of knowledge which he has accumulated over many years of experience and observation. The twenty-four chapters cover subject matter which ranges from Sir James Brooke to the Dayak character, head-hunting, burial rites, native remedies, religion, sport and the future of Dayaks in the region. A significant number of Sea Dayaks still live in Brunei. A review of this work by A. C. Haddon appears in *Man* (vol. 11, no. 60 (1911), p. 91-92).

558 **The status of social science research in Borneo.**
Edited by G. N. Appell, Leigh R. Wright. Ithaca, New York: Cornell University, Department of Asian Studies, Southeast Asia Program, 1978. 117p. bibliog. (ITS Data Paper, no. 109).

In 1974, the Borneo Research Council held a symposium at the annual meeting of the Association for Asian Studies in Boston, Massachussets on the status of social science research in Borneo. This volume presents the results of that symposium. It includes thirteen papers and comments on several papers. The focus of the symposium was not only to assess the status of research but also its contribution to the knowledge about the cultures in Brunei, Sarawak, Sabah and Kalimantan. Whenever possible, the authors addressed the present goals of research, the problems still to be solved and the direction of future research. The disciplines covered include archaeology, social anthropology, oral literature, political science and geography. This is a valuable tool for researchers concerned with socio-cultural changes of Borneo. An extensive bibliography is included.

559 **Studies in Borneo societies: social process and anthropological explanation.**
Edited by G. N. Appell. De Kalb, Illinois: Northern Illinois University, Center for Southeast Asian Studies, 1976. 158p. 3 maps. bibliog. (ITS Special Report, no. 12).

This anthology contains seven research papers, some of which are based on original field investigations. In general, they illustrate how an adequate understanding of Bornean society requires the perspective of various social sciences and theoretical approaches. Several case-studies have employed anthropological data, others have used historical information to develop hypotheses on the nature of social processes. In Chapter 3 (p. 44-50) *Social structure, history and historiography in Brunei and beyond*, by D. E. Brown, the author combines archival research with field data to test hypotheses relevant to stratified societies, plural societies characterized by ethnic dominance (such as Brunei) and societies beyond the region, including Chinese and even European.

560 **Urang Darat, an ethnographic study of the Kadayans of Labu Valley, Brunei.**
Allen Richmond Maxwell, Jr.   PhD thesis, Yale University, New Haven, Connecticut, 1980. 272p. 5 maps. bibliog. (Available from University Microfilms, Ann Arbor, Michigan, 1980).
The objective of this ethnic study is to examine the traditional patterns of social and cultural activities in a Kadayan village. An analysis of household structure and marriage customs is related to the demographic and sociological characteristics of the community. Kadayans are still heavily involved in subsistence production in agriculture, fishing and hunting. The continuity and change of Kadayan culture in the 20th century is the subject of the last chapter. The field research was carried out between 1968 and 1971 in a rural settlement some thirty miles from Brunei's capital, Bandar Seri Begawan.

**Borneo scene.**
*See* item no. 3.

**Essays on Borneo societies.**
*See* item no. 26.

**Ethnic groups of insular Southeast Asia. Vol. 1: Indonesia, Andaman Islands, and Madagascar.**
*See* item no. 27.

**Natural man: a record from Borneo.**
*See* item no. 34.

**Life in the forests of the Far East.**
*See* item no. 42.

**Brunei, the structure and history of a Bornean Malay sultanate.**
*See* item no. 150.

**Brunei forms of address, titles and government officials.**
*See* item no. 247.

**Hereditary rank and ethnic history: an analysis of Brunei historiography.**
*See* item no. 266.

**The Kedayans.**
*See* item no. 267.

**The Sea Dayaks before white Rajah rule.**
*See* item no. 274.

**The long house and Dayak settlements in British Borneo.**
*See* item no. 283.

## Culture and Society

**Borneo medicine: the healing art of indigenous Brunei Malay medicine.**
*See* item no. 455.

**'Kalupis' – a delicacy of Brunei.**
*See* item no. 571.

**'Makan tahun': the annual feast of the Kedayans.**
*See* item no. 573.

**In the shadow of Kinabalu.**
*See* item no. 582.

**Museum development in Brunei, Borneo: 1953-1973.**
*See* item no. 610.

**Panduan dewan pameran.** (Guide to the gallery.)
*See* item no. 611.

# The Arts
# and Folklore

561 **An account of a Berhantu ceremony called 'perakong' by the Orang Belait of Brunei.**
H. R. Hughes-Hallet. *Brunei Museum Journal*, vol. 5, no. 1 (1981), p. 41-47.

The Belait people are a rapidly disappearing minority of some 800 individuals living along the lower reaches of the Belait River near the Sarawak border. Rarely seen and only performed every few years, the Belait *perakong* ceremony is a form of pagan harvest festival which marks the successful completion of a rice harvest. The author, believed to be the first European ever to have witnessed a performance, describes the setting, the musical instruments, the sacrifice and the dancers of this two-day ritual. The festival is performed with much attention to detail and involves objects of great antiquity; two factors which indicate that the custom has its roots in a well-established culture. This article is reprinted from the *Journal of the Malayan Branch of the Royal Asiatic Society* (vol. 16, no. 1 (1938), p. 102-08).

562 **Asal usul sungai Si-Amas, a folktale. (Origin of the Si-Amas River).**
Johari Haji Nasir. Bandar Seri Begawan: Dewan Bahasa dan Pustaka, 1979. 16p.

This sample of the various Bruneian folk-tales is part of a series of short stories.

563 **Borneo folktales and legends.**
Compiled by G. E. Saunders, illustrated by Lulu Taylor.
Kuching, Sarawak: Borneo Literature Bureau, 1976. 75p.

Presents a glimpse of Borneo's wealth of local legends and folk-tales. This work comprises a selection of twenty-six folk-tales extracted from longer stories. Of particular reference to Brunei is 'Nakoda Ragam' (p. 13-16), a story of a boy travelling on foot from Sambas to Brunei, and adapted from 'Nakoda Ragam: from Sambas to Brunei', by A. Bolang and T. Harrisson (*Sarawak Museum Journal*, vol. 6, no. 4 (1956), p. 58-60).

564　**Brunei brass: the traditional method of casting.**
J. S. Lim, P. M. Shariffuddin. *Brunei Museum Journal*, vol. 3, no. 4 (1976), p. 142-66. bibliog.

For centuries Brunei has been famous for its craftsmanship in silver and brassware. In fact, brass cannons and gongs became items of currency and barter in exchange for agricultural products from people in the interior. In the introduction to this article the authors speculate on the reasons for the renewed interest in brass casting, and raise questions as to the origin of this art form and the metals used. The process of casting is then documented in five stages: preparation of the wax; preparation of the clay mould; the manufacture of the crucibles; casting of molten brass; and, finally, polishing and decorating. These steps and some finished products are illustrated in thirty-six black-and-white plates.

565　**Brunei silver.**
H. Hickling. *Corona: The Journal of Her Majesty's Overseas Service*, vol. 7 (Aug. 1955), p. 294-96.

In this survey of silversmithing in Brunei the author states that the craftsmanship is almost wholly traditional, having been handed down through generations, and the artist is closely bound by the rules of the trade, leaving little opportunity for originality in design and method. A suggestion is made to send representatives to England to learn different techniques in silverware manufacturing.

566　**Cerita tradisi Brunei Darussalam.** (Brunei Darussalam's folklore.)
Taha Abdul Kadir. Petaling Jaya, Selangor, Malaysia: Pelanduk Publications, 1985. 113p.

This collection of ten seldom heard short stories is here published in Malay for the first time.

567　**The craft of the silversmith in Brunei.**
Pg. Haji Ismail bin Pg. Ibrahim. *Brunei Museum Journal*, vol. 6, no. 1 (1985), p. 89-104.

Treats the art of silver jewellery from the point of view of its origin, history and method of production. It is stressed that the Brunei craftsmen have not yet been influenced by new technical innovations and continue to pursue their traditional methods and designs. Thirteen photographs are included.

568　**Dua sahabat.** (Two friends.)
Sabtu Ampuan Safiuddin, Pengiran Tengah Bte. Pg. Mohd. Salleh (narrator), Chong Fu (artist). Bandar Seri Begawan: Dewan Bahasa dan Pustaka, [n.d.]. 23p.

This profusely illustrated children's story of two friends is written in Malay.

569   **Dusun tribal dances.**
Abdul Latif bin Haji Ibrahim.   *Brunei Museum Journal*, vol. 1, no. 1 (1969), p. 10-14.

'Dusun' is a term widely used to describe the non-Muslim inhabitants of the Belait and Tutong rivers. This article deals with some of their little-known customs, particularly the *alai* or 'tribal dance' which is believed to lift taboos. Three forms of *alai* are mentioned: *alai padi*, the rice harvest dance; *alai tahun* and *alai bulan*, the year and moon dances; and *alai buah*, the fruit dance.

570   **Folklore in Borneo: a sketch.**
William Henry Furness.   Wallingford. Pennsylvania: (privately published), 1899. 30p.

An essay which briefly discusses various accounts of creation according to the beliefs of the Dayaks and Kayans of the Baram River in northwestern Borneo. Also covered are the possible origin and reasons for the head-hunting tradition. The action of taking a head is necessary in order to obtain entrance into the 'pleasant region' of the departed spirits. The kind of life after death is, therefore, determined by the cause of death, such as sickness, old age, or becoming a victim of head-hunters.

571   **'Kalupis' – a delicacy of Brunei.**
Allen R. Maxwell.   *Brunei Museum Journal*, vol. 6, no. 1 (1985), p. 75-81. bibliog.

*Kalupis* are individually packaged steamed sweet rice cakes which appear to be a unique food item prepared by the Kadayans in Brunei, primarily for festivals and rituals. At some point in the past the dish became integrated into the customs and protocol surrounding the royal court and, even today, it retains an important place in the festival life of the rice-growing Kadayans. In this article, based on research carried out in Brunei in 1968-71, the author explains the production, history, and cultural and social significance of *kalupis*.

572   **Kedayan rafts.**
Thomas H. Harrisson.   *Brunei Museum Journal*, vol. 2, no. 1 (1970), p. 52-60.

A short description of the *gaman* used by Kedayan fishermen along the Brunei coast. Emphasis is on the structural characteristics of this simple raft, and the special paddle and gear associated with it. The type of timber required for the construction of this floating device is also mentioned. The author published his observations in the hope that the skills of making the Kedayan *gaman* may survive as a concept of merit.

573   **'Makan tahun': the annual feast of the Kedayans.**
P. M. Shariffuddin.   *Brunei Museum Journal*, vol. 2, no. 1 (1970), p. 61-66. bibliog.

The annual feast of the Kedayans in Brunei and elsewhere which is closely associated with the growing of rice and honouring the dead, is symbolic of family unity and the continuity of tradition. The author describes the cultural background, the stages of preparation and the activities of this three-day ceremony. Cooking *kelupis* is a major activity and remains central to many festive occasions in Brunei today. The author concludes that the problem of finance, time and provision of materials explains the fact that, nowadays, *makan tahun* has become more of a social function than an expression of concern for crop fertility or ancestor worship.

574  **Nakoda Ragam; from Sambas to Brunei.**
Alexander Bolang, Thomas Harrisson.  *Sarawak Museum Journal*, new series, vol. 6, no. 4 (1954), p. 57-60.

Sultan Bolkiah, also known as Nakoda Ragam, was the fifth Sultan of Brunei (1473-1521). He has been credited with expanding the empire over much of Borneo. A tale collected by Alexander Bolang and translated by Thomas Harrisson provides the first evidence of any knowledge of Nakoda Ragam in Sambas, near the Indonesian border. This paper contains a translation of this informal story and provides some evidence of linkage to historical events.

575  **The Royal *nobat* of Brunei.**
P. M. Shariffuddin, Abdul Latif Haji Ibrahim.  *Brunei Museum Journal*, vol. 4, no. 1 (1977), p. 7-17. bibliog.

The *nobat* is an assembly of drum and gong instruments used specifically for the coronation ceremonies of sultans and other important royal events. The authors discuss the possible origin of the Brunei *nobat* and the arrangement of instruments for orchestras in various Malaysian states. The ceremonial opening and closing of the *nobat* performance is also described in some detail.

576  **Seni-lukis yang masih berkembang maju. Art – nascent and latent.**
*Petroleum di Brunei*, (Jan. 1985), p. 19-29.

The Brunei Artist Association, founded in 1967, has some 150 members who work in a variety of mediums. In this bilingual report several artists discuss their uphill struggle for recognition, while others relish the notion of nurturing a natural state of art development. Most artists in Brunei are teachers or work for the government, which gives them limited time and opportunity for individual expression and artistic freedom.

577  **Some Bisaya folklore.**
D. Headly.  *Sarawak Museum Journal*, new series, vol. 5, no. 2 (1950), p. 187-92.

Presents a legend, translated from a Jawi script, which describes the early contact between the Bisayas of the Klias Peninsula opposite Labuan Island and the people of neighbouring Brunei. According to this story the contact between the two groups which had started with a casual meeting of hunting parties led to total domination by the Brunei Raja over the Bisayas some years later.

578   **Taman Indera: a royal pleasure ground. Malay decorative arts and pastimes.**
Mubin Sheppard.   Kuala Lumpur: Oxford University Press, 1972. 207p. bibliog.

This comprehensive study of Malay decorative arts and leisure activities is suitable for the general public. The author certainly deserves credit for having successfully collected information, largely unwritten, from recognized authorities, which otherwise would have vanished with the passage of time. Many coloured and black-and-white photographs accompany the written material on dance, drama, shadow play, textiles and pottery. The art of *kris* making, top spinning and kite flying, also practiced in Brunei, reveal the skills and tradition of Malay artistry.

579   **Two Brunei charms.**
G. T. MacBryan, Mohd. Yusof Shibli, translated from the Malay by Thomas H. Harrisson.   *Journal of the Malayan Branch of the Royal Asiatic Society*, vol. 29, no. 2 (1947), p. 48-59.

This article, in Malay and English, is concerned with two charms (known in Brunei as *pugay*) used to cast spells of love or hate on an individual. The text is a striking example of detailed documentary information about the little known Kelabit branch of the Murut and their association with the Malays.

**The birds of Borneo.**
*See* item no. 97.

**In the grandest tradition, the new Istana is today's Versailles.**
*See* item no. 250.

**The traditional economic activities in Kampung Air, Brunei.**
*See* item no. 287.

**A *Sebob Dirge* (sung on the occasion of the death of Tama Jangan Jau by Belawing Kupa).**
*See* item no. 533.

**The aims, approaches and problems in the study of folk literature or oral tradition with particular reference to Malay culture.**
*See* item no. 536.

**Brunei cannon.**
*See* item no. 539.

**Brunei cannon: their role in Southeast Asia (1400-1900 AD).**
*See* item no. 540.

**A critical and annotated bibliography of Philippine, Indonesian and other Malayan folk-lore.**
*See* item no. 645.

# Tourism and Recreation

580 **Brunei Darussalam in brief.**
Broadcasting and Information Department. Bandar Seri
Begawan: Broadcasting and Information Department, Ministry of
Culture, Youth and Sports, 1986. 63p. 2 maps.

This pocket-sized handbook, covering all aspects of life in Brunei, is aimed at the
general public. Subjects covered include the geography, the people, history and
important dates, the government, trade and industry, banking, social services,
transportation, press and broadcasting, international relations, visas and places of
interest. It is handsomely illustrated with coloured photographs.

581 **The Brunei beauty, *Betta mecrostoma*.**
Herbert R. Axelrod. *Tropical Fish Hobbyist* (June 1982),
p. 68-83; (July 1983), p. 68-79.

This two-part article decribes the species, *Betta mecrostoma*, and a journey to the
Mendaran River where samples of this tropical fish were collected. Its habitat is
shallow pools in rivers at 3,000 to 4,000 feet elevations. This is a popular
aquarium fish because of its unique spot on the dorsal fin. Also mentioned is the
Hassanal Bolkiah Aquarium in the capital containing forty-seven exhibition tanks.

582 **In the shadow of Kinabalu.**
Cyril Alliston. London: Robert Hale, 1961. 191p. map.

An intimate account of the work and travels of two missionaries set against the
background of the various ethnic groups living in the shadow of Borneo's famous
peak and Southeast Asia's second highest mountain. Brunei is mentioned
throughout the book. During a period of nine years between 1950 and 1959, the
Christian couple travelled through Brunei and Sabah recording their personal
impressions.

182

583 **Looking at Brunei.**
Kuala Belait, Brunei: Brunei Shell Petroleum Co. Ltd., Trade
Relations Department, 1980. 36p.
A pocket-book tourist guide which describes various trips and visits to major
attractions in Brunei, including Kampung Ayer (water village), the Lapau (Royal
Ceremonial Hall) and the national mosque.

584 **Malaysia, Singapore and Brunei: a travel survival kit.**
Geoff Crowther, Tony Wheeler. South Yarra, Australia;
Berkeley, California: Lonely Planet, 1985. 2nd ed. 295p. 51 maps.
An updated version of the 1982 edition. The introduction to this book provides
relevant facts about each country, its people, geography and culture; together
with important information for the visitor to Brunei, regarding entry visa,
language (including helpful phrases), and food and customs. Readers are also
provided with extensive travel information about getting to these countries by
rail, sea or air and, once they have arrived, what possibilities exist for local
transportation by bus, taxi or 'rent-a-car'. Each country is treated in some detail
with descriptions of places to stay, places to eat and visitor attractions in each
major city. The chapter on Brunei (p. 277-87) presents a summary of the
country's history, economy and cultural attractions for the tourists, including the
water village, the national mosque, the Brunei Museum, ancient tombs and the
Handicraft Centre.

585 **Malaysia, Singapore, Brunei: traveller's handbook.**
Stefan Loose, Renate Ramb, translated by David Crawford.
Berlin: Stefan Loose Publications, 1986. 332p. 2 maps. bibliog.
A general description for the first-time visitor to Brunei. A list of principal
attractions in Bandar Seri Begawan, hotel accommodation and day trips outside
the capital is included. A short history of Brunei and two maps provide additional
background for the potential traveller to Southeast Asia's only Sultanate. Brunei
is covered on pages 267-72.

586 **Muhibbah (Goodwill), Inflight Magazine of Royal Brunei Airlines.**
Bandar Seri Begawan: Royal Brunei Airlines, 1982-. bi-monthly.
A highly colourful and well-illustrated journal with feature articles about life and
culture in Brunei, as well as other tourist spots. The articles are short, usually two
pages in length, and written for the general public.

587 **Polo di Brunei Darussalam. Polo in Brunei Darussalam.**
*Petroleum di Brunei*, (July 1984), p. 25-33.
The popularity of polo with the royal family has made it the most rapidly
developing sport in Brunei. Since 1976, when the game was introduced, Jerudong
Park has been developed, the Royal Brunei Polo Association formed and the
Brunei team has participated regularly in tournaments overseas. Today, the royal
stables are among the world's best equipped facilities for the 200 playing ponies
imported from Argentina.

588 **Selamat Datang. Welcome.**
Bandar Seri Begawan: Broadcasting and Information Department,
Ministry of Culture, Youth and Sports, 1986. rev. ed. 45p. 2 maps.

This information booklet contains chapters on Brunei's history, people, economy, transportation, communication, mass media and social services, and is supplemented by forty coloured photographs. In addition, it outlines the family tree of the sultans, the origin of the flag and national crest, and the structure of the administration. For the visitor, the booklet lists public holidays, stipulates visa and health requirements, and describes the facilities at the Brunei Museum and the Handicraft Centre.

# Statistics

589 **Annual Report.**
State of Brunei.  Kuala Belait, Brunei: 1906-. annual.
The first government report on the State of Brunei was published in 1906 by the British Resident, Mr. S. McArthur. It was a 15-page document which described the introduction of a settled administration and the initial efforts of collecting statistics on trade, population, revenues and public services. By 1920, data on land use, education, the court system and census procedures were included. Up to this time the document was published as *House of Common Parliamentary Papers (Colonial Report);* later it became known as *State of Brunei, Annual Report.* For the next 50 years the reports expanded in terms of both subject matter and data analysis. Since the 1950s the report has come out as a hardbound copy. For the period 1963-68 a short bibliography on books and technical studies was included. The 1974 and 1975 editions appeared in both English and Malay. Most recent reports contain at least one map and several black-and-white illustrations. The 1977 edition, an extensive 507-page report, contains 13 chapters: 'General review which looks at the progress for that year; 'Physical features', which also covers physical planning, including the national master plan; 'Population', an assessment since the last census in 1971; 'Industrial structure', which provides statistics on employment, occupation, wages and types of industry; 'Public finance and taxation', which describes the system of accounting and provides data on revenues, expenditure, duties and currency circulation; 'Commerce', which shows annual figures for import-export trade; 'Production' gives annual output in forestry, fisheries and agriculture'; 'Social development' which assesses the status of education, health, religion, youth and sports; and 'Law and order' which describes the activities of the police department and shows statistics on crime, accidents and prison expenditure. 'Communication' includes a description of postal services, radio and television, land transport, civil aviation and port activities; 'Public utilities' provides information on infrastructure developments, such as road construction, building maintenance, land reclamation, water supply and drainage problems, and electricity supply. The last two chapters usually

185

provide a brief history of Brunei and a summary on the constitution and administration. Since 1960 various lists are shown in an appendix of members of the Privy Council, the State Legislative Council, the Council of Ministers and the British Residents. Some editions also provide a chronological list of Mohammedan sovereigns and their antecedents. The 1946 issue, for example, lists the names and dates of 27 Sultans and British Residents from 1906-46. Clearly, this series of reports is probably the most complete and continuous record, since 1906, of the physical and human developments in Brunei. This report is highly recommended as a research tool.

590 **Brunei.**
In: *The Europa year book 1985: a world survey.* Vol. 1, part III.
London: Europa Publications, 1985. p. 1,320-25.
The *Europa year book* is an authoritative reference work which, since 1960, has appeared in annual two-volume editions, providing a wealth of information on the political, economic and commercial institutions of the world. The information is collected from a variety of sources, such as national statistical offices, government departments and diplomatic missions. The entry for Brunei consists of three parts. The first part describes the geography, history, economy and social conditions of the country. Part two provides a variety of statistics primarily available from the Economic Planning Unit, Ministry of Finance, in Bandar Seri Begawan. The data entail population figures, production in agriculture, mining and industry, finance, external trade, transport, communication, health and education. Finally, a directory is presented of the most up-to-date addresses and heads of organizations. They include cabinet ministers and ministries, political organizations, the judicial system, embassies, publishers, trade unions, banks, civil aviation, tourist offices and the news media.

591 **Brunei: report on the housing census held in four towns, May-August 1960.**
Laurence Walter Jones. Kuching, Sarawak: Government Printing Office, [1961]. 47p.
An analysis of housing data for Brunei Town (now Bandar Seri Begawan), Tutong, Seria and Belait. This was Brunei's first housing census to be carried out only in urban areas. Information is given on type of building, ownership, rate of occupancy, number of rooms and facilities (such as water and electricity supply). Statistical tables and photographs illustrating typical housing styles are appended.

592 **Brunei Statistical Yearbook.**
Economic Planning Unit, Statistics Section, Brunei. Bandar Seri Begawan: Brunei Ministry of Finance, 1965/66-. annual.
This year-book is prepared for the purpose of providing the most current data available on Brunei. Most of the tables are compiled from published copies of the Brunei *Annual Report*, materials supplied by various government departments and some private sector companies. Each year, where necessary, some statistics have been amended and updated. All figures on production, except petroleum, natural gas, petroleum products and electricity, are only estimates. Statistics are also issued for population, labour, primary production, external trade, transportation, finance, education, health and national accounts.

186

593 **Brunei: statistischer Gesamtüberblick und neuer Entwicklungsplan 1986-1990.** (Brunei: statistical overview and the new development plan 1986-1990.)
Günter Siemers. *Südostasien Aktuell*, vol. 5, no. 2 (March 1986), p. 172-82. map.

Provides (in German) statistical information (up to 1984) under the following headings: climate, population, education, health, mass media, crime, economy, labour and wages, transport, agriculture, fisheries, mining and energy, communication and trade. Also included is an assessment of the latest five-year National Development Plan. In its long-range objectives this plan tends to pursue the same goals outlined in the previous two plans. A comparison is made between the plans in terms of GNP, the restructuring of the economy and investment activities.

594 **Report on the buffalo census and survey in Brunei 1980/81.**
Thomas Lee Kok Cho. Tutong, Brunei: Sinaut Agricultural Training Centre, 1982. 45p. map. bibliog.

In order to reduce its dependency on imported beef Brunei is trying to exploit more fully its own buffalo population to meet domestic meat requirements. Hence, this buffalo census which provides some base data could not be more timely. Sixty per cent of a total of 977 farmers were interviewed and the results are presented in this report. Data were collected on animal distribution, herd size, grazing area, feed resources and some management practices. The report makes some recommendations to improve the productive performance of this potential resource.

595 **Report on the census of population 1971.**
State of Brunei. Bandar Seri Begawan: Star Press, 1973. 260p.

The 1971 census was the fifth population count to be held in Brunei, but the first to be conducted by Brunei alone. This census was organized, conducted and analysed by the State Secretary of the Economic and Statistical section. This volume deals only with population characteristics; information on housing is dealt with in another volume. The data are presented in nine chapters which cover: population by district; ethnic groups; age, sex and marital status; literacy and education; religion; place of birth; employment; occupation and industry. The text of these chapters is also summarized in Malay. The analysis of these characteristics is enhanced by comparative data of previous census enumerations. Forty-four tables represent the statistical section of this report.

596 **The statesman's year-book: statistical and historical annual of the states of the world for the year 1987-1988.**
Edited by John Paxton. New York: St. Martin's Press, 1987. 124th ed. 1,695p.

'This annual publication, which started in 1864, is a concise and reliable manual of descriptive and statistical information about the governments of the world'. Recent issues have included a section on international organizations. For Brunei (as for most other countries) the following topics are briefly covered, supplemented with dates and statistics: history, area and population, climate, constitution and government, ruler, defence, economy, international relations,

**Statistics**

energy and natural resources, industry and trade, communication, justice, religion, welfare and diplomatic representatives.

597   **Statistics of External Trade.**
Economic Planning Unit, Statistics Section, Brunei.   Bandar Seri Begawan: Brunei State Secretariat, [n.d.]. annual.
Reports (in English and Malay) trade statistics registered by customs at Brunei ports, airports and other entry stations. The commodities include food, beverages, chemicals, minerals, manufactured goods and machinery. The import-export commodities are classified according to the standard international trade classification adopted by Brunei in 1964. This year-book was previously published by the Department of Customs and Excise.

**Brunei: report on the census of population taken on 10th August, 1960.**
*See* item no. 263.

**Laporan banchi pendudok Brunei 1971.** (Report on the census of population 1971.)
*See* item no. 268.

**Sarawak and Brunei: a report on the 1947 population census.**
*See* item no. 273.

**Ranchangan kemajuan Negara yang kelima, 1986-1990 – Fifth National Development Plan, 1986-1990.**
*See* item no. 367.

**Report on the 1964 census of agriculture.**
*See* item no. 444.

**Brunei housing needs, 1986-2000.**
*See* item no. 456.

**Annual Report.**
*See* item no. 589.

# Philately and Numismatics

598 **Brunei.**
Frederick John Melville. Pavia, Italy: Giorgio Migliavacca, 1980.
Reprint from the London Philatelic Inst., 1932 ed. 37p.
This booklet, authored by the President of the Junior Philatelic Society, details
the importance of stamps in the history of Brunei itself. Each chapter provides the
political and social setting for the issuance of special stamps. Other aspects of
philatelic publishing, such as colour changes, overprints, watermarks and designs,
are also discussed.

599 **Brunei: the definitive issues and postal cancellations to 1974.**
E. Thorndike. Newbury, England: Cockrill, [1983]. 52p. 2 maps.
bibliog. (Cockrill Series Booklet, no. 34).
This booklet brings together and updates previous publications on Brunei postage
stamps and cancellations. The text describes, chronologically, six important stamp
issues.

600 **Brunei coinage.**
J. A. Davidson. *Brunei Museum Journal*, vol. 4, no. 1 (1977),
p. 43-81. bibliog.
A history of the type and usage of coins and banknotes in Brunei from 1460 to
1977. The earliest coinage appears to have been Chinese, made of bronze and
pierced in the centre. Silver and gold has never been used in Brunei coinage.
16th- and 17th-century money was made of soft tin lead alloy which did not keep
well over a long period of time. Islamic coins, therefore, present a greater
problem of identification than the older Chinese ones. Many of these early coins
were found at Kota Batu. In the 19th century a kind of dowry money in the form
of miniature bronze cannons was issued. About 150 years ago pieces of iron strips
came into circulation, locally known as *duit besi* (iron cash). After Brunei became

**Philately and Numismatics**

a British Protectorate in 1888, the main coinage in circulation was that of the Straits Settlements. Less common were coins from Malaya, Sarawak and British North Borneo. In the 1960s Brunei issued its own banknotes for the first time. These notes illustrate the steady reassertion of Brunei identity, bearing the head of the current Sultan and his signature. The currency presently in circulation consists of several denominations and is decorated with illustrations of the state crest, cannons, the great white mosque and portraits of sultans. A recent notable numismatic occasion was the striking of magnificent medallions to commemorate the visit to Brunei of Her Majesty Queen Elizabeth II of England on February 1972. The article is supplemented by 74 illustrations of coins and 14 of banknotes.

601 **The coinage of the Sultanate of Brunei, 1400-1980.**
Saran Singh.  *Brunei Museum Journal*, vol. 4, no. 4 (1980), p. 38-103. map. bibliog.

An excellent coverage of the numismatic history of Brunei. As background to this history the author felt it necessary to include a short introductory survey of the spread of Islam in the region. A classification and chronology (with pictures) of coins and the sultans' genealogy accompany the text.

602 **The coins of Malaysia 1845-1967, including Straits Settlements, Malaya, British North Borneo, Sarawak, Brunei, Singapore, British trade dollars.**
Kevin F. Kavanagh.  Adelaide, Australia: Mitchell Press, 1969. 95p. 4 maps. bibliog.

A standard guide to the coinage of Malaysia, Brunei and Singapore. The author believes that in order for collectors to understand the history of coinage, one must know something about the history of the country. Each chapter, therefore, begins with a concise country history followed by a catalogue of selected coins. Brunei's coins are covered on pages 75-78.

603 **A few notes on the stamps of Brunei.**
Leonard A. Gibbens.  *Stamp Lover*, vol. 17, no. 1 (June 1924), p. 1-2.

A description of Brunei stamp series issued at different times in 1902 and from 1908-16. Useful information for stamp collectors is provided.

604 **Old Brunei coins.**
E. Wodak.  *Sarawak Museum Journal*, new series, vol. 8, no. 11 (1958), p. 278-92.

This article reports on a series of Brunei coins that is quite unique amongst Malayan soft metal issues. They include types picturing various animals and inscriptions of legal titles. Other coin collections, such as those discovered at Kota Batu, are also referred to for comparison.

605   **Paper currency of Malaysia, Singapore and Brunei: 1849-1970.**
William Shaw, Md. Kassim Haji Ali.   Kuala Lumpur: Muzium
Negara, 1971. 124p. bibliog.

Traces the numismatic history of the region including the manufacture and
counterfeiting of paper currency. Brunei is dealt with in part nine. Five currency
notes are reproduced and discussed.

606   **The postage stamps of Brunei 1895-1941: a philatelic outline.**
Brian J. Cave.   *Brunei Museum Journal*, vol. 3, no. 1 (1973),
p. 127-45.

The first adhesive postage stamps issued in Brunei date back to 1895 when the
official post office opened in the capital. Since that time new designs and new
denominations, different colours and sizes of stamps have appeared for specific
issues. Among them is the 1895 issue; the provisional issue of 1906; the Brunei
River stamps of 1907; the Malaya–Borneo Exhibition in 1922 and the Kampong
Ayer series of 1924. The objective of this survey of the pre-World War II stamps
of Brunei is to give the layman an insight into these issues and their background.
Other post-war definitive issues are of no less philatelic value, while the
commemorative issues trace the development of the state. Much has been
published about stamps in Brunei, but the story is still far from complete. For a
history of the postal service in Brunei see 'A study of Brunei postage rates and
changes, 1895-1985' by E. Thorndike (*Brunei Museum Journal*, vol. 6, no. 2
(1986), p. 128-147). Arranged chronologically, this article covers the concessionary
mail service (1895-1906) and rate changes in 1923-26, 1931, 1940 and the post-
Second World War period.

# Libraries and Museums

607  **Comparative notes on museum exhibits in Singapore, Malaysia, Indonesia, Brunei, Macao, and the Philippines.**
Mamitua Saber, Dionisio G. Orellana.   Marawi City, Philippines: Aga Khan Museum, Mindanao State University, 1977. 177p. map.

Provides a 'report to the Ford Foundation on a travelling symposium for Southeast Asia museum development, April-May 1971.' An analysis of the Brunei Museum's contribution to the enrichment and preservation of local culture is included (p. 78-86). The Sultan's government gives maximum support to the museum's development as a valuable cultural, scientific and historical centre for present and future generations. The present museum facilities which date back to 1968 and the official journal, the *Brunei Museum Journal*, first published in 1969, testify to the recent efforts in the preservation of Brunei culture. The collections of classic ceramics, jade articles, cannons, brasswork, musical instruments and textiles are described in some detail. The Brunei Museum is regarded as the fastest growing rival to its counterparts, the Malaysia Muzium Negara in Kuala Lumpur and the Sarawak Museum in Kuching, Sarawak.

608  **Dewan tembikar Musium Brunei di-Kota Batu: satu pendahuluan mengenai sejarah tembikar dagangan di-Borneo. The Ceramic Gallery of the Brunei Museum at Kota Batu: an introduction to the history of trade ceramics.**
Barbara V. Harrisson, translated by Abdul Latif Haji Ibrahim.
Kota Batu, Brunei: Brunei Museum, 1972. 54p. bibliog.

A detailed description (in Malay and English) of the museum's stoneware and porcelain collections, many items of which date back over thirteen centuries. Harrisson catalogues all artefacts and traces their origin back to several Chinese dynasties.

609 **Libraries and librarianship in Brunei.**
Nellie Haji Sunny. Master's thesis, Loughborough University of
Technology, England, 1980. 129p. 2 maps. bibliog.
Represents a preliminary attempt to assess the status of library services in Brunei
and to make recommendations for future progress toward internationally
recognized standards in information science. Special emphasis is given to public
and special libraries. Although many of these services only began to operate in
the late 1960s, their progress since then is truly noteworthy.

610 **Museum development in Brunei, Borneo: 1953-1973.**
P. M. Shariffuddin. *Brunei Museum Journal*, vol. 3, no. 1 (1973),
p. 51-61.
Commemorates the completion of the first museum in Brunei, ceremonially
opened in February 1972 by Queen Elizabeth II of England. Archaeological
discoveries at the ancient site of Kota Batu between 1953 and 1956 encouraged
the development of museum services in Brunei. During subsequent years efforts
were directed toward: (a) the training of personnel; (b) the acquisition of
historical sites; (c) the development of collections for exhibition; and (d) the
construction of the museum building itself. The facilities and permanent exhibits
in the building are briefly explained. Current research results are published in the
*Brunei Museum Journal* and are also used to prepare lectures and exhibitions for
the education of the public, especially the young.

611 **Panduan dewan pameran.** (Guide to the gallery.)
Bandar Seri Begawan: Muzium Brunei, 1972. 4 vols. bibliog.
(Penerbitan Khas-Muzium Brunei, bil. 3-6. [Brunei Museum
Special Publications, nos. 3-6]).
Although these guides are produced primarily for the visitor to the Brunei
Museum, they also provide background information for students and researchers
interested in local anthropology and archaeology. Each booklet is richly illus-
trated with black-and-white photographs of the museum's exhibitions. The four
guides respectively describe the Ceramic Gallery (by Barbara Harrisson – see
item no. 608), the Cultural Gallery and the Gallery of Natural History (by Erika
Birkenmeier and Lim Jock Seng – see item no. 612) and the Exhibition Gallery of
Native Houses.

612 **Panduan rengkas Dewan Ilmu kejadian alam. Dewan Pameran 3. A
brief guide to [the] Natural History Gallery. Exhibition Gallery 3.**
Erika Birkenmeier, Lim Jock Seng, translated by Abdul Latif Haji
Ibrahim. Kota Batu, Brunei: Brunei Museum, 1972. 34p.
(Penerbitan Khas-Muzium Brunei, bil. 5. [Brunei Museum Special
Publications, no. 5]).
A detailed bilingual explanation of the various showcases in the Natural History
Gallery of the Brunei Museum. It features typical scenes of Brunei's animal life,
ranging from insect habitats to those of the larger mammals.

613  **Penyata Muzium Brunei 1965-1970. Brunei Museum Report 1965-1970.**
Brunei Museum.  Bandar Seri Begawan: Brunei Museum, (1965-70). 63p. (Penerbitan Khas-Muzium Brunei, bil 1. [Brunei Museum Special Publications, no. 1]).

A comprehensive treatment of the development of the Brunei Museum, its history, construction and administration. In addition, this work reports on the museum's activities, which include the acquisition of specimens, the archaeological excavations and the development of ethnographic collections.

614  **Research collections for the study of Borneo in Sabah, Brunei and Sarawak.**
George Miller.  *SEARMG (Southeast Asian Research Materials Group) Newsletter*, no. 27 (Aug. 1984), p. 18-21.

An introduction to local collections developed by libraries, archives and museums of Sabah, Sarawak and the Sultanate of Brunei. Written by a librarian from the Australian National Library, the description is intended to highlight certain repositories and their collections. In the case of Brunei, for example, the Language and Literature Bureau, the Brunei Museum, the Brunei Department of Information and the Brunei Department of Religion are briefly described.

615  **Some problems of getting materials for the Brunei Museum.**
P. M. Shariffuddin.  *Brunei Museum Journal*, vol. 2, no. 1 (1970), p. 1-16.

Describes the need for a comprehensive museum as a centre of research and a place in which to display ancient remains of the country. The author, the first curator of the museum, describes the historical value of many cultural artefacts since they are no longer used and produced in the country. Also modern influences and foreign occupations have caused these materials to be taken out of the country. The author urges the authorities to exert every effort in recapturing these lost items even if it means paying a high price for their return.

**Guide to modern archives and manuscripts found in the United Kingdom relating to Brunei, Sabah and Sarawak.**
*See* item no. 647.

# Mass Media, Periodicals and Directories

616 **Asiaweek.**
Hong Kong: Asiaweek, 1975-. weekly.
*Asiaweek* is the equivalent of *Time* or *Newsweek* for all of Asia. Correspondents stationed in many countries throughout the region contribute news and in-depth reports on politics, economics, social affairs and culture. Editorials and literary reviews reflect a definite Asian point of view. This publication is a valuable resource for educators, scientists, researchers and others interested in Asian society.

617 **Bahana.**
Bandar Seri Begawan: Dewan Bahasa dan Pustaka, 1966-. monthly.
Established by the Language and Literature Bureau to support Brunei's national identity, this journal is mainly devoted to language, literature and linguistics. All articles are in Malay.

618 **Berita. Malaysia–Singapore–Brunei Studies Group, Southeast Asia Council.**
Philadelphia: Temple University, Journalism Department, 1975-. tri-annual.
Represents the official organ for the Malaysia–Singapore–Brunei Studies Group, which is a country division of the Southeast Asian Council, Association for Asian Studies, in the United States. The purpose of *Berita* is to serve as a forum and bulletin board for scholars concerned with these three countries. Each issue contains announcements of new publications, a bibliography, the content of recent periodicals, relevant information on conferences, information on the Southeast Asian Studies Summer Institute, and articles pertaining to travel, research and impressions relevant to Malaysia, Singapore and Brunei.

195

Mass Media, Periodicals and Directories

619  **Borneo Bulletin.**
Kuala Belait, Brunei: Brunei Press, [1953]-. weekly.
The *Borneo Bulletin* supposedly has the largest circulation of any newspaper in Brunei, Sarawak and Sabah. Published and printed in Kuala Belait, the feature stories, editorials, and sports section focus primarily on local issues, events and conditions. Each issue also presents cultural, religious, social and political news in Malay. The *Borneo Bulletin* is the most regular and current English-language source of information on all aspects of Brunei, available to students and researchers.

620  **Borneo Research Bulletin.**
Williamsburg, Virginia: Borneo Research Council, 1969-. semi-annual.
A scientific journal devoted to further research activities on Borneo and which coordinates information from many different sources. Articles, research news, book reviews and a bibliography of recent publications are included.

621  **Broadcasting development in Brunei.**
Glyn Alkin.  *Comboard (Commonwealth Broadcasting Association)*, no. 46 (Jan.-March 1980), p. 39-42.
Prior to 1974 Brunei had two radio networks, one broadcasting in Malay and the other dividing its time between English and Chinese. Television was receivable in monochrome from neighbouring Sabah. In 1974 the decision was made to introduce a television service to Brunei. A year later a new broadcasting facility known as Radio Television Brunei (RTB) began transmitting for four to five hours each day. The opportunity to view high-quality programmes in colour, coupled with an imaginative news service quickly reversed the general direction of across-the-border viewing. The service has continually expanded and with a new television complex in full operation by 1980, Brunei had one of the best equipped commercial television centres in Asia. A main problem cited throughout the entire enterprise has been, and still is, the shortage of trained local staff. The impact on isolated villages of a sudden exposure to Western culture was no less startling and confusing. The development of television in Brunei has also forged some important linkages with the BBC and Television Singapore both of which assisted in the development of RTB.

622  **Brunei: television in a rich ministate.**
John A. Lent.  *BMIE's World Broadcast News*, (March-April 1979), p. 10.
In 1975, within less than nine months, a national colour television service had been established in Brunei. Such a feat is only feasible in a rich country such as Brunei where the government had decided that installing a television network was one of its top priorities. Even the creation of an audience was instantaneous as the government provided interest-free loans to purchase television sets. Indeed, people were buying them so quickly that the shops could not keep the shelves stocked. In a country of 180,000 people in 1977 an estimated 100,000 colour television sets existed. Radio Television Brunei (RTB) is financed almost wholly by the government and, therefore, carries a very small amount of advertising.

196

623   **Brunei Museum Journal.**
Kota Batu, Brunei: Muzium Brunei, 1969-. annual.
This is the official scholarly journal of the Brunei Museum. Original papers cover history and prehistory, ethnography, ethno-biology, geology, demography, culture, language and linguistics. The series also includes an occasional monograph. Starting with volume three, each volume has four numbers, which are published in consecutive years. The majority of the articles are in English. The *Analytical index to the Brunei Museum Journal 1969-1984*, published in 1985, provides access to the contents alphabetically by both author and by title.

624   **Buku panduan badan-badan perusahaan perniagaan Negara Brunei Darussalam.** (Directory on business undertakings, Brunei Darussalam.)
Bandar Seri Begawan: Unit Perancang Ekonomi Kementerian Kewangan (Economic Planning Unit, Ministry of Finance), 1985. 89p.
The National Planning Unit has produced surveys and census data on businesses and companies since 1978. Much of that data, which is published in the *Brunei Statistical Yearbook*, has revealed a steady growth in the business community in recent years. This prompted the publication of this directory which consists of names and addresses of enterprises registered as limited companies, together with those with ten or more employees. The classification follows the International Standard Information Classification system.

625   **CORMOSEA Bulletin. Committee on Research Materials on Southeast Asia.**
Ann Arbor, Michigan: Association for Asian Studies, 1975/76-. irregular.
This bulletin contains progress reports on research projects, announcements on grant support, notes of reference material, guides and bibliographies, comments on computer technology, new publications, conference announcements and minutes of the annual meeting of the committee.

626   **Far Eastern Economic Review.**
Hong Kong: Far Eastern Economic Review, 1946-. weekly.
A business weekly containing news, editorials and feature articles on economic, political and social issues throughout Asia. Brunei is covered with some emphasis on the Sultan, oil and ASEAN and cover stories on independence. Informed, comprehensive and perceptive, this is an essential source for those who wish to keep abreast of political, economic and commercial developments throughout Asia.

627   **Journal of Southeast Asian Studies.**
Singapore: McGraw-Hill Far Eastern Publishers (1970-77); Singapore University Press (1978- ); 1970-. semi-annual.
This periodical, successor to the *Journal of Southeast Asian History* (1960-69), takes a multidisciplinary approach to the study of Southeast Asia as well as a

social science perspective. It aims to increase people's understanding of how the past interacts with current forces which are at work in the region. Full-length articles on Brunei are featured periodically.

628 **Journal of the Malaysian Branch of the Royal Asiatic Society.**
Kuala Lumpur: Malaysian Branch of the Royal Asiatic Society, 1923-. semi-annual.

This well-established journal specializes in the history, literature, culture, anthropology, natural history and archaeology of the Malay world. From 1878-1922 the journal was known as the *Journal of the Straits Branch, Royal Asiatic Society*, and from 1923-63 it was known as the *Journal of the Malayan Branch of the Royal Asiatic Society*. Three indexes to the journal have been published so far: *Index Malaysiana. An index to the Journal of the Straits Branch Royal Asiatic Society and the Journal of the Malayan Branch Royal Asiatic Society, 1878-1963*, by Lim Huck Tee and D. E. K. Wijasuriya (Kuala Lumpur, 1970. 395p.); *Index Malaysiana. Supplement I. An index to the Journal of the Malaysian Branch of the Royal Asiatic Society and the JMBRAS monographs, 1964-1973*, by D. E. K. Wijasuriya and Lim Huck Tee (Kuala Lumpur, 1974. 66p.); and *Index Malaysiana. Supplement no. II, 1974-1983*, by D. E. K. Wijasuriya, Lim Huck Tee (Petaling Jaya, 1985. 72p.). This is an essential source for the study of Malaya/ Malaysia and general region.

629 **Malaysia, Singapore and Brunei studies – personnel, programs, resources: directory.**
Joseph A. Weinstock.    Ann Arbor, Michigan: Malaysia, Singapore & Brunei Studies Group, SEA Regional Council, Association for Asian studies, 1978. 62p.

A source book for individuals interested in research activities and academic programmes for several Southeast Asian nations. It provides details on research faculties and their specialization, American and foreign institutional programmes, resources and libraries. Information is also provided on the personnel and funding sources for many programmes both in the United States and Southeast Asia. Although somewhat dated, this directory is still quite useful.

630 **Mass media in East Malaysia and Brunei.**
John A. Lent.    *Gazette: International Journal for Mass Communication Studies*, vol. 30, no. 2 (1982), p. 97-108. bibliog.

Mass media in East Malaysia (Sarawak and Sabah) and Brunei has undergone rapid changes since the 1960s, resulting in a decrease in person-to-person communication and a dependence on colour television. The print media, on the other hand, is suffering from problems endemic to the press in many Third World nations: lack of capital, staff and material as well as overdependence upon governmental sources for information. Certainly, in Brunei the print media has not had a long history or a dominant role. The country is served by only three weekly newspapers, the *Borneo Bulletin, Pelita Brunei* and *Salam*; the dailies from Malaysia are available, sporadically, but are expensive. In 1975 Brunei television went on the air. The keywords in the system were 'instant' and 'important' – it was installed in six months at a cost of US$15 million. The government needed a system that could effectively compete with Television Malaysia and open up communication with remote areas, especially the Limbang River settlements. Much of the programming, however, is still foreign and this has profoundly affected the cultural integrity of the country.

631   **Media directory: the 13th media directory incorporating the creative services.**
Singapore: Association of Accredited Advertising Agents, 1987. 512p.

This directory presents updated media information for Singapore, Malaysia and Brunei. A large portion is devoted to details on newspapers and periodicals. The section on audio-visual data covers cinema, broadcasting, advertising and television. A guide to creative services includes art supplies, photography, recording services, graphic design, trade shows, publishing companies and printers.

632   **Newspapers published in the Malaysian area, with a union list of local holdings.**
Patricia Lim Pui Huen.   Singapore: Institute of Southeast Asian Studies, 1970. bibliog. (Institute of Southeast Asian Studies Occasional Paper, no. 2).

Lists all newspapers published in Malaysia, Singapore and Brunei from 1827 to 1968 in any language or script. A chronological arrangement by date of issue, within language groups, has been adopted. Publication dates, and the location of hard copies and microfilms within the area is also provided. Brunei and East Malaysia are covered on p. 191-96. There is no index.

633   **Pelita Brunei.** (Official Bulletin of the Government of Brunei.) Bandar Seri Begawan: Information Section. Ministry of Culture, Youth and Sport, 19?-. weekly.

This free government-sponsored publication represents the official viewpoint on domestic and foreign affairs. It includes information with some emphasis on religion, the news media, national politics and the economy. Periodically, it covers sports, school examination results and trips to Mecca.

634   **Sarawak Museum Journal.**
Kuching, Malaysia: The Museum, Sarawak, 1911-37; 1949-. irregular.

One of the oldest and most authoritative publications of scientific literature for Sarawak, Brunei and, indeed, all of Borneo. The journal has played an important role in providing a medium for the distribution of original research in history, anthropology, archaeology, ethnology and the natural sciences. Prior to the founding of the *Brunei Museum Journal* (in 1969), at least one article on Brunei appeared in each issue.

635 **Southeast Asia Business.**
Ann Arbor, Michigan: University of Michigan, Center for South
and Southeast Asian Studies, 1984-. quarterly.
As the title indicates, the journal is heavily geared to the business world. It
includes, per issue, one feature article and a series of brief country reports. Other
information includes notes from abroad and industry news extracted from the
*Asian Wallstreet Journal*, the *Singapore Straits Times* and other Asian newspapers.
A bibliography, and a calendar of events are also provided.

636 **Southeast Asian Affairs.**
Singapore: Institute of Southeast Asian Studies, 1974-. annual.
Each volume contains two kinds of contributions, those which highlight the
political, economic and social developments of the year for individual countries
and those which deal with topical problems concerning the region as a whole. The
coverage of Brunei focuses on issues of current interest and mostly pertain to the
year under review. The goal of this collection of essays is to give the enquiring
reader a broad grasp of current affairs in the region. This is an invaluable source
of information.

637 **Südost Asien Aktuel.** (Southeast Asia Today.)
Hamburg: Institut für Asienkunde, 1982-. six times a year.
Provides (in German and English) current information and statistics on every
nation in Southeast Asia and ASEAN. The material ranges from in-depth reports
to short news items and even holiday schedules. For the researcher and
administrator there are announcements of national development plans, relevant
social issues and bibliographical references to recent publications. Banking
information in the form of exchange rates of the German Mark and the US dollar
is shown. All issues are divided into three parts. Part I covers current political
issues for each nation. Part II includes themes/topics, and usually two to three
major articles, and part III consists of a news/information column. The March
1987 issue, for example, reported (for Brunei) the visit of the US aircraft carrier
'Kitty Hawk', the reorganization of the banking system and plans for an
underwater cable to Singapore.

**Petroleum di Brunei.**
*See* item no. 16.

**Illuminating the path to independence: political themes in *Pelita Brunei* in
1983.**
*See* item no. 237.

# Bibliographies
# and Indexes

638 **Bibliografi mengenai Brunei. (Bibliography concerning Brunei).**
Bandar Seri Begawan: Dewan Bahasa dan Pustaka, [n.d.]. 12p.
This mimeographed document (in Malay and English) includes mostly govern-
ment publications and some English monographs by such authors as Nicholas
Tarling and Robert Nicholl. It lists the annual report starting with 1958.

639 **Bibliography of English language sources on human ecology:**
   **Eastern Malaysia and Brunei.**
Complied by C. P. Cotter with the assistance of Shiro Saito.
Honolulu, Hawaii: University of Hawaii, Department of Asian
Studies, 1965. 2 vols.
A voluminous bibliography of 6,203 unannotated entries pertaining to all of
Malaysia, including Sabah and Sarawak, and Brunei. Although somewhat dated
this work is still very valuable. It includes material dating from the earliest
European accounts through to the year 1964, and covers the social sciences,
humanities, human ecology and the sciences. The bibliographical entries are listed
alphabetically by author. A subject index and extensive appendixes are included.

640 **A bibliography of the demography of Malaysia and Brunei.**
Saw Swee-Hock, Cheng Siok-Hwa. Singapore: University
Education Press, 1975. 103p. bibliog.
The scope of this bibliography is 'restricted to published works in the English
language in the form of books, booklets, reports, articles and ordinances'. To
facilitate access to topics among the 644 titles, the publication is classified into 18
sections according to subject matter, ranging from housing, migration, urbanization, fertility and family planning, to population policy. An author index is
included.

Bibliographies and Indexes

641    **British Malaya and British North Borneo: a selected list of references.**
Compiled by Florence S. Hellman, Library of Congress, Division of Bibliography.   Washington, DC: Library of Congress, 1943. 103p.

The subject matter is arranged geographically according to the states of Malaya, Straits Settlements and British North Borneo, including Brunei. Topics range from economics, natural history and population, to politics and government. General reference sources, and author and subject indexes are included.

642    **Brunei in the *Sarawak Museum Journal*.**
Thomas H. Harrisson.   *Brunei Museum Journal*, vol. 1, no. 1 (1969), p. 180-89.

The *Sarawak Museum Journal*, has made a significant contribution to the advancement of knowledge about Brunei in the period before the country opened its own museum (1965) and then began to publish the *Brunei Museum Journal* (BMJ) in 1969. This annotated list contains forty articles which deal with Brunei and were published from 1949-69. This compilation should prove useful to researchers interested in historical and archaeological sources published between these dates.

643    **A checklist of English language fiction relating to Malaysia, Singapore and Brunei.**
Compiled by Lewis Hill.   Hull, England: University of Hull, Centre for Southeast Asian Studies, 1986. 89p. (Bibliography and Literature Series, Paper no. 2).

A comprehensive checklist of 737 bibliographical entries of novels, works of fiction, plays and short stories related to Malaysia, Singapore and Brunei. Half a dozen references refer to Brunei and adjacent cultures. Each entry is accompanied by several abbreviations indicating literary form, subject matter, period setting and geographical location. The work is arranged alphabetically by author. There is no index.

644    **Checklist of holdings on Borneo in the Cornell University Libraries.**
Michael B. Leigh, with the assistance of John M. Echols.   Ithaca, New York: Cornell University, Department of Asian Studies, Southeast Asia Program, 1966. 62p. (ITS Data paper, no. 62).

An exhaustive checklist of monographs, pamphlets and serials (excluding articles) on Borneo, as of May 1966, available at the Cornell University Libraries. The contents are organized under the headings: Borneo, General; Indonesian Borneo; and East Malaysia and Brunei. For additional sources (from May 1966) Cornell's monthly *Southeast Asia Accessions List* should be consulted.

645 **A critical and annotated bibliography of Philippine, Indonesian and other Malayan folk-lore.**
Gabriel Adriano Bernardo, edited by Francisco Demetrio Y. Radaza. Cagayan de Oro City, Philippines: Xavier University, 1972. 150p. bibliog. (A Museum and Archives Publication, no. 5).

Professor Bernardo has painstakingly gathered and arranged all the material on Philippine, Indonesian, Malayan and allied folklore available in three major public libraries in Manila in 1923. Selected additions from regional journals have been added up to the 1950s. In the annotations the author has frequently quoted from leading authorities in order to shed light on the character and value of a given entry. The table of contents is made up of general works, myths, legends, fairy tales and miscellaneous texts, arranged by culture. An author and title index is included.

646 **Dialek Melayu Brunei: catatan bibliografi.** (Brunei Malay dialect: a bibliography.)
James T. Collins. *Dewan Bahasa*, vol. 28 (June 1984), p. 390-411. bibliog.

This critical bibliography contains 151 annotated entries, 73 of which are English sources; but all are annotated in Malay. The text points out some of the unique characteristics and the need for more linguistic investigation of the Malay Brunei dialect. The selection of entries is primarily based on writings in the *Brunei Museum Journal*, *Bahana*, the *Sarawak Museum Journal* and the *Journal of the Royal Asiatic Society* (the Straits and Malayan/Malaysian branches). In addition to ethnographic and language studies, the author has also included some scientific papers in which the Malay–Brunei dialect is used, as well as material in the Kedayan dialect. This bibliography was compiled with the assistance of the Tun Seri Lanang Library at the University of Malaysia.

647 **Guide to modern archives and manuscripts found in the United Kingdom relating to Brunei, Sabah and Sarawak.**
Chua Sui Gim. *Brunei Museum Journal*, vol. 5, no. 1 (1981), p. 56-77.

This indispensable source for the researcher covers specific repositories in the United Kingdom which hold archives and manuscripts relating to Brunei, Sabah and Sarawak for the pre-1963 period. Some details on Borneo's link with the United Kingdom and the historical relationship between Brunei, Sabah and Sarawak are presented at the beginning of this article. The types of repositories covered include: general guides, official archives, business archives, missionary archives, private papers, general archives and literary manuscripts.

648   **Index Malaysiana. An index to the** *Journal of the Straits Branch Royal Asiatic Society* **and the** *Journal of the Malayan Branch Royal Asiatic Society*, **1878-1963. [Supplement I: 1964-73; Supplement II: 1974-1983].**
Edward Lim Huck Tee, D. E. K. Wijasuriya.   Kuala Lumpur, Malaysia: Malaysian Branch Royal Asiatic Society, 1970, 395p. Supplement I: Kuala Lumpur, 1974. 66p. Supplement II: Petaling Jaya, 1985. 72p.

A comprehensive index which covers the entire run of the *Journal of the Straits Branch Royal Asiatic Society* (JSBRAS) and the *Journal of the Malayan/ Malaysian Branch Royal Asiatic Society* (JMBRAS) up to 1983. All articles, long or short, notices, views, book reviews and obituaries are indexed. The only categories of material omitted are those pertaining to the activities of the Society, which are printed annually, such as a list of members and annual reports . The index is in two parts: an author and title index and a subject index, which is mostly based on the Library of Congress subject headings, with ample cross references.

649   **Index to periodical articles relating to Singapore, Malaysia, Brunei, ASEAN: humanities, social science.**
Humanities/Social Sciences/Management Reference Department. Singapore: University of Singapore, 1980-.

This index is a by-product of PERIND, an on-line data base maintained by the National University of Singapore Library. It includes articles relating to Singapore, Malaysia, Brunei and ASEAN. The first volume, published in 1984, covers the years 1980-82. The 1985 supplement covers the years 1983-84 and one quarterly issue (1985) is also available covering articles published in 1985 as well as older articles not covered in the previous issues. The core list includes 115 journals of which 102 are published in Singapore, Malaysia and Brunei. In addition twenty-four indexes were scanned for selection of articles outside the core list. It is divided into three sections: a subject listing, arranged according to the Library of Congress subject headings; book reviews; and authors.

650   **The Malay world of Southeast Asia: a select cultural bibliography.**
Patricia Lim Pui Huen.   Singapore: Institute of Southeast Asian Studies, 1986. 456p.

A comprehensive bibliography on all aspects of the Malay-speaking region of Southeast Asia. The work is divided into four parts: I. Reference and general works; II. The setting (geography and history); III. The people; IV. The culture (subdivided into five parts: language; ideas, beliefs, values; institutions [social organizations, education, political, law/justice]; creative expression [literature, art and performing arts]; and social and cultural change [communications, industrialization, urban]). All parts are again subdivided by country.

651 **Malaysian studies: archaeology, historiography, geography and bibliography.**
Edited by John A. Lent, Kent Mulliner. De Kalb, Illinois: Northern Illinois University, Center for Southeast Asian Studies, 1986. 240p. bibliog. (ITS Monograph Series on Southeast Asia, Occasional Paper no. 11).

Contains five papers which focus on the evaluation of the literature on archaeology, history and geography. Each paper includes extensive, partially annotated bibliographies, and suggestions for further research. Pertinent information for Brunei is found in chapter one, which covers periods of distinct activities and results in archaeological research.

652 **North Borneo, Brunei, and Sarawak: a bibliography of English language historical, administrative and ethnographic sources.**
Conrad P. Cotter, Wilhelm G. Solheim II, Thomas R. Williams. [s.l]: [n.p.], [1963] 33p. bibliog.

A reference listing of English-language sources in the social sciences concerning published material up to 1962 for North Borneo, Brunei and Sarawak. The section entitled 'North Borneo and Brunei' (p. 1-10) covers 186 references on the history, government, education, religion, language, economy, exploration and folklore of the area. The bibliography is not annotated but serves as a useful guide to the literature.

653 **Official publications of Malaysia, Singapore, and Brunei in New York libraries.**
Margaret Roff. New York: Columbia University, 1970. 45p. (Southern Asian Institute. Columbia University. Occasional Bibliographical Papers, no. 1).

Publishes official materials emanating from the area itself and available in New York libraries. The materials date back to the 19th century and are available up to the date of compilation. Arrangement is by state or territory and alphabetically by corporate entity.

654 **The overseas empire in fiction: an annotated bibliography.**
Compiled by Winifred Hill. London: Oxford University Press, 1930. 66p.

This selected list of the best representative fiction is aimed at the general reader, rather than the expert. Some works have been chosen for their descriptions of scenery; others for their delineation of national characteristics and for the light they shed on political, economic or social problems. A short annotation and, where possible, a brief biographical note of the author, have been added to each citation. Eighteen works are listed under British Malaya and the Far East, including Brunei.

655  **Prehistory and archaeology of Malaysia and Brunei: a bibliography.**
Monica Kuak Sim Joo, Puteh binti Ismail.   Kuala Lumpur:
Perpustakaan Universiti Malaya, 1982. 41p.

An updated and expanded edition of an earlier preliminary list entitled *Archaeology in Malaysia*, published by the authors. It provides an excellent collection of archaeological studies carried out in Sarawak, Brunei and Sabah between the 1950s and the 1970s. As can be expected, Thomas Harrisson features heavily in this bibliography, with 105 papers published during the 1950-78 period, not to mention numerous others which he co-authored. This work is divided into three sections: I. Western Malaysia; II. Eastern Malaysia and Brunei (p. 23-39); and III. Review articles, arranged alphabetically by author and subdivided chronologically.

656  **Reading list of English language materials in the social sciences on British Borneo (with critical annotation).**
Conrad P. Cotter, prepared with the assistance of the Legislative Reference Bureau of the University of Hawaii.   Honolulu,
Hawaii: University of Hawaii, 1960. 88p.

This reading list contains occasional informal annotations of English-language material on British Borneo. Brunei is included in Part I: North Borneo and Brunei (p. 1-28). Many references are derived from regional periodicals and newspapers, as well as the annual reports for Brunei, North Borneo and Sarawak. Geographically, the bibliography emphasizes Sabah and Sarawak, but selected material for general background reading on Brunei is also included.

657  **Singapore Periodicals Index.**
Singapore: National Library, 1969-79. biennial. 1979-. annual.

The material in this index is arranged into 37 broad inter-disciplinary subject headings, and is enhanced by an author and subject index as well as a separate author index for Chinese entries. The Dewey Decimal classification system is used for the period from 1973 to 1980; after that date, entries are indexed according to the Library of Congress subject headings. In general, the index covers articles from approximately 100 Singapore and Brunei periodicals in Malay, English and Chinese.

658  **Southeast Asia, Malaysia, Singapore, Brunei and including Hong Kong.**
Compiled by Roger Hughes.   London: Commonwealth Institute, 1973. 26p. (Selected Reading Lists for Advanced Study).

This annotated bibliography is divided into two parts: Southeast Asia, Malaysia, Singapore and Brunei in part one; and Hong Kong in part two. Both sections are subdivided by subject matter, including arts and literature, geography, economics, education, flora and fauna, history and biography, and government and politics. Emphasis is on general texts and reference sources up to the early 1970s.

659   **West Kalimantan: a bibliography.**
Jan B. Ave, Victor T. King, Joke G. W. de Wit.   Dordrecht, The
Netherlands: Foris Publications Holland, 1983. 260p. 4 maps.
(Koninklijk Instituut voor Taal-, Land- en Volkenkunde.
Bibliographical Series, no. 13).

A comprehensive bibliography, six years in preparation, which covers most of the
available literature on the Indonesian administrative division of West Kalimantan
(Kalimantan Barat) which borders Sarawak and is close to Brunei. This reference
work is truely interdisciplinary and covers subjects in the humanities, social
sciences and physical sciences. This bibliography is relevant to Brunei for various
reasons. A significant number of sources on the natural environment, early
expeditions and certain aspects of material culture cover not only West Borneo
but other parts of the island as well. Some coastal districts in West Kalimantan
have had intimate economic and political links with northeastern Borneo in the
past. Finally, a number of ethnic groups, such as the Iban, Kayan, Malays and
Chinese, are found in both areas as a result of extensive regional migration. This
bibliography of 1,855 (unannotated) entries also includes a lengthy introductory
chapter, four maps and an author index.

660   **Western language historical sources in the British Borneo
Territories.**
John Bastin.   Kuala Lumpur: University of Malaya, Department
of History, 1962. 27 leaves.

Provides a brief survey of manuscripts, court records, dispatches, letters, annual
reports and government gazettes of Sarawak and Brunei, available in the Sarawak
Museum, in Kuching, Sarawak.

**The demography of Malaysia, Singapore, and Brunei: a bibliography.**
*See* item no. 25.

**Die Insel Borneo in Forschung und Schrifttum.** (The island of Borneo in
research and literature.)
*See* item no. 30.

**Southeast Asian research tools: Malaysia, Singapore, Brunei.**
*See* item no. 36.

**Annotated bibliography on the climate of British Borneo (including
Brunei, Labuan Island, North Borneo and Sarawak).**
*See* item no. 38.

**European sources for the history of the Sultanate of Brunei in the 16th
century.**
*See* item no. 176.

**The languages of Borneo.**
*See* item no. 494.

## Bibliographies and Indexes

**Bibliografi sastera kreatif Melayu. Jilid I: Brunei, Malaysia dan Singapore 1920-80.** (A bibliography of Malay creative writings. Vol. I: Brunei, Malaysia and Singapore 1920-80.)
*See* item no. 507.

# Indexes

There follow three separate indexes: authors (personal and corporate); titles of books; and subjects. Title entries are italicized and refer either to the main titles, or to other works cited in the annotations. The numbers refer to bibliographic entry rather than page numbers. Individual index entries are arranged in alphabetical sequence.

# Index of Authors

For purposes of clarity, Malay names are listed under the first element as well as the last element of the name. For instance, 'Ibrahim bin Mohd. Jahfar' is listed under 'I' and also under 'J'.

# Index of Titles

## A

Abode of peace 514
Het adatrecht van Borneo 316
Agreement between Her Majesty the Queen of the United Kingdom of Great Britain and Northern Ireland and His Highness the Sultan of Brunei amending the Agreement of 29 September 1959 317
Analytical index to the Brunei Museum Journal 1969-1984 623
Annotated bibliography on the climate of British Borneo (including Brunei, Labuan Island, North Borneo and Sarawak) 38
Annual Report 357, 589, 592
Annual Report 1984 423
Archaeological excavations in protohistoric Brunei 123
Archaeology in Malaysia 655
Area handbook on British Borneo 537
Asal usul sungai Si-Amas, a folktale. (Origin of the Si-Amas River) 562
Asia and Pacific Review 351
Asian Wallstreet Journal 635

Asiaweek 616
Assessment of undiscovered conventionally recoverable petroleum resources of Malaysia and Brunei 395
Atlas of Southeast Asia 46
Australasia. Vol. II: Malaysia and the Pacific archipelagoes 19

## B

Background notes: Brunei Darussalam 1
Bahana 506, 617, 646
Bahana rasa: antoloji cherpen 506
Bandar Seri Begawan 47
Barbara Hansen's taste of Southeast Asia; Brunei, Indonesia, Malaysia, the Philippines, Thailand and Vietnam 20
Berita. Malaysia– Singapore– Brunei Studies Group, Southeast Asia Council 618
Bibliografi mengenai Brunei. (Bibliography concerning Brunei) 638
Bibliografi sastera kreatif Melayu. Jilid I: Brunei,

Malaysia dan Singapore 1920-80 507
Bibliography of the demography of Malaysia and Brunei 640
Bibliography of English language sources on human ecology: Eastern Malaysia and Brunei 639
Birds of Borneo 97, 114
Bloody revolt in Brunei: a brief study on the success and failure of the Party Ra'ayat of Brunei 183
Borneo and the Indian Archipelago: with drawings of costume and scenery 185
Borneo Bulletin 619, 630
Borneo folktales and legends 563
Borneo jungle: an account of the Oxford expedition to Sarawak 21
Borneo: the land of river and palm 520
Borneo medicine: the healing art of indigenous Brunei Malay medicine 455
Borneo – principal towns (outline map) 49
Borneo Research Bulletin 620
Borneo scene 3

220

# Index of Subjects

## A

Abdul Kahar, Sultan
528
Abdul Mumin, Sultan
159, 194
Academic programmes
directory 629
Accidents
statistics 589
Accommodation 585
Accounting 589
*Adat* 325-326, 518, 538, 554
Address, Forms of 247
Administration 30, 588-589
*see also* American
Embassy
Administrative policy
366
Advertising
directory 631
AFC *see* ASEAN
Finance
Corporation
Agricultural
development 355, 360, 451
Agriculture 11, 15, 19, 41, 112, 242, 354, 361, 368, 421-425, 427, 429-431, 434-437, 442, 444-448, 450-451, 453
and the economy 453
censuses 444-445
commercial 35, 421
experimental
435-436, 469
government policy
444
map 59
sedentary cultivation
421
self-sufficiency 453
shifting cultivation
283, 421-422, 437

small-scale 359, 430
statistics 445, 589-590, 593
subsistence 41, 421
technology 345
trade 381
*see also* Crops;
Ethnic groups and
individual ethnic
groups by name,
e.g. Kedayan;
Farmers; History;
Livestock
Airport
construction 78, 193, 355, 360, 379
radio-navigational
equipment 379
al Fayed, Mohamed
394
*Alai* 569
Alak Betatar, Sultan
169
*Amantis reticulata* 110
*Amathusia utana aglaza*
102
American Embassy 10
American Geographical
Society, New York
67
American Trading
Company 151
American University,
Washington, DC
15
Ammunition 540
Anak Hashim 216
Ancestor worship 573
Anduki 116
Anglicanism 521
missionary activities
534
Anglo–Brunei
Agreement (1971)
302
Anthologies 506
Anthropology 30, 123, 135, 267, 277-278, 537, 556, 559

periodicals 628, 634
*see also* Biological
anthropology;
Medical
anthropology;
Social
anthropology
Aquaculture 359, 452
*see also* Oyster
culture
Aquariums 581
Archaeology and
archaeological sites
122-147, 160, 167, 527, 558
artefacts 123, 125, 128, 147
beads 122, 138, 147, 549
bibliographies 642, 651, 655
bone remains 132, 549
bronze vessels 135
burial grounds 147, 549
carbon dating 128, 131, 144
caves 145
ceramics 125, 127, 138, 141-143, 147
ceramics (Chinese)
129, 133, 138
ceramics (Siamese)
129
charcoal remains 132
Chou Dynasty 135
classification 122
coins 132, 600
excavations 123
glass 132, 138
Han Dynasty 135
Iron Age 128
jars 125, 142-143
Kota Batu 126-128, 131-134, 136, 138, 147, 167, 171
Kupan 171
metal 132

Archaeology *contd.*
Ming Dynasty
134-135
Neolithic period 146
oriental classical
period 130
periodicals 623, 628,
634
photographs 135, 142
pottery 123, 132, 136,
142-143
quaternary sediments
144
Sarawak 137, 139,
147
Stone Age 137, 146
stone implements 146
Sungei Lumut 147
T'ang Dynasty 135
Tanjong Batu 141,
146
Architecture
conservation 289
traditional 289
*see also* Istana Nurul
Iman; Omar Ali
Saifuddin Mosque;
Public buildings
Archives 163, 647
local collections 614
Archivo General de
Indias 180
Armed forces 242, 321
Art 576
bibliography 650
decorative 34, 578
Artists 576
Arts 17, 34
bibliography 658
*see also* Ethnic
groups; History;
Islam
ASCOPE *see* ASEAN
Council on
Petroleum
ASEAN *see*
Association of
Southeast Asian
Nations
ASEAN Council on
Petroleum
(ASCOPE) 363

ASEAN Finance
Corporation
(AFC) 372
Association for Asian
Studies, Boston,
Massachusetts 558
Association of
Southeast Asian
Nations (ASEAN)
7, 23, 29, 230, 234,
236, 240, 242,
295-297, 300, 308,
334-336, 338, 345,
349, 352, 363-364,
372, 375, 408
Attorney-General 320
Australia
relations with Brunei
352
trade with Brunei 13,
381
Australian National
Library 614
Aviation, Civil 328,
397, 590
statistics 589
Azahari 219, 241, 299,
339

## B

Bacteria 425
Bagong 376
Bajau 550
Bajau Darat language
484
Bajau Laut 26
Balau Nyareng (cycle
of stories) 511
Bandar Brunei *see*
Bandar Seri
Begawan
Bandar Seri Begawan
14, 281, 585
housing 591
map 64
Bangar
map 64
Banknotes 600
*see also* History
Banks and banking 354,

375, 385-394, 580,
590
map 64
services 351
statistics 637
Baram District 553
Baram River 545, 570
expedition 103
*see also* History
Barisan Kemerdekaan
Ra'ayat *see*
People's
Independence
Party
Barter 564
Batu Marang 438
Bauxite 81
BBC *see* British
Broadcasting
Corporation
Beaches 359
Belait District 421, 444
housing 591
oil 52, 86, 410
*see also* History
Belait (people) 561
Belait River 549
and the postal service
464
valley 286
Belcher, Captain 13
Bendahara Sakam,
Raja 182
Berakas
coal deposits 87
Berbunut Island 357
*Betta mecrostoma* 581
Beverages 20, 597
BIA *see* Brunei
Investment Agency
Bibliographies 30,
638-647, 650-656,
658-660
*see also* Individual
subjects by name,
e.g. Geography
Bilingualism
in education 297
Biographies
bibliography 658
*see also* Names of
individuals, e.g.

Brooke, James
    Rajah
Biological anthropology
    140
Biology 30
Birds 95, 97, 103-104,
    109, 114, 117
    photographs 97
    see also Mythology;
    Rainforests
Bisaya 27, 499, 550, 577
    and the environment
    291
    culture 291
    sago production 447
    see also History
Bisayah language
    485-486, 499
BNDP see Brunei
    National
    Democratic Party
Boats 282, 376
Body tattoo 97
Bolkiah, Sultan 126,
    574
Borneo 3, 30, 32, 95,
    97, 105, 121, 130,
    137, 139, 184-185,
    219, 264, 270, 410,
    490, 494, 520,
    556-559
    folklore 570
    maps 48, 62,67, 69
Borneo, British 24, 38,
    155, 211, 271, 280,
    283, 285, 350, 359,
    410, 537
    bibliography 660
Borneo Literature
    Bureau 512
Borneo, North 2, 15,
    17, 31, 38, 76, 83,
    155, 188, 197,
    199-200, 209, 212,
    224, 269-271,
    280-281, 284, 343,
    350, 359, 376, 519,
    550, 554
    bibliography 641,
    652, 656
    maps 54, 61, 66
    see also Sabah

Borneo Research
    Council 558
Borneo Territories 184
Botany 106
    see also Forests and
    forestry
Boundaries 19
    international 49
    maps 51, 56, 66, 68
    see also
    Brunei–Sarawak
    boundary; History
Boxer Codex see
    History
Brassey, Lord
    traveller's account
    209
Brassware 564
    see also Cannons;
    Gongs
Brick production 369
Britain
    commercial interests
    332, 409
    in Southeast Asia 31,
    35, 49
    relations with Brunei
    331-333, 338, 409
    see also History,
    Labuan Island
    (British
    occupation);
    Treaties
British Broadcasting
    Corporation
    (BBC) 621
British Crown Agency
    387
British Malayan
    Petroleum
    Company 186
British Museum,
    London 67
British Navy 205
British Residents 246,
    295, 302, 589
    see also History
Broadcasting 580, 621
    directory 631
Brooke, Charles, Rajah
    60, 126, 193, 201,
    213, 216, 218, 220,

    228-229, 310, 313,
    342, 543
Brooke, James, Rajah
    13, 19, 22, 121,
    184-185, 191, 193,
    195-198, 201,
    203-205, 208, 211,
    213-215, 222,
    228-229, 293, 326,
    543, 557
    biography 206
    diaries and
    correspondence 28,
    203, 206
    personal rule
    philosophy 543
Brooke, Vyner, Rajah
    228
Brunei Artist
    Association 576
Brunei Bay 376
    agriculture 447
    fishing and fisheries
    426
    geology 75
    map 69
    minerals and mining
    75
    oil 410
    see also History
Brunei Coldgas 406,
    418
Brunei District 444
Brunei Education
    Commission (1972)
    474
Brunei Investment
    Agency (BIA)
    386-387
Brunei LNG 406, 418
Brunei Low dialect 499
Brunei Museum 126,
    135, 160, 289, 539,
    584, 588, 610,
    614-615
    administration 613
    butterfly collection 94
    cannons 607
    Ceramic Gallery 608,
    611
    ceramics 125, 130,
    607-608

Civil engineers 420
Civil service 323
  *see also* History
Clay deposits 369
Climate 19, 38
  bibliography 38
  maps 46, 56
  statistics 593, 596
Clothing 10
Coal 42, 81, 84, 87, 144
  *see also* Berakas;
    History
Coastal resources
  management 359
Coastal towns
  maps 65, 68
Coastal zone 45, 359
Cock-fighting 541
Coins 42, 601-602
  bronze 600
  commemorative 600
  *see also* Archaeology
    and archaeological
    sites; History
Colonial Office
  (London) 61,
  196-197, 199, 226
Colonization
  European 35
Commerce
  statistics 589
Commercial law 321
Commissioner of
  Labour 11
Committee on
  Research Materials
  on Southeast Asia
  (CORMOSEA)
  625
Communication 9, 11,
  350, 450, 588
  bibliography 650
  maps 46
  statistics 590, 593,
    596
Community services
  statistics 263
Companies 393
  directory 624
  *see also* Multinational
    corporations; Oil
    companies

Concubines 42
Conferences 618
Conservation 98
  *see also* Architecture;
    Forests and
    Forestry
Constitution 6, 12, 235,
  259, 295, 301, 309,
  314, 316-330, 589,
  596
  documents 320
  reform (1946) 324
  *see also* History
Construction 242-243,
  358, 361, 368, 386
  surveys 379
  *see also* Airport;
    Roads
Contras 295
Cookery books 20
Copper 81
Coral fish 440
CORMOSEA *see*
  Committee on
  Research Materials
  on Southeast Asia
Cornell University
  Libraries
  holdings 644
Corning Glass
  Museum, New
  York 138
Cottage industry 287
Cotton 445
Council of Ministers
  318, 589
Council of Succession
  318
Court records 660
Court system
  statistics 589
Cowie, W. C. 218, 224
Crafts and craftsmen 3,
  34
  *see also* Ethnic
    groups
Crime 42
  statistics 589, 593
  *see also* History
Criminal law 321
Crops
  fertility rituals 573

production costs 423
statistics 381, 444
yields 423
  *see also* Fruit; Rice;
    Vegetables
Cultural development
  32
Cultural Relics
  Preservation
  Committee,
  Nanking 260
Culture 4, 27, 233, 254,
  366, 536-560, 584
  bibliography 650
  periodicals 616, 623,
    628
  *see also* History;
    Individual ethnic
    groups by name,
    e.g. Kedayan;
    Political culture;
    Prehistory
Currency 10, 321, 390
  statistics 589
Customary law *see Adat*

### D

Dali Dusun language
  499
Dance 578
Datu Merpati 548
Datus *see* History
Dayak 26-27, 570
  *see also* History;
    Land Dayak; Sea
    Dayak
Deer 105
Defence 237, 241-242,
  295, 311, 321, 338,
  340, 363, 370, 386
  external 337
  internal 230
  statistics 596
  *see also* Gurkha
    Batallion, British
    Army; History;
    Royal Brunei
    Armed Forces
    (RBAF)
Democracy 308
  *see also* History

231

Demography 25, 32, 263, 270, 273, 276, 288, 537
  bibliography 640
  periodical 623
  statistics 25, 273
  see also Population
Dent, Alfred 200
Dent Brothers 223
Department of Agriculture and Fisheries 426, 430, 436, 439-440, 443, 451-452
Department of Customs and Excise 597
Department of Education 502
Department of Health 443
Department of Religion 529, 532, 614
Deramas jasada herdji 102
Development 12, 356, 359, 366, 382, 386, 589
  see also Agricultural development; Cultural development; Financial development; Industrial development; Infra-structure; Political development; Ports
Dewan Bahasa dan Pustaka see Language and Literature Bureau
Dialects 484-485, 490
  bibliography 646
  vocabulary 494
  see also Brunei Low Dialect
Dictionaries 36
  Malay–English 497, 504

Dido (vessel) 28
Diesel 403
Diocese of Labuan and Sarawak 520
Diplomatic relations 308, 596
  see also Embassies; History
Dipterocarp forests 37, 96, 101, 106, 108, 120
  photographs 101, 106
Directories 624, 629
  see also Media
Disease 465
  coronary artery 465
  see also Malaria; Smallpox; Typhus
Divorce 530, 535
Drainage
  statistics 589
Drama 578
  bibliography 507
Drugs 328
Duit besi 600
Dukun 455, 458
Dusun 26-27, 550
  health conditions 465
  settlement 283
  tribal dances 569

E

East India Company 190
East Indian Archipelago 61
East-West Environment and Policy Institute, Hawaii 417
EC see European Community
Ecology 37, 97, 107, 113
  see also Forest ecology; Human ecology
Economic development 29, 235, 311, 350, 353-354, 360, 378, 392, 408, 412
  see also History
Economic geography 284
Economic history see History (economic); History (economic development)
Economic Planning Unit, Ministry of Finance 590
Economic policy 366-367
Economic problems 31, 233, 367, 371
Economic relations 33, 375
Economics 30
  see also Macro-economics
Economy 1, 4, 6-7, 9-11, 15, 17, 30, 32, 35, 39, 230, 241-243, 245, 300, 305, 308, 311, 336, 338, 348-371, 382, 389, 397, 537, 584, 588-590, 593
  and employment 467
  and independence 386
  and nationalism 304
  bibliographies 641, 652, 658
  diversification 231, 235, 308, 337, 351, 355, 360, 364, 368, 430, 432
  periodicals 616, 626, 633, 636
  regional 280
  statistics 189, 273, 360, 365, 593, 596
  see also Ethnic groups; Finance; National Development Plans; Oil
Education 6, 10-11, 35, 242, 321, 360, 368, 470-483, 537

Fruit 425
Fungi 425

## G

*Gaman* 572
Gas, Natural 12, 52, 72,
    81, 354, 395-420
  dependency on 243
  exports 353
  statistics 592
  *see also* History
Genealogy 249,
    256-257, 519, 528,
    588, 601
Geochrom
    Laboratories,
    Massachusetts 128
Geography 1, 10-12,
    15, 17, 23, 30, 32,
    35-36, 38-69, 74,
    238, 284, 558, 580,
    584, 589
  bibliographies
    650-651, 658
  *see also* Economic
    geography;
    Geopolitics;
    History; Human
    geography;
    Regional
    geography;
    Surveys
Geologic Survey
    Department 73
Geology 19, 30, 32,
    70-93, 404
  Cainozoic period 77
  coastal sediments 80
  Cretaceous period 77
  Holocene period 87
  map 76
  Miocene period 87
  Neogene period 71
  offshore 73
  onshore 73
  periodical 623
  photographs 76
  Pleistocene period 71
  Pliocene period 71,
    88

post-glacial period 92
surficial 50, 76
Tertiary period 89
*see also* Brunei Bay;
    Engineering;
    Gravel deposits;
    History;
    Palaeontology;
    Regional geology;
    Rocks;
    Sedimentation;
    Stratigraphy;
    Volcanoes
Geomorphology 71, 74,
    76
Geopolitics 60,
    213-214, 244
Geosyncline 91, 93
Geotectonics 76-77
Gongs
  brass 564
Government 291-315,
    318, 351, 370, 580
  bibliographies 641,
    652, 658
  cabinet 319
  centralized 231
  corruption 296
  internal problems 234
  ministers 296, 590
  role of the royal
    family 296
  statistics 596
  traditional 41
  *see also* History;
    Individual Sultans
    by name; Local
    government
Government agencies
    72
Government
    expenditure 366,
    370, 384, 386
  statistics 368
Government policy 33,
    297, 308, 311, 456,
    467
  *see also*
    Administrative
    policy;
    Agriculture;
    Economic policy;

Education;
    Employment;
    Investment,
    Foreign; Medicine;
    Trade
Government
    publications
  bibliographies 638,
    653
Government revenue
    29
  oil 413
  statistics 358
Graphic design
    directory 631
Gravel 82
Great Khan of China
    163
Guides 36
Guns 540
  prohibition 98
Gurkha Batallion,
    British Army 242,
    295, 300, 409
  status 296
  withdrawal from
    Brunei 302, 340
  *see also* History;
    Tenth Gurkha
    Rifles Company

## H

*Halpe clara* 102
*Hammaleh* (vessel) 551
Handicraft Centre 584,
    588
Handicrafts 378
Hankin 'F' 415
Harrisson, Thomas H.
    124
Hashim, Sultan
    196-197, 228
Hassanal Bolkiah
    Aquarium 581
Hassanal Bolkiah,
    Sultan 40, 241,
    252, 258, 262, 315,
    317, 319, 348, 364,
    370

# M

McArthur, M. S. H. 313
Machinery 597
Macro-economics 29
Magellan, Ferdinand 69, 161, 173-174, 176-177, 179
works 69
Maharaja Karna mausoleum (Nanking, China) 260
Mahkota 215
*Majlis* 530
*Makan tahun* 573
Malacca 35
Malaria 458, 463-465
eradication 193, 462
Malaria Eradication Programme 462, 464
Malay Archipelago 343
'Malay Islamic Monarchy' 352
Malay language 58, 474, 476, 496-497, 499
as national language 487-488
standardization 487
terminology 35
vocabulary 499, 505
Malay migrants 364
coastal concentration 271
'Malaynization' 337
Malaysia
relations with Brunei 296, 337-340, 343, 546
trade with Brunei 380
*see also* History (trade)
Malaysia–Singapore–Brunei Studies Group 618
Malaysian Federation 219, 294, 301, 309
Malaysian parliament 312

Maloh 26
'Manaregarna' *see* Maharaja Karna
Mangroves 63, 359
Mantodea 107
Manufacturing 354, 358, 361
statistics 368
Manuscripts 647, 660
Maps, mapping and atlases 36, 46-69
collections 48, 61, 67
survey stations 51
*see also* Individual subjects by name, e.g. Geography
*Marchesa* (vessel) 22
Marine life 116
diatoms 441
Marine Police 23
Maritime activities 35
*see also* History
Maritime Museum, Rotterdam 67
Maritime security 23
coastal protection 23
Marketing 430, 444
Markets 3, 378
Marriage 278, 325, 327, 530, 535
*see also* Ethnic groups; Individual ethnic groups by name, e.g. Kedayan
Marudi 87
Marudu Bay *see* History
Media 588, 590
directory 631
periodical 633
statistics 593
Western coverage of Brunei 237-238, 242
*see also* Broadcasting; Newspapers; Radio; Television
Medical anthropology 465
Medical services 460, 462

*see also* History
Medicine 10, 321, 455, 458-460, 465
government policy 308
rural communities 459
*see also* Ethnic groups; Plants; Veterinary care
Melanau 27
Melanan
sago production 447
Mendaran River 581
*Menteri darat* 544
*Mentri Besar* (Chief Minister) 318
'*Merdeka Games*' 352
Meteorology 38
maps 45
Methodism
missionary activities 534
Micro-photography 90
Migration and migrants 265, 270-271, 276
bibliography 640
internal 272, 274
temporary resident workers 276
restrictive policy 276
*see also* Individual nationalities by name, e.g. Chinese; Individual ethnic groups by name, e.g. Iban
Mindanao *see* History
Minerals and mining 41, 70-93, 321, 359, 597
maps 46, 59
photographs 84
statistics 590, 593, 596
trade patterns 81
*see also* Bauxite; Coal; Copper; Gas, Natural; Gravel deposits; Hydrocarbons;

Nationality Enactment
(1961) 314
Nationality law 314,
322
Natural history 22
bibliography 641
periodical 628
Nepal
relations with Brunei
295
The Netherlands *see*
History (Dutch
policy); Treaties
New York Public
Library 67
Newspapers 237, 619,
630, 632
Chinese propaganda
331
directory 631
Nitrogenous fertilizer
414
*Nobat* 575
North Borneo
Chartered
Company 19,
151-152, 157, 190,
194, 196-197, 200,
213-214, 224, 228,
280, 326
North Borneo
Company
*see* North Borneo
Chartered
Company
North Kalimantan
National Army 339
Novels 507-508
bibliography 643
Numismatics 600-602,
504-605
*see also* Coins


O

Occupation 290
statistics 263, 268,
273, 589, 595
*see also* Chinese
migrants;

Employment;
Labour
Oceania 55
Oil 12, 16, 72, 83, 86,
88, 93, 334,
351-352, 368, 387,
395-420, 450
and the economy 72,
231, 233, 242,
336-337, 408, 412
and independence
363, 412
and public relations
406
and urbanization 285
concessions 84, 407
consumption 401
effect on
environment 72
engineering 398, 406
exploration 398,
400-401, 406, 420
exports 353, 400
fields 52, 74, 76, 82,
86, 89-90, 396,
402-404
government
involvement 407
legislation 72, 86
maps 52, 406
offshore 23, 72, 85,
359, 401, 407, 410
onshore 52, 402
production 398, 401,
420
refinery 405
statistics 368, 406
technology 72, 345
trade 401, 406, 411
wells 82
*see also* Hankin 'H';
History; Jasra
Jackson;
Petroleum
Oil companies 72
Oil palm 430
Old age pensions 193
Omar Ali Saifuddin
Mosque 193,
583-584
architecture 522
Omar Ali Saifuddin II,

Sultan 13, 198, 216
Omar Ali Saifuddin III,
Sultan 253, 259,
295, 309, 319-320
Ophioninae 113
Oral history 274
Oral tradition 536, 558
Orchestras 575
Organization of Islamic
Conferences 242
Organizations
bibliography 650
heads of 590
*see also* International
organizations;
Political
organizations;
Social
organizations
Overbeck, Baron
Gustav von 190,
200
Oxford Exploration
Club 21
Oyster culture 115


P

Padas Valley
geology 75
minerals and mining
75
*Padian* 552
Pagon Peak,
Temburong
District 79
Pagon Ridge 94
Palace of Religious
Light *see* Istana
Nurul Iman
Palaces 262
*see also* Istana Nurul
Iman
Palaeo-environmental
studies 86
Palaeontology 73
Palynology 87-88
Pandasan *see* History
Partai Ra'ayat *see*
People's Party

244

Revenue
  statistics 589
  *see also* Government
    revenue
Revolts 230
  *see also* History
Rhinoceros Hornbill 97
Rice 453
  cultivation 193, 421,
    429-430, 437, 469
  harvest festivals 561,
    569, 571, 573
  imports 381
  local varieties 446
  *see also* Kedayan
Rivers 3, 19
  maps 51, 64-65, 68
Roads 46
  construction 78, 193,
    355, 450, 589
  maps 47, 51, 57,
    64-65, 68
  statistics 589
  *see also* History
Rocks 77
  formation 75
  igneous 50, 76
  sedimentary 50
  source of oil deposits
    93
Ross, Captain 13
Royal Brunei Airlines
  11
Royal Brunei Armed
  Forces (RBAF)
  295
Royal Brunei Malay
  Regiment Flotilla
  23
Royal Brunei Polo
  Association 587
Royal Dutch Shell 76,
  418
  *see also* Shell Oil
Royal family 8,
  233-234, 238, 311,
  364, 370, 387
  *see also* History;
    Sultans
Royal Geographical
  Society, London 67
Royal weddings

traditional 254
*Royalist* (vessel) 203
RTB *see* Radio
  Television Brunei
Rubber cultivation 193,
  421-422, 427, 430
Rural areas 39, 41
  *see also* Settlement;
    Social conditions


S

Sabah 3, 15, 139, 145,
  151, 190, 194, 267,
  284, 292, 359, 447,
  512, 519, 537, 582,
  614, 647
  bibliography 639
  maps 66
  *see also* Borneo,
    North; History
Sabah, Western 76
*Saccostrea cucullata* 115
Sago palm 447
Saiful Rijal, Sultan 182
St. John, Spenser
  Buckingham 103
Sande, Francisco de
  178
Sarawak 3, 15, 31, 34,
  38, 74, 76, 83,
  124-126, 139, 144,
  188, 191, 197, 201,
  206, 221, 223,
  228-229, 265, 267,
  270-271, 273, 280,
  292, 350, 359, 447,
  463, 512, 537, 543,
  548, 550, 614, 647
  bibliography 652, 656
  maps 54, 60, 66, 68
  *see also* History
Sarawak Museum 607,
  660
Sarawak State Advisory
  Council 34
School of Oriental and
  African Studies,
  London 257
Schools
  impact on health

conditions 465
  *see also* Secondary
    schools
Schultz, George 295
Science
  bibliographies 639,
    659
  periodicals 620, 623,
    628, 634
Scottish Integrated
  Science
  programme 471
Sea Dayak 274, 519
  burial practices 557
  folklore 274
  head-hunting 557
  medicine 557
  migration 274
  religion 557
  settlement 283
  sport 557
  *see also* History
Seafood 443
  *see also* Prawns
Secondary schools 471,
  479
Security 334, 338, 409
  *see also* Internal
    security; Maritime
    security; National
    security
Sedimentation 73, 86,
  89, 91, 377
  *see also* Rocks
Seri Begawan, Sultan
  government 315
  obituary 253
  *see also* Omar Ali
    Saifuddin III,
    Sultan
Seria
  gravel deposits 82
  housing 591
  map 64
  oilfields 52, 82, 86,
    89, 396, 402-403
Settlement 19, 39,
  279-290
  maps 51, 64
  rural 284, 450-451
  urban 284, 288
  valleys 286

246

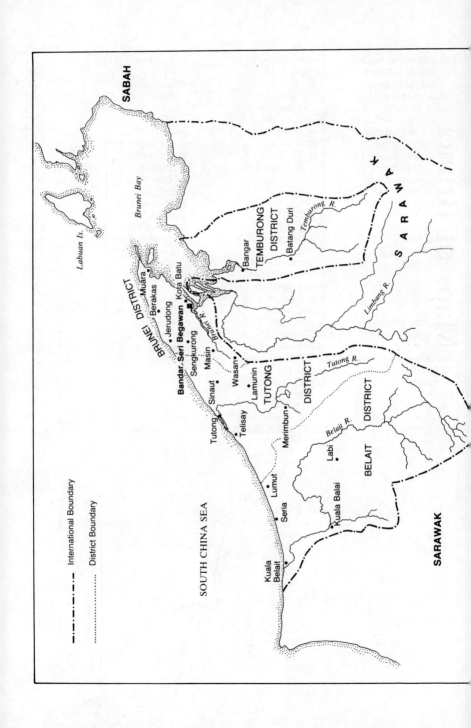

# Maps of Brunei

These maps show the more important towns and other features.

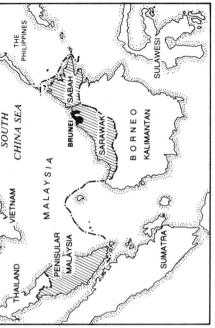

OIL FIELDS AND CONCESSIONS

○ Oil Fields

SARAWAK

BRUNEI

SABAH

Labuan Is

CHAMPION
MAGPIE
FAIRLEY
FAIRLEY-BARAM
SOUTH WEST AMPA
K'SERIA
Refinery
Lumut LNG Plant

Shell offshore — 1

Shell onshore — 2

Jasra Jackson — 3

Woods — 4

Sunray — 5

THAILAND

VIETNAM

SOUTH CHINA SEA

THE PHILIPPINES

PENISULAR MALAYSIA

MALAYSIA

SABAH

BRUNEI

SARAWAK

BORNEO

KALIMANTAN

SUMATRA

SULAWESI